IN THE CAUSE OF ARCHITECTURE

Frank Lloyd Wright.

IN THE CAUSE OF ARCHITECTURE
FRANK LLOYD WRIGHT

EDITED BY FREDERICK GUTHEIM

LARKIN BUILDING, BUFFALO, N.Y., 1904
DRAWING BY FRANK LLOYD WRIGHT

ESSAYS BY
FRANK LLOYD WRIGHT
FOR
ARCHITECTURAL RECORD
1908-1952

WITH
A SYMPOSIUM ON
ARCHITECTURE
WITH AND WITHOUT WRIGHT
BY EIGHT
WHO KNEW HIM

ANDREW DEVANE
VICTOR HORNBEIN
ELIZABETH WRIGHT INGRAHAM
KARL KAMRATH
ELIZABETH KASSLER
EDGAR KAUFMANN, JR.
HENRY KLUMB
BRUNO ZEVI

ARCHITECTURAL RECORD BOOKS ⒶR NEW YORK

The editors for this book were Hugh S. Donlan and Martin Filler.

The designer was Jan V. White.

The production supervisor was Susanne LanFranchi.

The printer and binder were Halliday Lithographic Corporation.

Published by Architectural Record,
A McGraw-Hill Publication,
1221 Avenue of the Americas,
New York, New York 10020

Library of Congress Cataloging in Publication Data
Wright, Frank Lloyd, 1867-1959.
    In the cause of architecture, Frank Lloyd Wright.
    The essays by Wright first appeared in the Architec-
tural record from 1908 to 1952.
    Includes index.
    1. Wright, Frank Lloyd, 1867-1959—Addresses, essays,
lectures. I. Devane, Andrew. II. Gutheim, Frederick
Albert, 1908-   ed. III. Architectural record.
IV. Title.
NA737.W7D37   720′.92′4   74-22707
ISBN 0-07-025350-1

Second printing, 1975

CONTENTS

IN THE CAUSE OF ARCHITECTURE

ESSAYS BY FRANK LLOYD WRIGHT
FOR
ARCHITECTURAL RECORD 1908-1952

PREFACE

BY FREDERICK GUTHEIM

CERTAINLY it is to his buildings that we first turn to discover the essential Frank Lloyd Wright. These are well supplemented by the *Autobiography*, the self-told story of a life that ranks with Henry Adams, Louis Sullivan and Lincoln Steffens; and those of his writings (fewer as the years went on) that rise above the polemic. Among those that do, the sixteen essays written for *Architectural Record* constitute the major effort Wright made to address fellow architects. While excerpts were published in *Frank Lloyd Wright on Architecture* and subsequent presentations, no apology is required for their republication in their entirety. They form the only written record of Wright's architectural theories and are clearly to be distinguished from his much later philosophizing, not to mention such efforts as his address to the 1949 annual meeting of the American Institute of Architects on the occasion of receiving their Gold Medal.

The editor of the *Architectural Record* who showed his faith in Wright was M. A. Mikkelsen, and to the end Wright always joked with *Record* editors that he "still owed them an article." This referred to the agreement in 1926 by which Wright received $7,500 for fifteen articles, of which only fourteen were produced. The sum was a large one, probably unprecedented for an architectural magazine, and it must have reflected an appreciation not only of Wright's genius but of his desperate financial circumstances that in a couple of years would bankrupt his professional corporation. While the period yielded some of Wright's most brilliant work (the Doheny Ranch project and the resort

FREDERICK GUTHEIM became a frequent visitor to Taliesin, the Spring Green, Wisconsin, home of Frank Lloyd Wright, in 1928. From office files that survived moves and fires, he then prepared the first comprehensive list of Wright's numerous speeches and writings. In 1941 Gutheim instigated the three-volume series comprising the revised and updated version of Wright's *Autobiography*, Henry-Russell Hitchcock's corpus on Wright's building, and his own edited collection entitled *Frank Lloyd Wright on Architecture*. Republished in paperback in 1959 (the year Wright died), this remains the most complete presentation of the architect's writings.

hotel, San Marcos in the Desert—neither of them realized) it was also a period in which Wright's fame was in eclipse. In short, a time for reflection and summing up, a time to write.

The fresh availability of these essays provides more than an historical document: it offers a view of architecture that returns to the fundamentals of physical design and materials. Today's preoccupation with new humanistic goals of architecture, with vernacular design, with "architecture without architects," with environmental objectives, with an anti-historicism that has rejected the "modern architecture" of functionalism—the architecture of LeCorbusier, Gropius and Mies van der Rohe—as firmly as that generation had rejected academicism and nineteenth century eclecticism, has left architects traumatized and bewildered. Let us hope that Wright's essays will provide an architectural landmark that will be welcomed as much as it is needed today.

In the essays republished here for the first time Wright addresses the architectural profession in its leading journal. These essays form the principal record of his deliberate and formal statement of his architectural philsophy. While it is to the man that we must look for an understanding of his creativity, and to the buildings that we must turn for the architectural language that Professor Zevi hopes will develop from Wright's work, it is in these writings alone that Wright has made any deliberate effort to formulate the principles of his art. Of course one approaches them with the full consciousness of their historical context. Reservations must be kept in mind in translating these thoughts to the contemporary scene. But the words themselves are valid evidence of Wright's philosophy, and they are of particular relevance to architects.

From 1908 when the first of these essays was published (and the internal evidence shows it was conceived even father back, in 1894) to the last of them in 1952, there is a notable continuity and consistency of thought. From the start, Wright is most impressively concerned with the total body of his architectural work, not with particular buildings. And he presents a concise design principle that changes little over the next

50 years. Here it is: "I have endeavored in this work to establish a harmonious relationship between ground plan and elevation of these buildings, considering the one as a solution and the other an expression of the conditions of a problem of which the whole is a project. I have tried to establish an organic integrity to begin with, forming the basis for the subsequent working out of a significant grammatical expression and making the whole, as nearly as I could, consistent. What quality of style the buildings may possess is due to the artistry with which the conceptualization as a solution and an artistic expression of a specific problem within these limitations has been handled."

What Frank Lloyd Wright means today, fifteen years after his death and far longer from the time when he ceased being a great creative force in architecture, must be determined by a new generation. His influence is conveyed in many ways—by his buildings, his writings, his teaching. Increasingly, however, these demand interpretation. In 1930, Henry Klumb and Takehiko Okami, then working in Wright's office, faced the problem of interpreting Wright's buildings to a new generation of European architects who would attend an international circulating exhibition of Wright's work. Their solution, published later in the Princeton Lectures, was a boldly shadowed yet simplified rendering—not what one would have drawn before the building had been executed, but one that well illustrated its final effect and significance. Something of this sort has been attempted by many of the authors of the essays in this volume. Together they provide a symposium of different opinions but with a common purpose.

An impressive unanimity emerges in the conclusions equally expressed by such divergent figures as Klumb and Zevi, that the forms of Wright's architecture should be set aside and instead one should return to his architectural language.

"No reminiscences," I adjured the contributors to this symposium. "Wright has been dead fifteen years. So what? Who needs him now? How can his value to architecture be communicated to those who can never know him as a living personality?" As I had suspected, "no reminiscences" has proved an impossible directive. Nothing more clearly demonstrates the overwhelming impact of Wright's personality than the inability of some of these authors, especially the creative, practicing architects, to escape it, and their compulsion to talk about it. Twenty, thirty or forty years later, the encounter with Wright is still unforgettable and unmatched in later experiences. Let it be so in the minds of those who had this experience. But it is not a transferrable experience, and to those for whom it is impossible the question is how else to place oneself in relation to this titanic figure. Here we owe a debt to these authors, for each has attempted (and I believe successfully) in his own fashion to make the creative architect they knew *available* to a new generation. They have demonstrated how inseparable the work is from the man, and how rooted the ideas are in both. In doing this, they have plumbed both the secrets of creativity and the processes of architectural history.

Frank Lloyd Wright's "Cause of Architecture" had not much to do with the business-like affair architecture has become today. More concerned with processes and with the very conditions of creative action, Wright's conception of architecture can now be seen as supremely relevant to the contemporary anxieties about architecture, both the art and the profession. The authors are full of the urgent present, and they address the current generation to whom Wright has become a legendary if not a forgotten figure.

The contemporary quality that illuminates the essays by Frank Lloyd Wright made available to the general reader in this volume, and which bemuses the distinguished contributors to the symposium that introduces it, cannot be denied. Both the problems faced by our world—the environment, technology, the human condition—and the problems faced by the creative architect—the plan, the organization of interior and exterior space, and use of materials and tools—were on his mind three-quarters of a century ago. Not only a man of the present, he still looks to the future. Hence, his thinking is so stimulating and relevant to today. Indeed, one suspects we can now understand what eluded Wright's contemporaries as they read the current issues of the *Architectural Record* in which his essays were first published.

F. LL. W. AT TALIESIN WEST, 1958

Photographs by Mildred F. Schmertz, AIA   Senior Editor *Architectural Record*

The concept of total design set forth in the architectural theory of Frank Lloyd Wright found practical application in the approach to his Western encampment in Scottsdale, Arizona, begun in 1938. From the first signpost (above, left), the visitor's way along a winding desert road is directed by Wright-designed pylons (above, right) that reflect the shapes of the cacti that punctuate the horizon. Arriving at the gatehouse (opposite, above), made from stone found in the surrounding desert, the spatial climax comes in the dramatic forecourt to the Taliesin West complex (below).

Regardless of the plan of Taliesin West, its true focal point during Wright's lifetime was always in the presence of the Master himself (right). Seated on his sheepskin under the watchful eye of his long-time associate, the late John Howe, F.LL.W. works in the drafting room, facing into the bright sunlight of a February afternoon.

Surrounded by young members of the Taliesin Fellowship, Wright puts his finishing touches on a presentation drawing of a project for a motor hotel. Along with seven others, this project was included in *Frank Lloyd Wright: A Selection of Current Work* in the May 1958 issue of *Architectural Record*. *Record* Associate (now Senior) Editor Mildred F. Schmertz visited Taliesin West in February 1958 to gather material for that article, the last portfolio of Wright's new work to be published in his lifetime. Her photographs of F.Ll.W., taken fourteen months before his death at 89, are a unique record of the Master at work near the end of a career that spanned nearly seventy years.

THE WHOLE MAN

BY ELIZABETH KASSLER

MUTILATED by the head trip of a conventional education and disappointed that study at the Bauhaus had been made impossible by depression here, politics there, I found my way to Wisconsin in 1932 after Fritz Gutheim told me that Frank Lloyd Wright was about to accept apprentices. Mr. Wright was then about sixty-five, Mrs. Wright at least thirty years younger, and Taliesin already timeless.

That winter was very strange, very uncomfortable. Physical austerities became acceptable, perhaps because they were shared by Mr. and Mrs. Wright. The lasting discomfort was simply that I understood nothing, nothing at all. Why was there no instruction, and no work in the drafting room other than when a hungry Chinese friend would accept my desserts in exchange for setting up a tracing job? If architecture is indeed the mother art, why was the execution of menial chores held equally important and subject to the same demand for attention? What was the unfamiliar quality of that attention, directed to every detail of living? Why the distrust of intellectuals? What was behind the strange compelling beauty of the place? Why did I feel so disturbed, so inadequate, and why couldn't I get my mind around it?. . . .

I left in the spring, with some relief but always to be haunted by the hint of another dimension, a potential that defied identification. Afterwards, in Europe and New York, the discomfort intensified. Gropius, LeCorbusier, and even the ambivalent Mies seemed laid out on a plate, gratifyingly "modern," and handsome fun to deal with. Wright was altogether different, yet certainly not to be dismissed as a pioneer who made the others possible—an assessment fashionable in those late days of the Age of Progress. If not that, then what else? The question could usually be avoided.

In these last years, it begins to come clear that what I was exposed to briefly in Wisconsin, in greater depth at Taliesin West in the later forties, was the startling experience of a whole man, evolving ways of living and building which would tend to express, implant, and support that state of being.

Whole man? Not the academic ideal of *mens sana* neatly packaged *in corpore sano*, and not the universal man of the Renaissance. Frank Lloyd Wright had it all together in quite another way. In him, body, feeling, thought, and spirit were one and indissoluble —an inner centering which released a wealth of creative energy to his lifelong search for processes and forms appropriate to his holistic vision. Organic man, he would have said.

Most of us walk as strangers on this earth, as out of touch with what is inside us as with what is outside, and caught up in that life-denying circle of cause and effect. If this,

ELIZABETH KASSLER lives in Princeton, New Jersey, and writes frequently about architecture and landscape design. Her contributions to *Architectural Record* have included a memorable series of articles "Water and Architecture." Her most recent book is *Modern Gardens and the Landscape*. As Elizabeth Mock she is the author of *The Architecture of Bridges*. She is former curator of the Department of Architecture, Museum of Modern Art, and sometime research associate of the School of Architecture and Urban Planning, Princeton University.

as we are told on every side, is the condition of modern man, then Wright was not a modern man. Secure in the knowledge of his own essence, he lived and built almost as though the dreary split of man from nature, reason from instinct, science from religion, work from life, art from meaning, practice from knowledge, had never happened. His alienation, such as it was, was not from himself, and not from the earth, where he was at home, not from advanced technology, which he welcomed early on as a supremely valuable servant, and not from the old dream of America as terrestrial paradise, but from a society dominated by values which diminish the individual present and threaten the collective future. A measure of loneliness was inevitable. Astonished to see him strutting with pride when he returned to Arizona in 1949 with the Gold Medal of The American Institute of Architects, I asked why he was so pleased with that absurdly belated honor. "One never outgrows the need for the recognition of one's peers," was his answer.

Mr. Wright preached "the gospel of work." Not unlike Karl Marx in this, he considered meaningful, varied work, integrated with all of life, as the base of wholeness and creativity. Farming and cooking, cleaning and repairing, were arts as biologically valid as the design and construction of shelter, and to be pursued with the same loving care, the same search for inherent rhythm. It was all a celebration of life, and even the elder statesmen of the studio would cheerfully correct plumbing failures or rise from bed two or three times a night to help a novice cook raise festive bread for Sunday breakfast. So far, nothing foreign to utopian communities, old or new, but Taliesin had some special twists besides, behind and beyond its unique physical beauty. Taliesin was devoted to the cause of architecture and to the idea that it takes an organic man to produce organic architecture. To be an architect, one must first be a man fully human in nature, an awakened man simultaneously aware of his inner being and his outward behavior and relationships; and contemplative action was the prime vehicle for the raising of consciousness. No activity was to be pursued mechanically. Whether one were peeling onions or making working drawings, dancing or laying up a wall, and whether one were raging or loving or quietly devoted to the task at hand, this two-way attention was asked for. The demand was rarely explicit, not always understood as such, and perhaps infrequently met, but it was always there. By the gospel, Taliesin life was designed as ritual support of an effort to be wholly present to the present and responsible for it. "What do we have but the present," he asked rhetorically. . . . The influence in these matters of Gurdjieff, the philosopher with whom Mrs. Wright had studied in France, can be overestimated. I would guess that Mr. Wright must have been well on his way to full self-consciousness before Mrs. Wright entered his life late in 1924 and long before he met Gurdjieff; when the two finally did meet, I imagine a mutually educational, extremely salty relationship.

How does a whole man build? He built as he was. Tuned to nature within and nature without, man and architecture were all of a piece and never more vividly so than at his own beloved places in Wisconsin and Arizona.

Believing that the limitations of a problem are the architect's best friends, he considered the specific nature of the site, the specific nature of the human purpose, and the specific nature of the materials appropriate to that site and that purpose, then worked "from the inside out" to develop an integrated structure with its own complex, principled life. Not the assemblage of separate design elements that commonly passes for architecture—much as an assemblage of separate selves commonly passes for a person—but an organism subject to the inner laws of its own being. Nothing was to be imposed from without: his response to LeCorbusier's paean to the Golden Section and the regulating line in *Towards a New Architecture* was, "Proportions come after the fact. Why can't these boys understand that?" And beauty comes from within, he could have added.

Because he knew the life principles of his structures, he was never afraid to add, subtract, change. When he strode most happily into the dining room at breakfast, it was usually to order a general turnout for drastic reconstruction of some part of Taliesin. A marvel would be lost, often without record. But no matter: other marvels would appear, and being is becoming. "Perfection" was not part of his working vocabularly, doubtless because perfection leads to stasis.

The unspoken word can be revealing. He avoided "scenery," a word dear to his generation, and was chary with "landscape," presumably because both terms imply a separation of the viewer from what is viewed. It is ironic that the "picture window" was probably derived from him by some circuitous route, for he had no interest in providing pictures. Instead, using his art to break down the barriers which man over the centuries has erected between himself and the rest of nature, he pulled the audience into the act as participant. Building and nature interpenetrate. The modulated flow of space continues. He erased the boundary between exterior and interior by drawing the low soffit of boldly projected roofs back over the glass and into the room, then extended sight-lines at the base by sweeping the floors out to become terraces and verandas. The sky enters in surprising ways, yet never to threaten the dominant, man-scaled horizontal, his "earth line of human life . . . the line of repose." At the Taliesins, by decentralizing the various functions and minimizing indoor passageways, he literally forced himself and his people out into the open for direct bodily sensation of the season of the year, the weather of the moment, the time of their lives. He worked to shock us, those of us who were ready for it, into recognition of our place in nature. But his first concern was to "harmonize his building masses with topography and typify his walls with the natural creation they consort with."

"I knew well," Wright wrote in his autobiography, "that no house should ever be *on* a hill or *on* anything. It should be *of* the hill. Hill and house should live together, each the happier for the other." That last sentence has many layers of meaning. It reminds us that Frank Lloyd Wright was the great form-giver of what Leo Marx calls "the symbolic middle landscape created by mediation between art and nature . . . the landscape of reconciliation," and perhaps more confident than Jefferson or Emerson, Thoreau or Whitman, that in the favorable conditions of the United States a happy resolution could be found to the conflict of artifact and natural fact, city and wilderness, technology and the rural ideal. Echoing Webster's definition of symbiosis as the intimate living together of two dissimilar organisms in a mutually beneficial relationship, he suggests that the life-giving, life-enhancing reality lies neither in the house nor in the hill, but in the place between—the realm of interaction and interchange where Martin Buber found the I-Thou relationship.

Wright's horizon lay beyond the boundaries of reason, and nowhere more so than in the meeting of house and hill at Taliesin in Wisconsin. There, as at Delphi—and, Mircea Eliade tells us, countless other ancient sites—is the navel of the earth and the axis of the world, where sky meets earth and a passing can occur from one cosmic zone to another.

Thirty years ago, on a fine summer morning as I sat talking with Mr. and Mrs. Wright in the old garden of the Museum of Modern Art, he said quietly and with no apparent provocation, "It's been five hundred years since there was an Architect. After me, it will be five hundred years before there is another." His famous New York arrogance had never been more outrageous, yet his assessment of the past seemed fair. Although medieval utopia may be a product of our imagination, and although medieval architecture was evidently designed in mysterious and wonderful anonymity, Wright's buildings are as alive in their various ways as those cathedrals were alive in their ways, while intervening centuries were times of mounting drought as man started worshiping his own sweet marketable Reason and began the long cultural skid into alienation and potential extinction. But Wright's prophecy of the future was unacceptable: arbitrary, and out of line with my need to believe.

Optimism was far more typical. In *Our House,* Mrs. Wright quotes him as saying that "men of stature . . . will come from those who have not divorced themselves from nature. Art, then, will acquire magnitude again." Here no time is set; but we know now, much better than he could have known when he made the pronouncement, that time runs out. If we are to redirect our technology and way of life to deal with emerging crises of energy, food, land, air, water, population, poverty, bombs, war and psychosis, we must collect ourselves in wholeness, quickly.

Frank Lloyd Wright, fortunately, was not a reflection of his splintered society. He was not a modern man. He was a man of the future, if there is to be a future. But architecture in that hypothetical time, when men will again be at lively peace with themselves and the earth and when each hearth will be penetrated by the *Axis Mundi,* will not necessarily be cast in his precise terms. Will our enlightened grandchildren (the day of reckoning closes in) raise up from among themselves great trusted Architects?—or will there once more be a festive anonymity of folk architecture, soaring here and there to cathedral stature?

WRIGHT, THE MAN

BY HENRY KLUMB

THE WORK of Frank Lloyd Wright continues to be convincing evidence of the creative powers latent in America, and indeed that the proclaimed high aspiration of our basically free democratic society can be achieved, and that by achieving, our society will also contribute to the cultural enrichment of other peoples.

Every word written, every building built by Frank Lloyd Wright, expresses the surge for creative truth to bring to earthly efforts spiritual values and an awareness that man belongs to and is an inseparable part of nature. But those who knew him as a whole personality have an obligation to communicate this experience, for it is from the behavior of the man, as well as from his architecture and his writings and ideas, that his significance for our times is to be understood.

Material success achieved at the expense of higher values, eclecticism and emulation as a substitute for creativity he despised. These he always fought, and he considered them, with deep conviction, detrimental to the American ideal.

He saw in the machine a tool to develop new techniques. He visualized the unlimited contribution the machine could make to enrich the art of architecture and the quality of life when in the hands of free creative men. He cautioned against its abuses, warned us that "until we master the machine, the machine will master us"—a statement made at the beginning of this century, as valid today as it was then.

During Frank Lloyd Wright's long evolutionary journey, he succeeded in distilling the workings of his philosophy into realities which defy the passage of time. His work triumphs poetically over commonplace reality, it leads technology, materials, methods, and the work of man into a humane and balanced relationship with beauty. It is the humanization of architecture. It is the concept of organic architecture brought into form.

The personalized characterization of his ideas, combined with an indulged-in joy of human playfulness, obscure, to the uninitiated, the inner forces of creation. The optical only is seen, the irrelevant of it analyzed, a single element of the whole praised or criticized. The encounter with its basic idea, living it, sensing the joy contained in doing it, what made it what it is, to obtain an eternal state of becoming, is missed. To consider its form in a frozen state, an object to be copied or to be emulated, will not liberate one's imagination, stimulate or bring forth the creative possibilities dormant within the viewer, nor will "cutting open the drum, to see where the sound comes from," do anything for the young aspiring to be architects.

All this may be important to the historians and the analyst, but it cannot ignite the spark that awakens deep desire to be involved, to make us aware that in being involved only the Doing matters, not emulation; that *in* Doing, one must give the self the chance to grow, starting at the beginning and adhering to the patterns of growth in nature.

The greatest homage we who knew him could give to Frank Lloyd Wright today is

HENRY KLUMB, FAIA is Puerto Rico's outstanding architect, designer of the principal buildings of the University of Puerto Rico, churches, schools and laboratories, and many examples of social architecture. Born and educated in Germany, he emigrated to Wisconsin to become Wright's "right bower," and lived in the western states until 1944 when he was called to Puerto Rico by then Governor Rexford Tugwell.

to detach ourselves, for a while at least, from the forms of his creations. Drink from the spring of his creative sources, absorb his philosophy and let that spirit which is his flow forcefully through to fill us with his ideas—of which there are so many that, for generations to come, just *one* would be sufficient to achieve one's life fulfillment and to develop in one's *own* right that which one honestly possesses.

Today more than ever before, Frank Lloyd Wright's work and personality are being scrutinized and dissected in minutest detail. Friends try to explain away his human frailties. Detractors deny him his human playfulness, label him a man without social concern, a romantic, an escapist: forgetting, or not knowing, that Frank Lloyd Wright was the first to design steel furniture, a wall-hung toilet, shop-produced pre-cut homes of medium cost, just to call attention to a few of his inventions. He used the new technology and urged the use of it to further the advancement of architecture. That ''Man is the Measure'' he never forgot. The new technology, to be beneficial to men, had to be in the service of man; side by side with advanced methods, the simpler architectural problems of immediate and daily need would remain with us, and should be solved architecturally in simple ways, best accomplished by bridging the dual existence of work and living of the architect.

''The art of work and the art of living,'' the merging of his private life with his architecture, was deeply centered in Wright's being. Architecture he never considered just a profession or a business the architect should indulge in. Architecture needed to be lived, fully, every minute of one's life.

Observation of the organic processes of nature, a deep understanding of the interdependence of all living things with each other and nature, and a realization that all that grows comes ''out of the ground into the light''—this understanding he felt to be essential to any architect worth his calling.

My fortunate introduction to this life, his life, a simple, natural and healthy life, was given me and a few other young architects of different nationalities in early January, 1929. We were trying to escape from the sterile concepts of an international style. At that time he was preparing to leave for Chandler, Arizona, to produce the drawings for San Marcos in the Desert, a resort hotel to be built for Dr. Chandler in the desert of Arizona.

Soon after arriving in Chandler, and after being quartered in a corner of a loft space, with cots brought in to spend the first night, we visited the site, a few miles out of town, on which the hotel would rise. A small hill, allowing a full view of this site, was chosen on which to build our working-living quarters. Sketch layouts for the camp were made that night on improvised drafting tables. Next morning, studs, boards, battens for walls, for rafters and the enclosure of the compound; white canvas to stretch between the rafters, to keep out the elements, also to give light; plywood for drafting tables; and other needed miscellaneous items were bought and taken to the site to carry out the plans put on paper the previous night. Working from sunrise to sunset, Camp Ocotillo, as it was named, came into existence. There it was, rising overnight, sitting dignified, human in scale, on a rocky rise of the desert floor, interwoven into the Arizona landscape, belonging to it, in form interwoven with the geometric triangular-shaped mountains and rock formations, sparkling in the sun with its white canvas roof surfaces, rose-painted lumber walls and the coral-painted flaps providing ventilation, arousing a joyful thankfulness in being alive to every one who came upon it.

All this achieved with bare hands, locally available materials and inexpensive hand tools. Here we experienced in a couple of weeks Frank Lloyd Wright's principle applied. A lesson to be taught without teaching, taking architecture from its pedestal and putting it to a simple task in solving a minor, immediate and pressing need to provide a temporary shelter for work and living, all accomplished within limited economic means, with low cost materials and, of course, with willing hands. Where are the architects today whose dignity would not suffer when called upon to use their hands for menial tasks? This was not below Frank Lloyd Wright's dignity. At the age of sixty he worked side by side with us, showed us how to hammer, how to saw with least exertion, how to coordinate action with rhythm, or to rake patterns on a gravel path with a twist of the wrist.

After a couple of weeks of being subjected to this most basic lesson implied in his concept of organic architecture, work began on San Marcos in the Desert. We worked under the diffused light of white canvas during the day, at night under gasoline pressure lanterns suspended from the rafters until an electric generator was installed (rattlesnakes and sidewinders stayed outside the compound thanks to the wooden fence enclosing it; within the compound by scorpions, enormous spiders, other insects and strange desert creatures, most harmless, some poisonous, congregating by the hundreds on screens placed to keep them off the drafting boards: this nightly assembly Frank Lloyd Wright introduced us to, called it the exuberance of desert life) and his ideas for the desert resort hotel grew, unfolded and were put on paper. By the end of May the work was done, the projected building ready for construction.

In actually living and doing organic architecture I had found, as a 24-year-old, a deeper meaning than that contained in intellectually conceived formulas, imposing frozen solutions without concern to emotional needs of living beings. Here I experienced how Frank Lloyd Wright achieved an architectural and structural unity by devising a simple standardized part made on the site, by hand, of simple easily available materials, in its basic concept also adaptable to future machine tool application.

The structural concept was a double shell of concrete blocks to form a hollow wall, the periphery of the blocks forming a thickened and cored rib to be filled with a concrete mix after vertical and horizontal steel reinforcement bars were placed. The inner and outer shells held in place by tie rods to become a monolithic structure achieved without forms or falsework, woven of standard concrete units, needing no finish inside or out after being placed. Floor and ceilings were formed of single blocks braced until integrally anchored to a structural slab. Needed concentrated structural elements were produced by special reinforcing and filling with concrete hollows between the shells. The size of blocks determined to retain a human scale, the weight by the need of easy handling. Shapes and texture either plain or ornamented to lighten, perforated to give light or ventilation, all depending on the function each part was to serve, on the requirement of spatial needs, intent and interrelations; architectural form, texture and color on the merging with the spirit of the chosen natural setting and not least on the creator's indulgence in his personal poetic playfulness.

By following a modular system, its dimensions and geometric shapes determined by the architectural scale to be maintained, a discipline was established to keep all in harmonious relationship, growing into a related entity, without one element dominating another.

This principle of organic growth will work for any architectural problem and can be applied to any material or structural system. It is as valid to apply to a humble economically limited and undemanding problem as it is to apply to the most demanding complex one. The tapestry can be woven with the same material, except the warp and woof adapts itself to each particular problem. The same stuff is used, the same creative efforts are devoted to its solution, providing a basic human bond holding the pattern created together. By respecting the needs and rights of everyone, architecture as an isolated work of Art, as well as the dehumanization of architecture, becomes impossible.

This is the meaning, to me at least, a lesson to be learned, contained in the humble character of Ocotillo Camp, a temporary structure, and in contrast, the permanent luxurious San Marcos in the Desert. Both were given the right to exist, each in its own way, side by side, and considered worthy of the workings of an organic architecture, its principle applied with equal concern to each.

This lesson was given us in 1929! In 1974, fifteen years after Frank Lloyd Wright's death, we find ourselves deprived of architectural leadership and the voice of conscience. Ever since, on the whole, we have been in a void, we lack a guiding philosophy, a dedication to principles. Ethics and a sense of dedication are absent. We have lost the emotional attachment to architecture, have taken the easy way out and made architecture a business.

No one has voiced so vividly and so clearly the state of today's architecture as Ada Louise Huxtable. She points out, astutely, the causes of the dehumanization of architecture.

We must stop being impressed by bigness. We must question the self-seeking architectural exhibitionism, the use of technology to do the impossible because it is possible. We must end the ostentatious display of superwealth widening the gap between the poor and rich.

But, more than anything else, we must put to work the piercing wit, the inexhaustible spiritual exhuberance, the love and reverence for life of Frank Lloyd Wright that saturated his life, his writings and his buildings.

In his essays "In the Cause of Architecture"—essays long unheeded, now appearing as a timely publication—Frank Lloyd Wright goes to the source from which the basic ideas of organic architecture spring. They appear crystal clear, in simple terms.

Frank Lloyd Wright's genius is alive.

WRIGHT: THEN AND NOW

BY ANDREW DEVANE

OVER twenty-seven years ago, I flagged a truck on a dirt road in the blistering heat of the Arizona desert.

For me it was the last step of a sleepless three-day journey, which started with a miserable March day in Shannon, Ireland; thence by Constellation (at that time the piston-engined queen of the airways) to a blizzard night in a Labrador hut; on to a winter's day in Newfoundland; and from there to a spring evening in New York. A quick change of planes, to the first of a series of those inimitable DC3's—crossing America for the first time, and for the first time realizing the vastness of a continent measured against the small scale of my native Ireland. Finally the heat and glare of the tarmac at Phoenix airport, and the somewhat premature anticipation of my ultimate destination—Frank Lloyd Wright and Taliesin West.

I had written some months before, asking if he would allow me to come and work for him. It was a heartfelt letter, but in retrospect it must have been revoltingly brash and ignorant, worthy only of the wastepaper basket. With student ego, I wrote that I was distressed that there seemed to be so few architects, and so many media-men (even then!)—so many paper tigers, whose words and images far outstripped the sad reality of the architectural eggs they laid. Was he—F.LL.W.—the real architect I had believed in above all others, or was he just another phony?

Incredibly—to my eternal gratitude—he cabled, out of the blue: "Come along and see, Wright."

And so I came, with many difficulties in that postwar period, to Phoenix—with no luggage, and total assets of under two dollars, looking for "Frank Lloyd Wright, Taliesin West." It never even occurred to me that a postal address might be needed. He was one of America's most famous men—for me anyhow—and everyone would know about him. In fact no one did! I checked everything I could think—airlines, post office, telephone, police, hotels and finally people on the streets. No one had ever heard

---

ANDREW DEVANE is an architect who practices in Ireland and lives near Dublin. He studied with Wright in the Taliesin Fellowship, one of many young architects from all over the world who were drawn to Wright's office.

of him, much less of Taliesin. My hopes and expectations sank, with tiredness, to zero, and I realized acutely the meaning of a prophet in his own land. He was that—he certainly still is—some day in more truthful times he will be honored as befits him.

A bus in the street marked "Scottsdale" suddenly jogged my memory; and without any certainty—the bus driver knew nothing—I spent most of my capital on a one-way ticket.

Scottsdale was an outpost, saloon, gas station, a scatter of houses, on the fringe of the desert furnace. There, in the gas station, I met the first American who had heard of F.LL.W. He pointed to a road which ran straight and shimmering into an apparent infinity of desert, and told me that there was no transport in Scottsdale and no telephone in Taliesin.

I started to walk, wondering if I would get there before either sunstroke, nightfall or both, and if I did whether it would have been worth it all.

There were three persons in the truck, which was dun-red under the dust, and loaded with provisions. They were going to Taliesin, and it was the most welcome hitch of my life.

A dark, strikingly beautiful young woman drove with speed and skill. She was F.LL.W.'s stepdaughter and the wife of Wes Peters, Svetlana Peters, who was to die so tragically before the year was out.

Suddenly the truck was slamming diagonally towards a rhythm of white sails, raked beams and stone walls viewed through passing cacti and desert scrub. A long, low magnificent ship anchored securely in a sea of desert, stone masses and tilted white plans counterpointing the mountains, spiking the haze behind it.

I remember, but I could never describe, the release and joy I felt as I walked through these truly wonderful buildings. Here, for me, was—and I hope, still is—the purest architecture that it has been my good fortune to see, and, in part, to help build. Nature, material and space, fused and distilled, with indescribable variety and discipline, by the sure hand of a master. For once, here, for me, there was, between the ideal and the reality, no shadow, no doubt.

Under a low deck, into a beautiful luminous space built with canvas, redwood and stone, a space that flowed into courtyard and desert and which was contained by vistas, mystery, and pools of light and shade. A scatter of artifacts, Eastern and Indian, some obviously priceless; water splashing outside and the sound of children playing . . . An incomparably lovely living space still, in my mind's eye, and still supreme in comparison with all those places and spaces seen since.

A man white-haired, head high, small yet somehow standing tall and relaxed. Keen, questing eyes, formidable, friendly. A gentle resonant voice, words flowing easily. An extraordinary face, that I came to know so well in a short time. Gentle and reflective, humane and ruthless, sad and proud. A succession of faces, moods, characters—a tilt of the head, for all the world a conquistador or a pirate; a dreaminess of speech—then pure, withdrawn, like a contemplative close to the ultimate; a row, argument—a brazen word and a sidelong look, face and actions as willful and hard as a spoilt tycoon; sometimes a face shining with love, humanity, and humility when he touched truths in life and nature and released them in words or crayon.

This, so poorly and personally told, is how I first found a true architect—and true architecture—in Taliesin West.

I owe Frank Lloyd Wright, and all in Taliesin at that time, a great deal—more particularly because I was unable to give them anything worthwhile in return—lacking ability or anything else which would have been useful to him. He was a titan, a genius, a very great architect, but much more to me he was a warmhearted human being, and a dear friend—always remembered with honor.

It seems trite, but it is true to say that he gave me—and others like me—an appreciation of our varying personal philosophies of life, such as we never had before; and in addition he gave us a deep understanding of what I, for one, believe to be the true nature of architecture—an understanding which has been used well or badly by all his apprentices and followers according to their natures and their talents—inevitably in his shadow.

The Taliesins, East and West, were wonderful and stimulating places for the young in heart, always changing, developing, building, all work culminating in the space and peace of the two drafting rooms—a luminous barque in Taliesin West, a dark forest in Taliesin East. The wisdom, management and the all-seeing eyes of Mrs. Wright, dealt with the restless tireless spirit of her master, and at the same time with the mix of apprentices—wise and foolish, young and old, of many creeds, nationalities, disciplines, forming a fascinating human pattern, and needing skill, tact, and a rhythm of daily life that at times would have taxed the ingenuity and the ruthlessness of a commissar!

The deep and lasting friendships that were formed in those dedicated carefree days were, and still are, a source of remembrance and gratitude for many.

And now they say Wright and Corb and Mies—and of course God—are dead, and technology and the media are alive and procreating: wildernesses of words and oceans of waste. Creation is this month's glassy innovation, plus P.R. is genius—strictly for the words. All systems go and come again under new management. Each and all for the golden art. Critics are architecture, and architects have become media men—like crossing sweepers covering holes with dead leaves, or managers, or sociologists.

I cannot speak for Le Corbusier or for Mies Van der Rohe; but there can be little doubt that Frank Lloyd Wright was a genius, and an American, which sets him apart. He can be criticized, reviled, imitated, possibly emulated, but never equalled. Like other men of genius, past, present and to come, he was the child of his time and at the same time master of the past and the future. The hallmark of a genius is not innovation; it is his God-given ability to see, sense, or understand, more clearly than his fellows, the immutable laws and rhythm of creation, mankind, and nature, and the power to fuse this understanding, with reason, passion and imagination, into incomparable reality.

This I believe Frank Lloyd Wright did—instinctively more than intellectually, perhaps, at times—but at Taliesin West, he achieved an incomparable excellence which was as close to perfection as any mortal may go.

The principles he worked to were both simple and profound—they are just as valid today as they will be a thousand years and a billion words from now. They were not his, they have been there since the beginning of time and will be there at the end, for those who have faith and the humanity to look for them, and use them well.

The realization of these principles with art and architecture is something each man must fight for, and forge, for himself alone.

NOW MORE THAN EVER

BY ELIZABETH WRIGHT INGRAHAM

IT WAS many years ago. Guests and apprentices had gathered in the living room of Taliesin, the home of Frank Lloyd Wright, for an evening concert. The musicians began with a Beethoven Trio. It was over all too soon and Mr. Wright asked to have it repeated. It flowed forth again, a beautifully sensitive composition. The musicians finished and Mr. Wright asked to have it repeated yet again. Not quite so lovely this time, the quality of the music a little compromised by the repetition. The end came and with it a silence out of which I could hear the yet unspoken words, "All right, boys, let's try it again." Suddenly, however, a clear voice spoke out, "Enough, not again, it is just too much." Mr. Wright chuckled softly and said, "Well, there's a courageous voice. If you don't speak up, don't expect to change anything."

To Frank Lloyd Wright, the hope for man lay in the ability to change and to speak out on behalf of that change. His own qualification for change lay in the nature of his work, an architecture which embodied forms fashioned as a part of the landscape; a concept of a living environment for human beings. Its first thrust was felt at the turn of the century.

Other men sitting on the verge of that 20th century spoke out strongly. They had a prescience about the course of human events. They suspected that man's inventions would overwhelm him, that man would lose control of his technology. It was not the development of the tools that worried them, it was their use and effect on human beings. It was a time when men were questioning society's directions and rejecting laws which forced people to march blindly together. The thunderous surge of Richard Strauss's music rose to meet the oncoming age. Nietzsche cried out in anger against the abandonment of passion and proclaimed the wasteland. Theodore Roosevelt hammered home the need to conserve natural resources and Walt Whitman wrote powerfully of the grandeur of nature. The voice of John Dewey could be heard defining an education in which reason was applied to everyday life and out of which a human being would remain master of his tools; Clarence Darrow in the courts attempted to bring law into focus and provide truly equitable remedies.

With these men Frank Lloyd Wright rose in the cause of architecture to capture what appeared to be the spirit of a new man in a new shelter. He was to live a long time, a man of many distinct historical occasions who remained prodigiously productive; a man of many and different seasons.

While ideas in these turn-of-the-century men differed, they all optimistically envisioned the 20th century as an opportunity for a greater exercise of reason. Their vision was a man in control of powerful new tools, one who could see his history, his world and his future. Eventually, this optimistic prospect began to lose its shape under the increasing pressure of the more profit-minded prophets, for whom the vision was a man

ELIZABETH WRIGHT INGRAHAM is a granddaughter of Frank Lloyd Wright, architect and director of the Wright-Ingraham Institute, an innovative environmental studies center at Colorado Springs, Colorado.

of power. Scientific achievement, with all its integrity and golden moments of truth was caught in the flames of a burning desire on the part of people to acquire "things." New heroes were found in the movies; in real life we gave them medals and pensions. The arts floundered. The age which refused many of its artists was being left with followers who were caught up in a material world without the dignity that arises from an example that "talks back." And dialogue floundered, too.

Frank Lloyd Wright once said that he would rather have honest arrogance than dishonest humility. He meant, I think, that it is better to stand up and fight for something which offers man a meaningful life than to tolerate a state where indolence and lassitude sit in contempt or ignorance of aspiration. I remember once seeing that graceful, white-haired figure immersed in work over his drafting table while a fire crackled in the fireplace; he seemed timeless. But, no man is timeless and I was seeing instead the timelessness of his ideas, the enormous vitality of his commitment. He was to produce some 500 buildings, hundreds of design projects, a school for architects and a host of published writings. Historians like to suggest the Puritan work ethic as an explanation of such energy; but Michelangelo, for example, lying on his back painting the Sistine Chapel, was no Puritan descendant. Creative fervor is a phenomenon which surpasses such narrow causal explanations; a phenomenon which remains a keystone, indeed, perhaps the entire arch, through which a productive society might walk.

Today, some handle on the past is needed to root ideas; something of that vision in the cause of humanity that endowed the productive work of those men at the turn of the 20th century. A sense of this vision began to rise in the sixties in the United States. Battles raged as young people strove to deflect the obsequious wheels of power. But in itself, the newly drawn constitution of the rising generation was all but a blank page, an unclear future without a past. The civil courage to say "no" which was gained in the sixties had to be turned to the individual courage to say "yes" to the human potential. Yes, to those ideas which would help to examine the questions at the interface of man and environment, redefine education, assess natural resources, question social systems, review community and maintain the long view for a productive human being in a finite world where constructive work would not be consigned to oblivion by being made the remedy for an eleventh hour tragedy.

Frank Lloyd Wright, along with other men of his time, seems very much alive today. The fears which he and they expressed are manifest in the living present, and the hopes that their work embodied are still the future. Now, more than perhaps ever before, it is important to give productive expression to that future community of man and the biosphere; to keep the individual in view, and to realize that "when the legends die, the dreams end, and when the dreams end, there is no more greatness"; and, that without greatness, the hope for a future is left to those whose vision is power rather than the promise of human dignity on a small planet.

TOWARD AN AMERICAN ARCHITECTURE

BY KARL KAMRATH

FRANK LLOYD WRIGHT'S influence and significance to architecture today has only recently begun to make itself felt. However, for years his design attitude has been noticeable on the American scene, as in the popular horizontal American "ranch house," the widespread emphasized use of natural materials such as stone, brick, wood and concrete, the use of corner windows, and the use of the more open plan letting the outside and inside become more nearly unified.

What Wright really gave us was a democratic architecture, an architecture that expressed for the first time unabated freedom, an American architecture. It more fully expresses the individualism, freedom, and democratic way of life of our country than any other architecture. Often Wright referred to it as "Usonian," meaning "United Statesonian," a word coined by Samuel Butler.

We all know that Wright drew upon nature itself for his design inspiration. Organic, as he termed it, simply means a natural architecture. Several times he mentioned to me that nature (in design) was difficult to improve upon.

Nature, in itself, has the inherent quality of the third dimension, or depth. The fascinating quality of depth expressed so strongly and beautifully in Frank Lloyd Wright's work is one of the outstanding qualities attained in his designs. The significance of this aspect of depth is beginning to show itself in current architecture. However, the vast difference in Wright's designs and the designs of the current architects is clearly shown by the beautiful and mysterious way Wright achieved depth in his work compared to the rather clumsy way today's architects attempt to achieve it. The difference, in my opinion, lies in the unusual ability of Wright as a talented and gifted designer. Perhaps as time passes, designers will improve on their ability to achieve balance and depth to the point of producing more beautiful and individual structures; and American architecture could be the great leader, in the same way we have achieved the highest standard of living.

The quality of mystery developed by Wright has always intrigued me. He almost always shunned the obvious to create the mysterious. He often placed the entrance to a structure where one had to look for it, and upon finding it, realize it was tucked into the plan in a very logical and protected manner. Therefore, the beauty and talent of his design became even more apparent as a delightful discovery. An achievement of the beholder.

Further significance of Wright's work for architecture today is seen in the way he conceived a project in the whole. A happy union of exterior landscaping expressed on through to the sensitive development of all interior design is what made his projects so completely and beautifully integrated. It is often difficult to discern where the building stops and the landscape begins, as the outside seems to flow on into the inside. His sensitive use of materials and textures and color are beginning to have some influence on current design.

KARL KAMRATH, FAIA practices architecture in Houston, Texas. He is former chairman of the Texas Planning Commission and for many years has been a leader in the development of the arts in Houston.

It would be well for designers to analyze Wright's organic architecture carefully and fully but not copy it; this, according to Wright, is the worst form of flattery. Instead, he urged designers to apply the principle of organic architecture. This is tedious learning for today's architects, but none the less more meaningful when a designer finally begins to achieve the knowledge that lets him understand the meaning of organic architecture and can experience the thrill of developing his own expression of these principles.

Until about a decade ago, contemporary architecture flourished in every type of project. Unfortunately, the average American designer was turning out work that was very mediocre, uninspired and often downright ugly—all in the name of modern architecture. It wholly lacked the character of livability and good design. Such debased and self-proclaimed modern or contemporary architecture did not fill the need of most clients. After World War II newer materials were developed which too often resulted in the flimsy flat-chested architecture commonly known as curtain wall construction. This was the antithesis of organic architecture and its essential ingredient of depth.

At last, about a decade ago, the American people began to rebel against the so-called modern architecture. It lacked the comfortable feeling and warmth contained in many traditional designs. This was primarily the result of modern architecture ignoring the public craving for a coziness, a warmer, more meaningful character in its structures. Some of the modern houses, churches or business structures were cold and forbidding, and bright raucous colors were not at all easy to live with on a permanent basis. Contemporary architecture had generally become so sterile and offensive and lacking in character that the public sought the more comfortable and pleasing designs offered by the various traditional styles. In came the mansard roof era with all its many ramifications. Traditional design was in again! Modern buildings were and are being remodeled to traditional styles by sticking on mansard roofs and false columns.

Here is where Wright's organic architecture showed itself so well. It was individual, warm and friendly, was realized with natural materials, contained an air of mystery, and blended so well with the site it rested on and became a part of.

If American designers can capture, without copying, the basic spirit and integrity of Wright's organic architecture in all types of projects, large and small, we may yet see the rise and more universal development of an individual American architecture. It will take great time and sacrifice along with unusual talent and dedication of young designers to accomplish this. But consider the titanic effort of Wright. He never gave up and was working harder near the end than ever before. He knew he had a message for America. A favorite 1954 quote of Mr. Wright's was: "Integrity is not something to be put on and taken off like a garment. Integrity is a quality WITHIN and OF the man himself. So it is in a building." The least we can do is to carry on his great effort with courage and talent. He showed us the way and I trust we have enough good young talent that one day we will truly achieve a known and recognizable American architecture, democratic, beautiful, useful, and full of American spirit.

A HUMANE AND ENVIRONMENTAL

BY VICTOR HORNBEIN

THE American Institute of Architects' Honor Awards Program juries in 1973 and again in 1974 gave the 25-year award to buildings designed by Frank Lloyd Wright. The first of these, Taliesin West, was Wright's own home and school near Phoenix, Arizona, begun in 1938. The following year, the jury selected his buildings for the Johnson Wax Company in Racine, Wisconsin, built 1946-47. The award is given annually to a building of "enduring significance at least a quarter-century old."

The awards for each year presumably represent the best work done in America during the preceding three to eight years. These award-winning buildings are not necessarily a fair sampling of contemporary American work; but along with those published in the architectural journals of the past few years, they provide an overview of contemporary architecture which makes it clear that, regardless of the "enduring significance" of much of Wright's work, his influence is not widespread, and his architectural philosophy, as expressed in his buildings, has few followers.

The paradox of the simultaneous recognition of Wright and of works antithetical to his philosophy suggests the question of the validity of the past in solving today's problems. It also suggests that while current work, generally, viewed in the context of today, may be excellent, viewed from a longer, more objective distance, and keeping society as a whole within the frame, there are serious shortcomings.

Consciously or not, each generation strives to express its own times, and leans generally to the idea that works of the past are of little value in supporting the solutions necessary for today. There is some validity in this approach to functional problems: Life is not lived in the fashion of the past, business is conducted quite differently today, and products, services and institutions exist with no earlier counterpart. Wright developed the open plan, in response to such changing needs.

Still, generations are indefinite periods of time; the medieval period did not suddenly change and give way to the Renaissance. Time is continuous and each man's life is built on the lives of those who went before him. The long struggle for freedom, still not completely won, built each small victory on the successes and the failures of earlier

VICTOR HORNBEIN, FAIA practices in Denver. Among his important projects is the Conservatory of the Denver Botanical Garden. A native of Denver, he has developed an outstanding regional style, expressed in many institutional buildings, which have received widespread recognition and awards.

ARCHITECTURE

years. All of the great innovations in politics, in science, in architecture, would have been impossible without the work of preceding statesmen, scholars and architects.

Given the functional changes and technologic advances which have provided new materials and constructional techniques, architectural expression changes as a matter of course. But there are principles at work in the architect's mind, verbalized or not, which determine the conformation of plan, the relationship between elements—in sum, the total building, encompassing change and meeting the physical needs of the occupants.

Adherence to a set of fundamentals does not necessarily produce great architecture, but their absence produces buildings which appear to have designed themselves. The world is full of such buildings, and their existence derogates man.

Based on his philosophy of man and man's relation to the environment, Wright developed a set of principles governing functional and esthetic solutions. The principles are of a sufficiently high order of generality that they direct, rather than determine, architectural characteristics; and they constitute a quality that identified Wright's buildings.

The idea of a personal architecture seems to be held in low esteem today. Certainly, the words carry a pejorative connotation. Whether this is negatively derived from the accepted technique of team design is not clear. It may be an expression of the influence of the steadily increasing size and power of bureaucratic structures which characterize contemporary society. Bureaucracy has little room for individual effort, and its functioning is dependent upon conformity. Its values are not consanguine with personal or individual effort or expression. It is clear that the work of most architects today is indistinguishable, one from the other. It seems clear, also, that the mass media constitute the most influential design partners.

Wright's vocabulary grew out of his principles logically and inevitably and all with a particular quality that gives his buildings a semblance of life—"the form and the function are one." It is this quality, primarily, that has made his work enduring, with every part, as well as the whole, expressing its function as a symbolic organism.

Architectural symbolism as well as vocabulary derive from fundamental principles, and the absence of symbolism in current work seems indicative of the absence of basic philosophy. The old symbols have been rejected and when new ones have been tried they have been confused, as when Marshall McLuhan's concepts were transposed to architecture. For example, a building was recently designed as an abstraction of the working parts of a television set as a means of symbolizing electronic communication. The building happened to be a university library. It mistook an abstract representation for a symbol. Furthermore, it elevated the communication technique rather than man communicating. It signified a confusion of the container with the thing contained. For the most part, the conceptualization of today's buildings does not appear to include symbolic content. The expression of a workable plan is confused with the symbolization of functional existence. Wright used the word organic to describe a special quality of a building when it carries the image or semblance of life, the same quality one finds in a Cezanne painting.

Without symbolism there isn't much left. Indeed, the notions generating the "pop architecture" movement, a form of anti-architecture, have gained some acceptance and become something of a school. It is argued that buildings should express the "ordinary." By being ordinary they are a true expression of society. This is an acceptable argument if one's premise excludes the spirit of man as a requirement of the art of architecture. This argument assumes that the ordinary is the outermost limit of man's capability.

In recent months the architectural journals have published check lists of design means aimed at the conservation of energy. It is interesting to note that most of Wright's buildings have the characteristics recommended, characteristics which developed from his belief that nature is a determinant in the conceptualization of a human environment. Reading the checklists gives more than enough evidence to support the fact that current architecture has been nature's antagonist with technology as weapons; a would-be conqueror rather than a welcome guest. Because man *can* build is not sufficient reason for him *to* build buildings inappropriate to climate or terrain; there is even less reason when no esthetic purpose is served.

The glass building is an example. It is possible that it began with Wright's own attempts to abandon "the box with holes punched in the sides." His aim was to achieve an internal spatial quality that related to external space, a free flowing space uninhibited by closed corners, in section as well as in plan. Parallel with the spatial problem was the problem of fenestration which Wright and succeeding generations of architects solved with the strip window. The strip window was followed by the floor to ceiling window. Finally, by making the entire building a window the problem ceased to exist.

The difficulty, however, was that the solution created a new problem, that of extra-ordinary heat loss in winter and heat gain in summer.

Wright's solution in the Price Tower in Bartlesville, Oklahoma, was to shade the walls—horizontal shades on the south and vertical on the east and west. Screening the sun from the interior spaces reduces the radiant heat gain considerably. The typical solution is technological: larger mechanical systems, insulated and half mirrored glass which, while reflecting a considerable amount of heat, still admits more heat than would enter were the glass shaded externally. The price is extremely high energy consumption.

The unshaded, mirror-walled box has arrived. Large and small, it is appearing everywhere—in the city, the suburb and the country, from the rock-bound coasts of Maine to the sun-drenched deserts of California. It stands comfortably or soars with ethereal grace in a few lovely meadows and in some hospitable climates, but elsewhere it is remarkably unsuitable.

The glass box, along with the abandoned screened façade and tens of other already rejected fashions, good in some of the prototypes, wearily familiar in their mass replications, have become unintentional symbols of the faceless, undifferentiated society that produced them. The glamour of technological innovation is the only apparent objective.

The glass building is not at fault, nor is it the only architectural concept that has been abused by insensitive, unnecessary repetition. Indiscriminate use is not its worst fault. Generally, the glass building has been stripped of scale—any scale, suitable or not. It has been used for dormitories, office buildings, classrooms, hotels, apartment houses, factories, powerhouses, dwellings—and rarely does it identify itself. It has, most certainly, become the symbol of the period.

Indigenous architecture, buildings that express their function, are concepts of Wright that have been forgotten. Scale is another. Wright felt strongly about scale and man's place in the universe. His houses, particularly, express his feelings, but the larger institutional buildings also have that quality. The scale of Wright's buildings expresses his belief that man is elite among organisms, but that he is physically less than midway in stature between the smallest visible organism and the largest.

Until a few centuries or so ago, most important buildings designed by architects were built to acclaim the glory of God or the preeminence of the state, and their scale was enlarged, as much to diminish the stature of the common man as to express the magnificence of his gods or his government. Wright scaled his buildings to man. The result heightened the expression of humanism and gave to the building the feeling that its purpose was to shelter, rather than dominate.

Today, we have a triumvirate. Corporate Business joins God and Government to demand glorification, and so we continue to build buildings of Superman scale. Emulating these powers, contemporary houses and condominiums are of the same scale. The pretense of grandeur is a poor defense and does not render man invulnerable to the frustrations of encounters with intractable Government or Corporation computers.

We could manage reasonably well if our conflict with scale were limited to the scale of our buildings. Unfortunately, we are surrounded and beset by things of enormous scale—the city or, rather, the megalopolis, the endless cloverleafs, the bureaus, both public and private, and on and on.

Wright never really had a following in America. Many of his professional colleagues held his work in high regard; but for the most part, architects of his own and the following generation either shrugged him off as a student of the master, Louis Sullivan, or ignored him completely as an untutored rebel who had no aim in view except that of upsetting the establishment. Succeeding generations readily adopted the outward forms of Internationalism and the Bauhaus, without the underlying principles of philosophy indirectly influenced by Sullivan and Wright. Except for a handful of architects in each generation, little attention was given to either Wright's work or the philosophy that generated it.

Looking back through the eighty-odd years since Wright began his architectural career, there have been unprecedented technological advances. The boundaries of man's knowledge have expanded exponentially. Social thinking has kept pace, and modern society has little in common with those years. Then, as now, the climate of anti-intellectualism has clung to American society. The intellectual has always been viewed with distrust in politics and business. Socially, he has been banished as an impractical idealist. As has been noted by eminent historians, Americans have had little regard for philosophy and, instead, have revered pragmatism. It is this quality which has persisted into the space age and which has kept Wright outside of the mainstream of architectural thought.

By 1890 architecture had already become more business than profession. The architect-artist identity had lost its reality and was becoming a legend. Even though industry was beginning to show signs of its future role as the latter-day Medici, businessmen had little patience with the serious artist except as his work lent social prominence to the owner.

Wright entered this stage costumed as artist; and, to make matters worse, he spoke his own lines—an architectural philosophy written in terms of morality. For many of those today who read his essays or view his completed buildings, his act is as unacceptable as it was then, and for the same reasons. Buildings are thought of in terms of net return, minimum standards of construction, amenities where they show, and then something innovative to attract attention.

Wright may be honored as one honors an artist by housing his paintings in a museum, but his philosophy of architecture is overlooked or rejected. Population growth, the social unrest of the last decade, and related factors, led the present generation of architects to misinterpret his humanism as an expression of a socially select group. His architecture was viewed by those who espoused the then popular advocacy movements as conspicuous waste that probably had racism as a motive. The aims of those movements were good and just, but like so many other movements they were single-minded. They mistook the part for the whole and rejected without examination everything which fell outside the narrow path on which they had committed themselves.

The violence of the sixties seems to be quieting and there are indications that a few students have become interested in Wright and his architecture, but the economic climate still seems hostile to the idea of a single building expressing the individuality of humanism. As more and more people inhabit the earth, as international corporations grow bigger, as government continues to enlarge and play an ever increasing part in the lives of everyone, the need increases for, among other things, an architecture which speaks of and to individual man and becomes an organic part of what is left of the unspoiled earth.

WRIGHT: THE ELEVENTH DECADE

BY EDGAR KAUFMANN, JR.

IT IS NOW fifteen years since Wright died, in his ninetieth year. What is left of his work? What do we think of his architecture and its guiding principles? Do we think of these things at all?

Wright's very personal forms have not proved viable in other hands. Whenever they are echoed they have a strange ring. Wright's words survive, but most often as aphorisms applicable to every kind of architecture. We are stopped, challenged, chiefly by his designs and actual buildings. Subject to time's tooth or man's indifference, these still speak to us powerfully, in ways that are unexpectedly direct.

This is because Wright's work embodies three ideas ardently alive today, ideas that are bound to continue to influence architecture. Wright's intent was to make principles manifest; there surely will be more to discover in his designs as time goes on. But now, these three ideas appear clearly related to the current scene: *Territoriality, Clustering, Indeterminacy.*

Territory and environment are twin concepts that dominate our hopes today. In the exploration of these themes, we trust that a working relationship between man and society can be reestablished between society and the natural order. Here is the very source of Wright's architecture. From the start, as he told it, even before he became aware of his own direction, Wright struggled to formulate a particular kind of territoriality, one more responsive to the environment than was usual, or ever had been usual, in the art of building. He called it "the destruction of the box." In his works, beginning with his own home of 1889, he established territories, centered in kernels of matter or space, and extending responsively and, as shown in the Walter Gerts project, even more freely into the environment. It will be possible to show, I think, that in Wright's usage, clusters and indeterminacy are natural developments from this nuclear form. Thus it seems worthwhile to dwell a moment on the expression of territoriality Wright chose, and on its place among other patterns of territoriality recognized by scientists now at work.

When the American Association for the Advancement of Science held its 1968 annual meetings, one paper contributed by Glen McBride, professor of psychology at the University of Queensland, outlined four basic patterns of territorial activity found in animal life. These were not typical of species or genera, but rather of moments and situations in the lives of the animals; some patterns appeared during mating and rearing of the young, some during migration, etc. Certain of these patterns are very close to

EDGAR KAUFMANN, JR. is adjunct professor of Architecture and Art History at Columbia University, where he has taught since 1963. He studied with Frank Lloyd Wright in 1933-34, and soon after was instrumental in initiating the building of Fallingwater, his parents' country house at Bear Run, Pennsylvania, now open to the public.

Reprinted from *Architectural Forum*, June 1969, courtesy of *Architecture PLUS*.

human expressions we find incorporated in architecture. The patterns can be identified (in my words, not Professor McBride's) as the Defended Perimeter (stockade, moat, castle); the Domain Center or Hub (Wright's nucleus); the Center in Motion, affecting surrounding areas as it moves; and the Center in Motion Forward, with reduced influence to the sides and back. When architecture and design for nomadic living become more amalgamated—a moment perhaps not too far off—the two later patterns may come into play for architects.

So far, only the first two are pertinent. And it is clear that Wright opted for, and developed expressions for, the one pattern of territoriality that represents the individual and the group in receptive contact with the environment. Becoming more aware of the trend in his own work, the pattern came into his view. The fortified clearing, held despite inimical forces and creatures, was typified by its wall. The nucleus, receptive to the world around but able to be protected as needed, was typified by the central hearth and sheltering roof, with screens to direct movement and give privacy. Wright's "destruction of the box" was not an esthetic campaign waged to establish new shapes and details, but a struggle to sense an appropriate way for man to behave in the world around him, with the world around him.

As Wright developed this sense of territoriality through the 1890's and early 1900's, he began to consider the possibilities of grouping architectural nuclei. At first he played cautiously with groups not dissimilar to good residential development schemes of the day. But, even in designing for single commissions, he found opportunities to cluster functions expressively along axes of motion and at their intersections. This trend appeared well developed in the Martin house of 1904 in Buffalo (now remodeled to serve a university). The grid was rectangular, a field of modules within which major and minor nuclei and screens were spotted freely, rhythmically. None of Wright's early demonstrations of this mastery have survived in reasonable condition; but from fragments, drawings, and photographs it is possible to establish how he combined the ancient device of modules with his nuclear theme to enhance the vocabulary of an architecture of clusters dominating territories.

Modular designs carried into the third dimension was another device taken by Wright from older practice, and again he began his experiments in projects for estate development. The grandest of these was a scheme of 1921 for the Doheny ranch in California. Here Wright combined a system of concrete blocks, tied by networks of vertical and horizontal reinforcing rods, with a plan based on a spiral roadway circling over mountain gorges and, every so often, expanding into supremely romantic, nuclear habitations. His imagination, loosened from the thrall of rectangularity, began to play with arcs, and with angles of other than 90 degrees.

Wright developed modular grids based on 60 and 120 degrees—hexagons and equiangular triangles. A fluidity of plan emerged that required unusual care and judgment as the forms were projected spatially; an example is the Cudney project. By 1927, schemes for the San Marcos in the Desert hotel, and its related residences, showed nuclei woven in a new mesh of angular shapes and gliding pathways that had been evolved in the context of Arizona terrain and climate. Balked by the economic debacle from realization, this system waited until, ten years later, it could be adapted and launched at the Hanna residence of Palo Alto. With diagonal modules Wright's architecture accepted the motility of dance; it provided a structure for movement, endowing every-day existence with some of the expressive scope of ritual and ceremony. Wright's work, in a sense, became an architecture of happenings.

At this same time points and pools of repose appeared in other of Wright's projects. Clustered circles were loosely arranged, as in the scheme for Ralph Jester's house, or regularly ranged, as are the point supports of the newspaper plant projected for Oregon as early as 1931. In the 1940's, tangential circles formed the pattern of a co-operative development scheme, each house the nucleus of its circular plot, all embedded in jointly held forest land.

The interplay between nucleus and clustering showed Wright the rich rewards of a casual use of strict elements; he had found a way to that blending of simplicity and complexity which artists have always envied in nature.

In the later years of his life, Wright could not resist the challenge of transposing this experience to the realm of single geometric forms. Over a long period, primary solids had appeared in his designs: the cube of Unity Temple; the cone of the huge Inter-Faith Cathedral projected in steel; the curious sphere suggested as a vacation house for Huntington Hartford. Wright now pursued ways and means of enlivening these ideal forms, tempering their purity while maintaining wholeness in each case. A new level of indeterminacy made its appearance in his work. The mature early houses and build-ings had, as it were, led space around cores and between screen walls so ingeniously that an element of uncertainty, of adventure within the context of the composition, had been a distinguishing mark of this architecture. In clustering, this had been united with the reassurance of modular rhythms. Now safeguards were abandoned, platonic solids were lifted free of the ground, or nearly so, and inflected enough that space itself, and not just the inhabitants, seemed involved in the dance. Wright called this continuity, and of course its major expression is found in the Guggenheim museum, or would be were that museum ever to be completed with the varied illumination and screening that was meant to articulate the now barren, repetitive ramp. Within that spiral nebula of space as Wright planned it no star of art would seem blanched or blurred.

Continuity incorporated in a simple geometric solid (the cube, the cone, or the sphere) was also essayed by Wright in lesser but more fortunate works. The square block of space, which is so forthright at Unity Temple, was often varied—though never more subtly than at the Douglas Grant house, gleaming amid the hills near Cedar Rapids. A high sliver of space, defined by a square screen of glass and a flat roof, is entered down a swift, narrow gorge of stairs from the hilltop. Before the living space itself is reached, a platform breaks the rhythm, leading off to a raised dining area. Above, the main bedroom has panels opening onto the principal space. At ground level the sheer glass walls separate terraces from living room, though all share a level floor. Thus uncertainty and clarity are continually juxtaposed and ideality is refreshed, not denied, by incident.

Wright's great conic cathedral project was, much later, transposed into a smaller synagogue outside Philadelphia. Here the form is lifted up, allowing a sloping auditorium floor that is faceted to correspond to the faceting of the translucent roof. Below, subsidiary spaces are accommodated. Within the main room, approached by ramps, a space crystal seems suspended in eternity, ready to cradle the congregation in the unending motion of creativity.

So too, Wright modified the rigid enclosure of a sphere until it became paired upper and lower shells, a saucer dome over a stepped, concave floor form, as in the Bailleres project for Acapulco. Gently recurving and softly hovering around an ideal center, these cupped surfaces are linked by a film of glass, they let light in from a central skylight, and masses of stone anchor the movement in an inglenook of intimacy and warmth The same shapes are used to different advantage in the scheme for a Greek Orthodox church near Milwaukee (executed with some loss of refinement). In these designs the crushing self-centeredness of sphere and hemisphere has been overcome, tamed to the use of human living.

These late, mature statements of Wright's architecture transmute his exploration of territoriality and flowing space into concentrated paeans of purity in flux. Our modern sense of indeterminacy, of the constant interchange between energy and matter, between man and milieu, between aim and act, is given form. No other age has asked this of its architects, no other civilization has openly pursued these insights into the realm of living matter. So far, Wright has blazed a trail for our times.

A LANGUAGE AFTER WRIGHT

BY BRUNO ZEVI

IN THEORY a dilemma exists between mannerism and language. However, as mannerism is exclusive of an elite, only language sounds plausible. It is my contention that a democratic language can be elaborated on the basis of Wright's work; but a few words should perhaps be spent to show why mannerism, where architecture is concerned, offers no solution out of the present impasse.

Vasari used the term *maniera* to indicate the confluence of Michelangelo's and Raphael's styles, a contamination of signs in sixteenth century painting. Such an operation would have been inconceivable in architecture and, in fact, nobody ever attempted to find a meeting point between Buonarroti's dramatic "non-finito" and Sanzio's metaphysical spaces. In consequence, mannerism in architecture acquired a vague and ambiguous meaning: it stood for an intellectual, sophisticated process directed to unbind, decompose and humanize the classical rules, the *a priori* precepts, the ideological abstractions of a "universal architecture" which nobody really accepted, not even Bramante.

But what happened when classicism was not there to be abjured? Is it possible to have a mannerism from anti-classical trends, from Michelangelo, Borromini or Wright? The answer, most unfortunately, is negative. After Michelangelo, we had half a century of architectural platitudes, with only the exception of Giacomo del Duca's grotesque. A similar desert after Borromini, until he was resumed in a decorative sense during the seventeenth century. What about Wright, fifteen years after his death? Almost no trace, in spite of the efforts of his disciples and of ten or twenty fans of organic architecture scattered around the world.

Now, why is it that the great creative geniuses, all anti-classical, are so immediately erased from the architectural scene? This is a crucial question often discussed by semiologists to-day, also because the same does not seem to occur in literature and poetry, painting, sculpture and music. As is known, in verbal language De Saussure made a distinction between *langue* and *paroles*. The *langue* is what is commonly spoken, a codified instrument of communication. The *paroles* instead are devised by poets and artists who contest the prevailing code and suggest an alternative to it. Such a scheme could be pretty well applied to architecture, but it has been constantly misused because semiologists and critics, old and new, consider as *langue* not what is actually "spoken" or "written" in building, but what has been theorized by the academy, in the Beaux-Arts *trattati* of all ages. Thus misinterpreted, De Saussure's distinction loses its meaning; so much so that while, in verbal *langue,* the *paroles* are slowly assimilated

BRUNO ZEVI is the editor of *l'Archittetura* and author of an influential weekly column of architectural criticism in *L'Expresso.* He is professor of architectural history at the University of Rome. Since his publication of *Toward an Organic Architecture* in 1945, he has written many books of architectural history and is the leading European interpreter of the American architectural tradition of Richardson, Sullivan and Wright.

into the common code and transform it, in architecture no exception is legitimized in the official rules which remain abstract and superstructural, totally inelastic and impermeable. No *paroles* by Michelangelo or Borromini could enter the architectural code of classicism, which was there to negate all derogations and enrichments. Analogous phenomenon for Wright. His *paroles* were blows on classical livers. They were more or less tolerated while he was alive: as the heretic could not be killed, the attempt was made to institutionalize him with a couple of gold medals. Once dead, however, his ghost was exorcized. In the last fifteen years, we had all kinds of architectural fashions, Beaux-Arts revivals in pseudo-modern forms, anti-heroic attitudes, "modern architecture is dead" schizophrenias, even some late Corbu-mannerisms, but Wright was forgotten to the joy of those who cannot stand the very notion of genius.

Architects are indeed a strange and comic breed in the human zoo. One would expect that, when a creative mind has upset the codified building *langue* to a point of substituting it with a new language, the following generation would be busy in diffusing and popularizing it, also in order to free it from the "mortgage" of the genius' mystics. This would be logical (didn't it happen after Schönberg with dodecaphony?) but it is rare in architecture. Only a very few, selected people are manneristic in respect not to abstract principles, but to real masters; and in general these few are not concerned with simplifying and making available the master's *paroles,* so as to translate them in new language. On the contrary, usually they further complicate the *paroles,* they elaborate them more and more intellectually, until they get tired of such narcissistic exercise and abandon it.

A Wrightian mannerism is therefore an illusion, even if the attempts made by the Taliesin Foundation to realize some of the master's projects deserve appreciation. But to save Wright's heritage from total dissolution, a more radical and courageous operation is needed. To put it in paradoxical terms, we should be able "to extract new rules out of the exceptions," formulating a modern language of architecture based on *paroles* which can be used by all architects and builders, and understood by the public at large.

Some verbal languages developed just in this way. Leaving out the peculiar case of Yiddish which, as Kafka said, "the people never handed over to the grammarians," take the Italian. It was born out of the disintegration of Latin and was spoken by the non-literates much before it was by the intellectuals: the *volgare,* for some centuries, was an instrument of communication without being a formal, codified language. Then a genius appeared, Dante, and adopted the *volgare* in the *Divine Comedy,* disregarding Latin which, by this time, had become a rigid, artificial idiom. The Italian was codified after Dante: its genetic process started from the people, culminated through the greatest poet's intervention, and went back to the people. Could not something similar happen in architecture?

The *volgare* is here: it is all the "architecture without architects," from peasants' homes to barriadas, barracks, hippies' domes. It implies the refusal of all styles, principles, trends, laws and assumptions. It is perhaps the "zero degree" of architecture. Substantially, Wright started at this level, because he rejected the whole Hellenistic-Roman tradition (the architectural Latin) which had been dominant for almost two thousand years. However, he did not stop there: he created an alternative language, whose feedback and check-control was the zero degree, forms deriving not from preceding forms, but from behavior. Fallingwater, the Kaufmann House at Bear Run, Pennsylvania, may be considered his *Divine Comedy*. Now, the question is: are we ready to extract a language from Fallingwater?

Surely, many architects are not ready, and for a number of reasons: some prefer to indulge in aristocratic mannerisms; others are afraid that, formulating a new language, we would be slaves of a modern academy; quite a few simply do not care or they are in love with their own private crises. The majority does not want to become mature.

Prehistory is conventionally divided from history by the use of writing, that is by the formalization of a developed instrument of communication. Of course, people did communicate somehow even before the invention of writing, but the revolutionary turning point was caused by this objective, verifiable system. In the same way, today we do communicate (more or less) in architecture; however, in order to leave the infantile stage, we should develop a coherent language. To celebrate the fifteenth anniversary of Wright's departure, such an hypothesis could at least be discussed.

A language is based on some constant elements, often called "invariants." Tentatively, we could examine seven "invariants" for an architectural language derived from Wright and, in fact, from the whole experience of the modern movement:

1. list, or inventory of functions
2. dissonances
3. anti-perspective tri-dimensionality
4. four-dimensional decomposition or dismemberment
5. cantilever, shell and membrane structures
6. temporalization of space
7. building-town-territory reintegration

These invariants are much simpler than they sound, and perhaps better names could be found. They are connected with precise historic phases of modern architecture, all of them present in Wright's work. They do not dictate what you should do designing a building, but what you should not do. The rules of classicism are based on "orders"; those of anti-classicism are anti-rules, reject all "orders" of any kind, are seven votes of "no" against dictatorship and repression in life as well as in art. Let us examine them again.

The list method dates back to the Arts and Crafts movement, to the preaching of William Morris. It means "no" to all conventions, habits and ready-made phrases, "no" to all esthetic taboos such as proportion, equilibrium, balance, eurythmic and other trifles, "no" to all "orders" with or without columns. No more grammar, no more syntax, no more verbs. Rather, an honest lining up of functions in a free, descriptive way, without any worrying about their formal relationships, or the final effect. No *a priori*, no concluded process, and therefore no Hellenic, Roman and Rennaissance approaches. A building should grow, expand or contract, like an organism. The classical dogma of a perfect object, to which nothing can be added or subtracted, is refused. The usual "words" of architecture are re-analyzed in order to give them back their semantic value. A notion like "window," for instance, disappears, the problem being how to get light into a space. Strictly functional words, one after the other, changeable as human living may suggest, with no synthesis, neither *a priori* nor *a posteriori*. Morris was looking at the early Middle Ages, because then the invariant of the list prevailed as a result of the destructuring of the classical precepts and orders. The list incarnates the "zero degree" of architectural writing. It is the first and most important principle of the contemporary architectural language, the one that prevents retrogressions in the academy, old and new.

Dissonances. Classicism tries to rub out the individual character of architectural elements (a colonnade is important, not each single column; so a sequence of windows, not each single functional opening). The modern approach, through the list principle, gives back to each ingredient its specific physiognomy: supports, windows or doors may all be different, according to different uses. But how to get together the differentiated components derived from the list process? Classicism needs uniformity to achieve a rhythmical consonance for the whole. The modern approach, on the contrary, not believing in a static whole, emphasizes the dissonances. This principle was well expressed by Schönberg when he stated that, in contemporary musical language, dissonances were no longer piquant sauces of consonances, but autonomous alternatives to them. No dogmatic rules with a few derogations, but exceptions as a rule. Schönberg discovered this invariant after the experience of atonalism which is, in some ways, a parallel to the list. Atonalism meant total destructuring of the musical speech, and therefore the independence of each element from what comes before and after it. Dissonance was then the instrument to formulate a new grammar and syntax or, better, to control the scientific consistency of anti-grammar and anti-syntax. In European architecture dissonances were basic both in the Art Nouveau movement and later in the Bauhaus.

Anti-perspective tri-dimensionality. It involves cubism, the end of a privileged viewpoint, the moving of the observer around, under, above, inside the architectural object. As a consequence, it means the end of the façades and, even more, of the hierarchy of façades To obtain such dynamic tri-dimensionality, cubism destroys the building mass, but expressionism does not. Cubism denies the matter values. Expressionism discovers a kinetic factor in the very nature of materials and exalts it. Think of Gaudi and Mendelsohn. In both cases, the Renaissance perspective vision is surpassed, without reducing building materials to cardboard.

Four-dimensional decomposition. It is the nucleus of the "De Stijl" theory. Breaking up the building box into slabs, and then reassembling the slabs in such a way that they could never reproduce the box. In other words, to kill the perspective tri-dimensionality, go back to bi-dimensional elements, and then proceed to their dynamic assemblage. The "De Stijl" principle, which was the only conscious attempt to give a grammar and a syntax to modern architecture, derived from Wright's work, found its best representation in Mies van der Rohe's European buildings, and determined the Bauhaus design method from 1924 on.

Cantilever, shell and membrane structures. This invariant is the result of the nineteenth century engineering epic. Its real meaning is that all architectural members should be involved in the structural play, avoiding or limiting the tremendous waste of the traditional building fabric. To the classical dichotomy, structure/architecture, is opposed the principle of architectural elements which are structural.

Temporalizing space. Einstein's vision applied in architecture. Or, if you like, the "De Stijl" theory transferred from the box to the contents, from volumes to cavities. It took centuries and centuries for man to recognize the positive, creative meaning of space, because, from prehistory to the Pantheon, "voids" were looked upon with mistrust and fear. Then it took more centuries to free space from static conceptions, and in fact the whole architectural itinerary may be interpreted as a clash between dynamic conceptions (Late-Roman, Middle Ages, Brunelleschi, Michelangelo, Borromini, etc.) and revivals of static conceptions (Renaissance, neoclassic, Beaux-Arts, etc.). Static space is typical of authoritarian regimes: Fascism and Stalinism. Dynamic space is emblematic of the community life and of the democratic scene. Only during the one period was space annihilated in architecture and did time prevail: this was in the catacombs, miles and miles of underground streets with no landing-places and arrivals. In this peculiar epoch, dominated by a metaphysical philosophy, by the idea that real life was to come after death, time-architecture corrodes space-architecture (the monumental, static, spectacular, classical city of Rome) at its very foundations. But soon, as Norris Kelly Smith has shown in *Frank Lloyd Wright—A study in architectural content,* when Christianity leaves the underground and its Hebrew origin, we have a compromise between time and space, biblical and Greek approaches, with continuous academic temptations to privilege space. Sant'Ivo alla Sapienza's spiral by Borromini turns upside down the visual configuration of the cupolas: it goes up instead of going down. However, the

Guggenheim Museum's spiral does the same in human, functional sense, not merely on a symbolic level.

Reintegration or continuity between building and town/landscape, and between town and territory. End of architecture as pure, isolated object, which implies its availability to absorb the urban *Kitsch* and be contaminated by it. Pop-architecture is satisfied to absorb. Action-architecture is not, as it is based on a dialectic process of absorbing and intervening in a creative key. The principle of reintegration may be compared to Einstein's idea of ''field,'' which was adopted by some critics in relation to Taliesin West in Arizona.

These seven invariants, even if so schematically enunciated, make a language which is intrinsically antithetic to the abstract one of classicism. Of course, Wright did not always use all of them: some of his houses are symmetric, others do not temporalize space. This is quite natural. A new language is not born in one day, and keeps many elements of the old language that it rejects. The new *paroles,* at the beginning, are exceptions to the rule, dissonances added to the preceding code or *langue.* But then such *paroles* make a new *langue,* or perhaps do without it. Wright created this new language, although he did not formulate it in a systematic theory. Fallingwater embodied all the seven invariants to a dramatic tension—a poetic tuning-fork. What is capital, however, is that Fallingwater's language, like the one derived from the *Divine Comedy,* can be used commonly in everyday life, as an elementary means of communication.

This is probably our cultural task today: to formulate a language which may enable all architects and non-architects to ''speak'', ''write'' or, at least, ''read'' architecture in a modern, democratic way. Fifteen years after his death, we could proceed to translate Wright's message in a popular idiom.

I don't see any other way out of the present impasse. Up to the sixties, we could manage without a language, because we had a father—among the masters of modern architecture—who fed and supported us. Now we are like orphans, bewildered, not knowing what to do. Some vainly look for a stepfather, be it Louis Kahn or computer-architecture. Others try to take shelter in the mother-womb of an obsolete academy. Few of the best explore mannerism, studying, more than the masters, their early imitators like Terragni or Schindler: a fascinating but transient escape. The majority is skeptical and sometimes cynical. All this is, indeed, rather infantile, and becomes demagogic when it defers the responsibility of a new architecture to the apocalyptic rising of a new society.

By this time, however, people have begun to suspect that there is very little left that we can destroy. Perhaps the season of rebuilding is near. The seven invariants deduced from Wright's architecture offer a radical alternative to the present state of self-satisfied dissolution. His heroic figure suggests the path towards an authentic anti-heroic language which can enhance our daily communication.

DRAWINGS BY FRANK LLOYD WRIGHT

Selected for publication in "The Wright Legacy Evaluated"   *Architectural Record* October 1960

It was Frank Lloyd Wright's ability as a draftsman that first brought him to the attention of Louis Sullivan in Chicago in the 1890's. Although Wright himself used draftsmen (notably the talented Marion Mahony) even early in his career, he nevertheless made thousands of original drawings through the years that bear the unmistakable touch of his own hand. This portfolio of Wright drawings, originally selected by Frederick Gutheim, is not intended to represent the full breadth of his work, but merely to serve as a reminder of the genius that extended itself to every aspect of his art.

Wright's first conceptual drawing for La Miniatura, Mrs. George Millard's residence in Pasadena, California (1923), shows the entire scheme as it grew from the concrete block as the unit of structure. A rough plot plan appears in the upper right hand corner of the drawing. The textile block system was used in most of Wright's buildings executed between 1923 and 1930. To enrich the pattern, some of the blocks were pierced, giving the effect of a screen within. La Miniatura, in its use of concrete, its contained plan and its massing of elements, resembles such early LeCorbusier projects as the Citrohan House of 1922. (Other illustrations of La Miniatura appear on pages 209 and 221.)

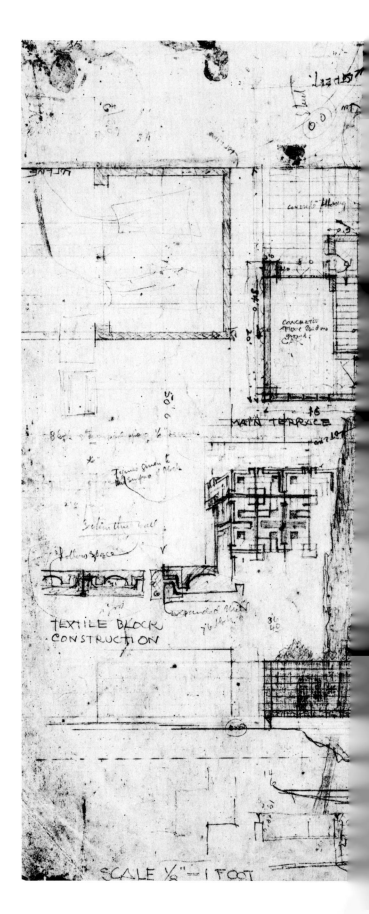

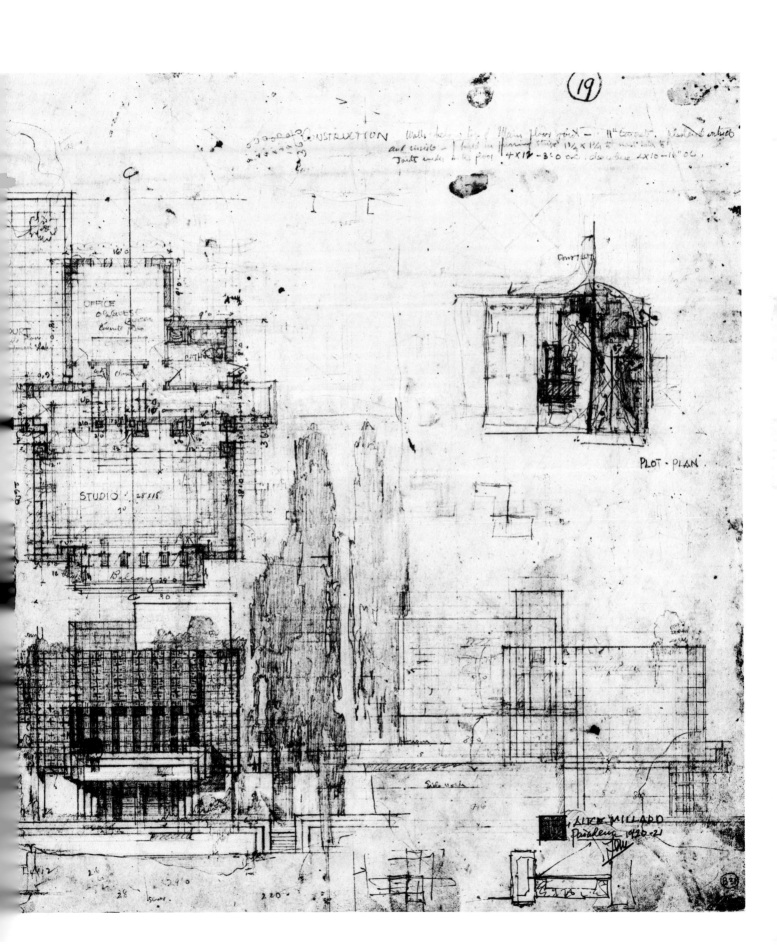

PLOT · PLAN

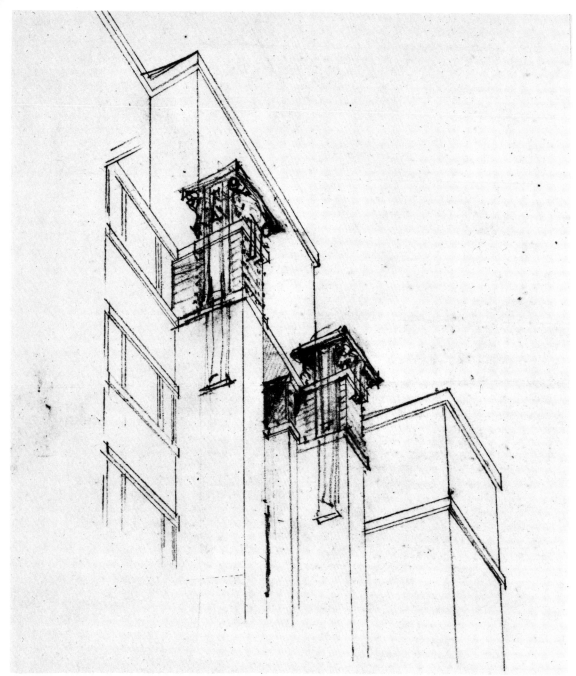

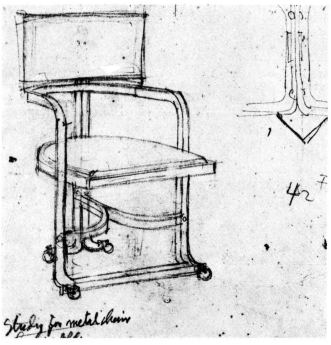

study for metal chair

In his *Autobiography*, Wright called the Larkin Building in Buffalo (1904) "a simple cliff of brick." His pencil study for the façade piers (left, above) shows ornamentation that was later removed. The building itself was razed in 1950. Wright also designed all the furniture and fixtures for the building as well. Another of his pencil studies (left, below) shows his design for a steel office chair. "All were designed," he wrote, "to simplify cleaning and make operation easy." (Other illustrations of the Larkin Building appear on pages 64-71 and 191.)

F.LL.W.'s study for roof supports (right) for his Unity Church in Oak Park, Illinois (1906), are similar to the details of the Larkin Building. But the monolithic massing first expressed there was carried out in Unity Church by Wright's first use of exposed reinforced concrete, used by him a half century later in his last major commission, the Guggenheim Museum. (Unity Church is further illustrated on pages 110-113 and 158.)

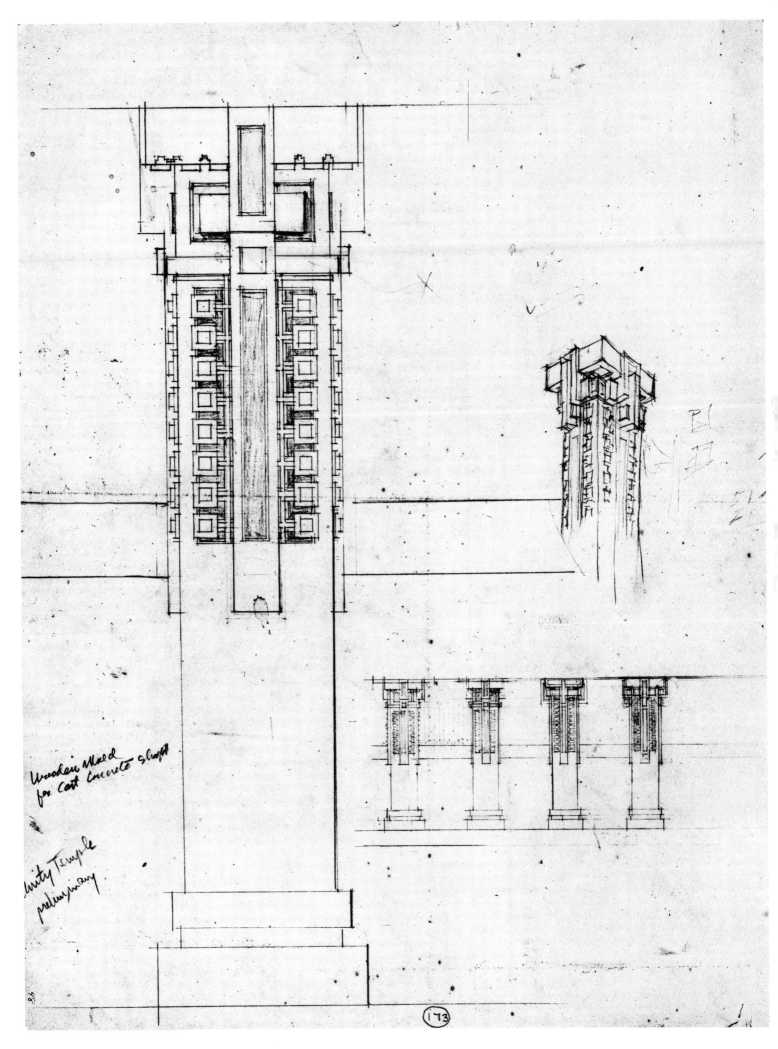

Wooden Mold
for Cast Concrete Shaft

nity Temple
preliminary

173

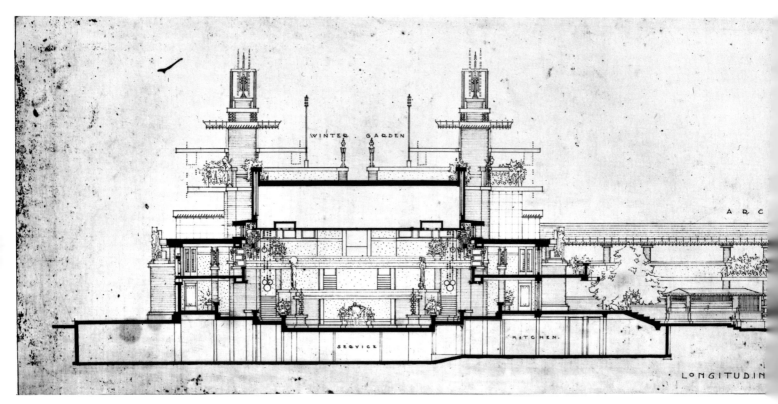

WINTER · GARDEN

ARC

SERVICE

KITCHEN.

LONGITUDIN

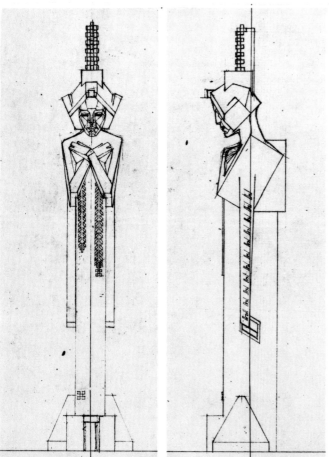

Wright's concern for total design found no more complete expression than in his Midway Gardens in Chicago (1913-1914). In this indoor-outdoor pleasure dome, inspired by the beer gardens of Germany, Wright "tried to complete the synthesis: planting, furnishings, music, painting, and sculpture, all to be one," as he wrote in *The Architects' Journal* in 1936. The longitudinal section (above) shows the orchestra shell at the right, which F.Ll.W. with characteristic candor noted was "a great success acoustically, astonishing everyone except the architect." Alfonso Ianelli's decorative figures were cast from studies by Wright (left), who also designed chairs, tables and table settings (right). Wright's last great work in Chicago, Midway Gardens was demolished during Prohibition.

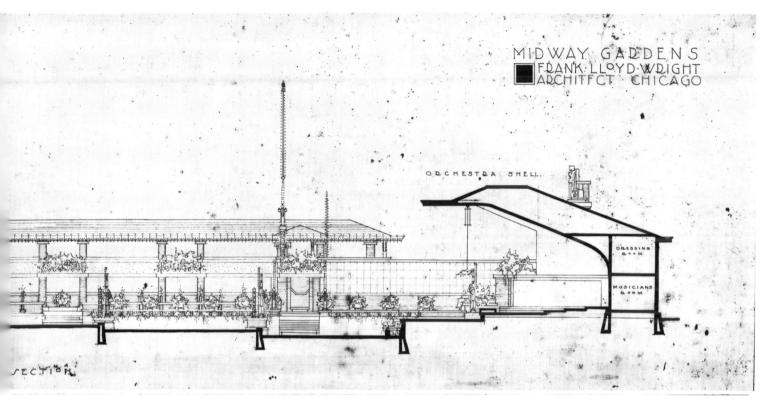

MIDWAY GADDENS
FRANK·LLOYD·WRIGHT
ARCHITECT CHICAGO

ORCHESTRA SHELL.

DRESSING
ROOM

MUSICIANS
ROOM

SECTION

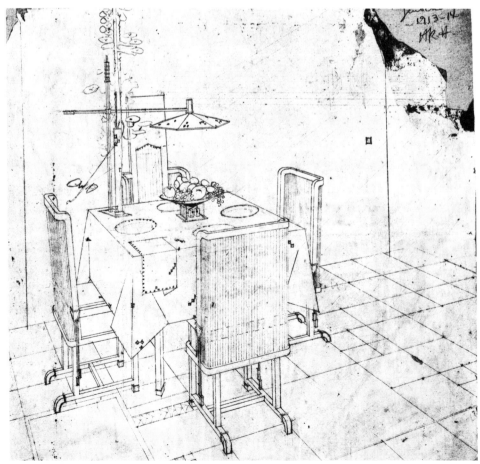

1913-14

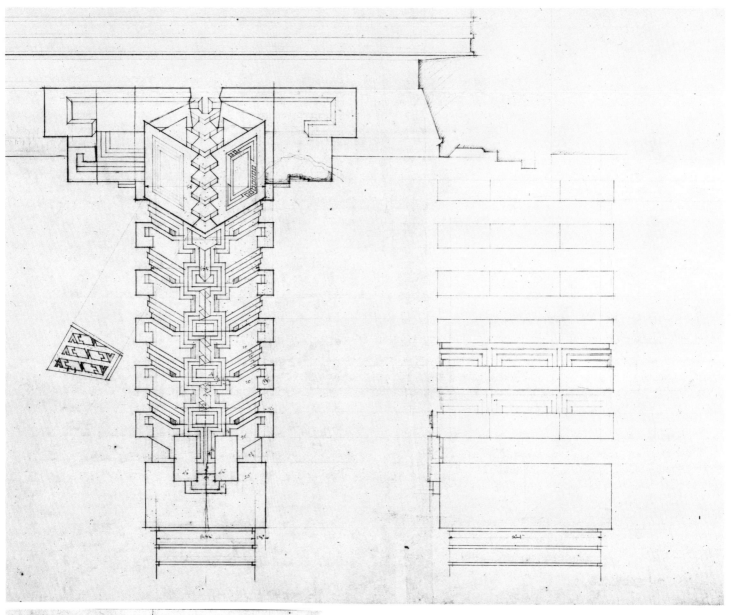

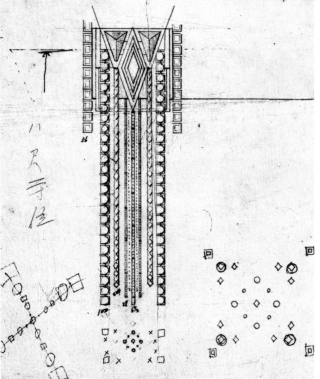

Wright's drawings for the Imperial Hotel in Tokyo (1915-1922) are among the most beautiful he produced. The decorative richness of his scheme allowed him to give full rein to his romanticizing manner in a way few other of his commissions could. His drawings for a pier cap (above), a light fixture (left) and a copper soffit of a beam in the hotel's theatre (right) are things of beauty in and of themselves. Torn down in 1969, the destruction of the Imperial Hotel was a grievous loss of a masterpiece of architecture. (Other illustrations appear on pages 172, 174, and 195.)

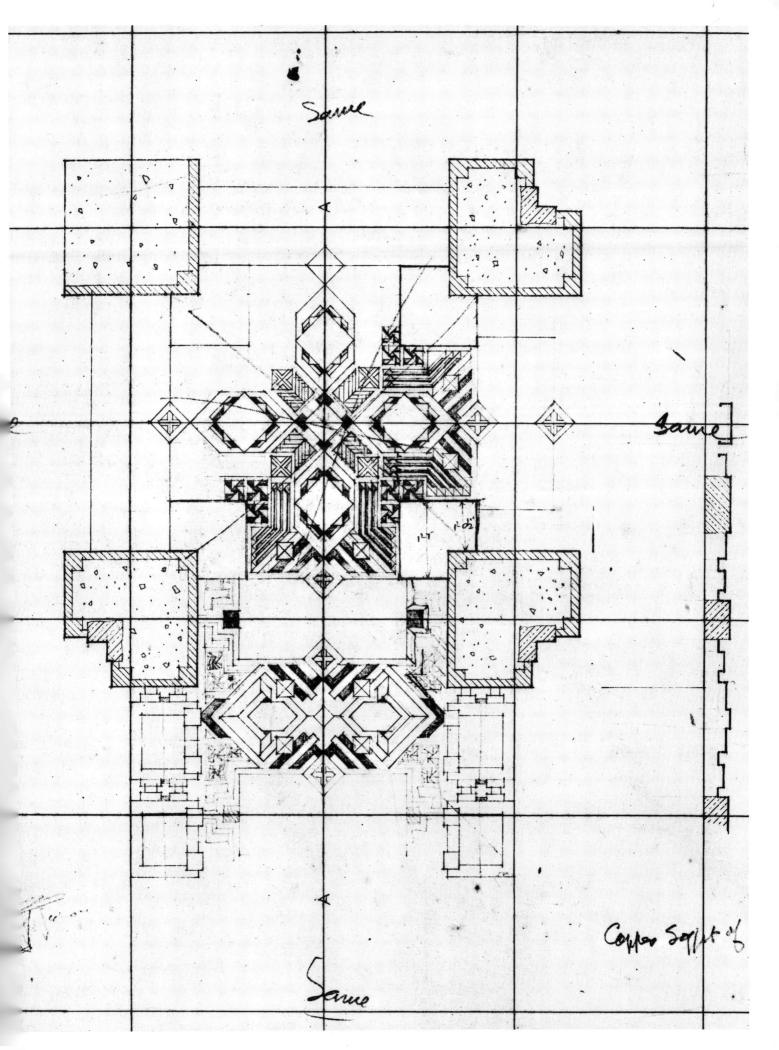

FRANK LLOYD WRIGHT 1869-1959

MAY 1959

Thinking of Frank Lloyd Wright, and remembering, is a kaleidoscopic kind of experience. At his death one turns naturally toward the eulogistic thoughts and noble phrases, but there is always the crackling interference of his personality. One did not talk to Wright in pious, sententious pronouncements; nothing like that is in the flashing images of remembrance. Nobody who ever observed the impish twinkle of his eyes while he peppered his audience with arrogant witticisms could remember Wright in complete solemnity—or wants to. There were always the tingle of wit, of interest, of penetrating insight, the emanations of creative energy.

Now that the current has been switched off, it is proper to get on with the sober task of evaluating the legacies he has left the world of architecture. And the ARCHITECTURAL RECORD staff will want to join in the work. All of this in due time; there is no need to hurry that monumental assignment. Immediate thoughts turn to more personal memories, and to more selfish thoughts of our own loss. Perhaps in trying to express this loss, we shall be adding something to the record.

Wright first appeared in the pages of the RECORD in 1905. That early article commented: "The attempt is to secure a more truthful relation between structure and design, a franker expression of the quality of the material in its treatment, and a basis for architectural ornament, less stereotyped and artificial . . ."

In 1908 came his first major article, a pronouncement about architecture. In it he gave his "propositions" about architectural design, which he had first written down in 1894 (reprinted in ARCHITECTURAL RECORD, May 1952). This first article was given the title: "In the Cause of Architecture," and this was the first of sixteen times that title was to appear over an article by Wright.

It was the blanket title for the famous series so often reprinted since, subtitled then "The Meaning of Materials" and later called "In the Nature of Materials."

The tale of that series was one of Wright's favorite stories. On meeting some new member of the staff, Wright delighted to tell how the then RECORD editor gave him the lift that was to rescue him from the depths of despondency, to start him anew on another great creative cycle.

It was in the twenties, when personal tragedy haunted him, and when the vagaries of stylistic fancies seemed to label him a "past" master, that M. A. Mikkelsen, RECORD editor, paid him the fabulous sum of $7,500 for a series of 15 articles. Wright always chuckled and said, "But I only wrote 14—I still owe you one."

With a great many friends believing in him, things gradually brightened for Wright. Publication of his work no doubt helped spread his influence, at least so it seemed to one subscriber: "Please cancel my subscription—that man Wright is having a baleful influence on my draftsmen."

Well, Wright contributed to our pages in the thirties, the forties, the fifties, through several eras of RECORD editors, over 54 years. Now we feel, with the world, the loss of its greatest architect, and, for ourselves, the loss of our greatest and most eloquent contributor. —*Emerson Goble*

ESSAYS BY FRANK LLOYD WRIGHT FOR

ARCHITECTURAL RECORD 1908-1952

IN THE CAUSE
OF
ARCHITECTURE

MARCH 1908

The
Architectural Record

Vol. XXIII   MARCH, 1908.   No. 3.

In the Cause of Architecture

The reader of architectural discourses encounters with increasing frequency discussions on American Architecture, Indigenous Architecture. These are generally to the effect that in order to establish a vital architecture in the United States, it is necessary for the architect to sever his literal connection with past performances, to shape his forms to requirements and in a manner consistent with beauty of form as found in Nature, both animate and inanimate. Articles in this strain have appeared, from time to time, in this and in other architectural journals, and have been in most cases too vague in their diction to be well understood, either by the lay reader or the architect.

The sentiment for an American architecture first made itself felt in Chicago twenty years ago. Its earliest manifestation is the acknowledged solution of the tall office building problem. An original phase of that early movement is now presented, in the following article and illustrations, the work of Mr. Frank Lloyd Wright.

—Editors of THE ARCHITECTURAL RECORD.

Radical though it be, the work here illustrated is dedicated to a cause conservative in the best sense of the word. At no point does it involve denial of the elemental law and order inherent in all great architecture; rather, is it a declaration of love for the spirit of that law and order, and a reverential recognition of the elements that made its ancient letter in its time vital and beautiful.

Primarily, Nature furnished the materials for architectural motifs out of which the architectural forms as we know them to-day have been developed, and, although our practice for centuries has been for the most part to turn from her, seeking inspiration in books and adhering slavishly to dead formulae, her wealth of suggestion is inexhaustible; her riches greater than any man's desire. I know with what suspicion the man is regarded who refers matters of fine art back to Nature. I know that it is usually an ill-advised return that is attempted, for Nature in external, obvious aspect is the usually accepted sense of the term and the nature that is reached. But given inherent vision there is no source so fertile, so suggestive, so helpful æsthetically for the architect as a comprehension of natural law. As Nature is never right for a picture so is she never right for the architect—that is, not ready-made. Nevertheless, she has a practical school beneath her more obvious forms in which a sense of proportion may be cultivated, when Vignola and Vitruvius fail as they must always fail. It is there that he may develop that sense of reality that translated to his own field in terms of his own work will lift him far above the realistic in his art; there he will be inspired by sentiment that will never degenerate to sentimentality and he will learn to draw with a surer hand the every-perplexing line between the curious and the beautiful.

A sense of the organic is indispensable to an architect; where can he develop it so surely as in this school? A knowledge of the relations of form and function lies at the root of his practice; where else can he find the pertinent object lessons Nature so readily furnishes? Where can he study the differentiations of form that go to determine character as he can

54

THE ARCHITECTURAL RECORD.

study them in the trees? Where can that sense of inevitableness characteristic of a work of art be quickened as it may be by intercourse with nature in this sense?

Japanese art knows this school more intimately than that of any people. In common use in their language there are many words like the word "edaburi," which, translated as near as may be, means the formative arrangement of the branches of a tree. We have no such word in English, we are not yet sufficiently civilized to think in such terms, but the architect must not only learn to think in such terms but he must learn in this school to fashion his vocabulary for himself and furnish it in a comprehensive way with useful words as significant as this one.

For seven years it was my good fortune to be the understudy of a great teacher and a great architect, to my mind the greatest of his time—Mr. Louis H. Sullivan.

Principles are not invented, they are not evolved by one man or one age, but Mr. Sullivan's perception and practice of them amounted to a revelation at a time when they were commercially inexpedient and all but lost to sight in current practice. The fine art sense of the profession was at that time practically dead; only glimmerings were perceptible in the work of Richardson and of Root.

Adler and Sullivan had little time to design residences. The few that were unavoidable fell to my lot outside of office hours. So largely, it remained for me to carry into the field of domestic architecture the battle they had begun in commercial building. During the early years of my own practice I found this lonesome work. Sympathizers of any kind were then few and they were not found among the architects. I well remember how "the message" burned within me, how I longed for comradeship until I began to know the younger men and how welcome was Robert Spencer, and then Myron Hunt, and Dwight Perkins, Arthur Heun, George Dean and Hugh Garden. Inspiring days they were, I am sure, for us all. Of late we have been too busy to see one another often, but the "New School of the Middle West" is beginning to be talked about and perhaps some day it is to be. For why not the same "Life" and blood in architecture that is the essence of all true art?

In 1894, with this text from Carlyle at the top of the page—"The Ideal is within thyself, thy condition is but the stuff thou art to shape that same Ideal out of"—I formulated the following "propositions." I set them down here much as they were written then, although in the light of experience they might be stated more completely and succinctly.

I.—Simplicity and Repose are qualities that measure the true value of any work of art.

But simplicity is not in itself an end nor is it a matter of the side of a barn but rather an entity with a graceful beauty in its integrity from which discord, and all that is meaningless, has been eliminated. A wild flower is truly simple. Therefore:

1. A building should contain as few rooms as will meet the conditions which give it rise and under which we live, and which the architect should strive continually to simplify; then the ensemble of the rooms should be carefully considered that comfort and utility may go hand in hand with beauty. Beside the entry and necessary work rooms there need be but three rooms on the ground floor of any house, living room, dining room and kitchen, with the possible addition of a "social office"; really there need be but one room, the living room with requirements otherwise sequestered from it or screened within it by means of architectural contrivances.

2. Openings should occur as integral features of the structure and form, if possible, its natural ornamentation.

3. An excessive love of detail has ruined more fine things from the standpoint of fine art or fine living than any one human shortcoming—it is hopelessly vulgar. Too many houses, when they are not little stage settings or scene paintings, are mere notion stores, bazaars or junk-shops. Decoration is dangerous unless you understand it

thoroughly and are satisfied that it means something good in the scheme as a whole, for the present you are usually better off without it. Merely that it "looks rich" is no justification for the use of ornament.

4. Appliances or fixtures as such are undesirable. Assimilate them together with all appurtenances into the design of the structure.

5. Pictures deface walls oftener than they decorate them. Pictures should be decorative and incorporated in the general scheme as decoration.

6. The most truly satisfactory apartments are those in which most or all of the furniture is built in as a part of the original scheme considering the whole as an integral unit.

II.—There should be as many kinds (styles) of houses as there are kinds (styles) of people and as many differentiations as there are different individuals. A man who has individuality (and what man lacks it?) has a right to its expression in his own environment.

III.—A building should appear to grow easily from its site and be shaped to harmonize with its surroundings if Nature is manifest there, and if not try to make it as quiet, substantial and organic as She would have been were the opportunity Hers.*

We of the Middle West are living on the prairie. The prairie has a beauty of its own and we should recognize and accentuate this natural beauty, its quiet level. Hence, gently sloping roofs, low proportions, quiet sky lines, suppressed heavy-set chimneys and sheltering overhangs, low terraces and out-reaching walls sequestering private gardens.

IV.—Colors require the same conventionalizing process to make them fit to live with that natural forms do; so go to the woods and fields for color schemes. Use the soft, warm, optimistic tones of earths and autumn leaves in preference to the pessimistic blues, purples or cold greens and grays of the ribbon counter; they are more wholesome and better adapted in most cases to good decoration.

*In this I had in mind the barren town lots devoid of tree or natural incident, town houses and board walks only in evidence.

V.—Bring out the nature of the materials, let their nature intimately into your scheme. Strip the wood of varnish and let it alone—stain it. Develop the natural texture of the plastering and stain it. Reveal the nature of the wood, plaster, brick or stone in your designs; they are all by nature friendly and beautiful. No treatment can be really a matter of fine art when these natural characteristics are, or their nature is, outraged or neglected.

VI.—A house that has character stands a good chance of growing more valuable as it grows older while a house in the prevailing mode, whatever that mode may be, is soon out of fashion, stale and unprofitable.

Buildings like people must first be sincere, must be true and then withal as gracious and lovable as may be.

Above all, integrity. The machine is the normal tool of our civilization, give it work that it can do well—nothing is of greater importance. To do this will be to formulate new industrial ideals, sadly needed.

These propositions are chiefly interesting because for some strange reason they were novel when formulated in the face of conditions hostile to them and because the ideals they phrase have been practically embodied in the buildings that were built to live up to them. The buildings of recent years have not only been true to them, but are in many cases a further development of the simple propositions so positively stated then.

Happily, these ideals are more commonplace now. Then the sky lines of our domestic architecture were fantastic abortions, tortured by features that disrupted the distorted roof surfaces from which attenuated chimneys like lean fingers threatened the sky; the invariably tall interiors were cut up into box-like compartments, the more boxes the finer the house; and "Architecture" chiefly consisted in healing over the edges of the curious collection of holes that had to be cut in the walls for light and air and to permit the occupant to get in or out. These interiors were always slaughtered with the butt and slash of the old plinth and corner block trim, of dubious origin, and finally smothered with horrible millinery.

That individuality in a building was possible for each home maker, or desirable, seemed at that time to rise to the dignity of an idea. Even cultured men and women care so little for the spiritual integrity of their environment; except in rare cases they are not touched, they simply do not care for the matter so long as their dwellings are fashionable or as good as those of their neighbors and keep them dry and warm. A structure has no more meaning to them æsthetically than has the stable to the horse. And this came to me in the early years as a definite discouragement. There are exceptions, and I found them chiefly among American men of business with unspoiled instincts and untainted ideals. A man of this type usually has the faculty of judging for himself. He has rather liked the "idea" and much of the encouragement this work receives comes straight from him because the "common sense" of the thing appeals to him. While the "cultured" are still content with their small châteaux, Colonial wedding cakes, English affectations or French millinery, he prefers a poor thing but his own. He errs on the side of character, at least, and when the test of time has tried his country's development architecturally, he will have contributed his quota, small enough in the final outcome though it be; he will be regarded as a true conservator.

In the hope that some day America may live her own life in her own buildings, in her own way, that is, that we may make the best of what we have for what it honestly is or may become, I have endeavored in this work to establish a harmonious relationship between ground plan and elevation of these buildings, considering the one as a solution and the other an expression of the conditions of a problem of which the whole is a project. I have tried to establish an organic integrity to begin with, forming the basis for the subsequent working out of a significant grammatical expression and making the whole, as nearly as I could, consistent.

What quality of style the buildings may possess is due to the artistry with which the conventionalization as a solution and an artistic expression of a specific problem within these limitations has been handled. The types are largely a matter of personal taste and may have much or little to do with the American architecture for which we hope.

From the beginning of my practice the question uppermost in my mind has been not "what style" but "what is style?" and it is my belief that the chief value of the work illustrated here will be found in the fact that if in the face of our present day conditions any given type may be treated independently and imbued with the quality of style, then a truly noble architecture is a definite possibility, so soon as Americans really demand it of the architects of the rising generation.

I do not believe we will ever again have the uniformity of type which has characterized the so-called great "styles." Conditions have changed; our ideal is Democracy, the highest possible expression of the individual as a unit not inconsistent with a harmonious whole. The average of human intelligence rises steadily, and as the individual unit grows more and more to be trusted we will have an architecture with richer variety in unity than has ever arisen before; but the forms must be born out of our changed conditions, they must be *true* forms, otherwise the best that tradition has to offer is only an inglorious masquerade, devoid of vital significance or true spiritual value. . . .

The trials of the early days were many and at this distance picturesque. Workmen seldom like to think, especially if there is financial risk entailed; at your peril do you disturb their established processes mental or technical. To do anything in an unusual, even if in a better and simpler way, is to complicate the situation at once. Simple things at that time in any industrial field were nowhere at hand. A piece of wood without a moulding was an anomaly; a plain wooden slat instead of a turned baluster a joke; the omission of the merchantable "grille" a crime; plain fabrics for hangings or floor covering were nowhere to be found in stock.

To become the recognized enemy of

57

IN THE CAUSE OF ARCHITECTURE.

the established industrial order was no light matter, for soon whenever a set of my drawings was presented to a Chicago mill-man for figures he would willingly enough unroll it, read the architect's name, shake his head and return it with the remark that he was "not hunting for trouble"; sagacious owners and general contractors tried cutting out the name, but in vain, his perspicacity was rat-like, he had come to know "the look of the thing." So, in addition to the special preparation in any case necessary for every little matter of construction and finishing, special detail drawings were necessary merely to show the things to be left off or not done, and not only studied designs for every part had to be made but quantity surveys and schedules of mill work furnished the contractors beside. This, in a year or two, brought the architect face to face with the fact that the fee for his service "established" by the American Institute of Architects was intended for something stock and shop, for it would not even pay for the bare drawings necessary for conscientious work.

The relation of the architect to the economic and industrial movement of his time, in any fine art sense, is still an affair so sadly out of joint that no one may easily reconcile it. All agree that something has gone wrong and except the architect be a plain factory magnate, who has reduced his art to a philosophy of old clothes and sells misfit or made-over-ready-to-wear garments with commercial aplomb and social distinction, he cannot succeed on the present basis established by common practice. So, in addition to a situation already complicated for them, a necessarily increased fee stared in the face the clients who dared. But some did dare, as the illustrations prove.

The struggle then was and still is to make "good architecture," "good business." It is perhaps significant that in the beginning it was very difficult to secure a building loan on any terms upon one of these houses, now it is easy to secure a better loan than ordinary; but how far success has attended this ambition the owners of these buildings alone can testify. Their trials have been many, but each, I think, feels that he has as much

house for his money as any of his neighbors, with something in the home intrinsically valuable besides, which will not be out of fashion in one lifetime, and which contributes steadily to his dignity and his pleasure as an individual.

It would not be useful to dwell further upon difficulties encountered, for it is the common story of simple progression everywhere in any field; I merely wish to trace here the "motif" behind the types. A study of the illustrations will show that the buildings presented fall readily into three groups having a family resemblance; the low-pitched hip roofs, heaped together in pyramidal fashion, or presenting quiet, unbroken skylines; the low roofs with simple pediments countering on long ridges; and those topped with a simple slab. Of the first type, the Winslow, Henderson, Willits, Thomas, Heurtley, Heath, Cheney, Martin, Little, Gridley, Millard, Tomek, Coonley and Westcott houses, the Hillside Home School and the Pettit Memorial Chapel are typical. Of the second type the Bradley, Hickox, Davenport and Dana houses are typical. Of the third, Atelier for Richard Bock, Unity Church, the concrete house of the Ladies' Home Journal and other designs in process of execution. The Larkin Building is a simple, dignified utterance of a plain, utilitarian type with sheer brick walls and simple stone copings. The studio is merely an early experiment in "articulation."

Photographs do not adequately present these subjects. A building has a presence as has a person that defies the photographer, and the color so necessary to the complete expression of the form is necessarily lacking, but it will be noticed that all the structures stand upon their foundations to the eye as well as physically. There is good, substantial preparation at the ground for all the buildings and it is the first grammatical expression of all the types. This preparation, or watertable, is to these buildings what the stylobate was to the ancient Greek temple. To gain it, it was necessary to reverse the established practice of setting the supports of the building to the outside of the wall and to set them to the inside, so as to leave the necessary support for the outer base. This was natural enough and good enough construction but many an owner was disturbed by private information from the practical contractor to the effect that he would have his whole house in the cellar if he submitted to it. This was at the time a marked innovation though the most natural thing in the world and to me, to this day, indispensable.

With this innovation established, one horizontal stripe of raw material, the foundation wall above ground, was eliminated and the complete grammar of type one made possible. A simple, unbroken wall surface from foot to level of second story sill was thus secured, a change of material occuring at that point to form the simple frieze that characterizes the earlier buildings. Even this was frequently omitted as in the Francis apartments and many other buildings and the wall was let alone from base to cornice or eaves.

"Dress reform houses" they were called, I remember, by the charitably disposed. What others called them will hardly bear repetition.

As the wall surfaces were thus simplified and emphasized the matter of fenestration became exceedingly difficult and more than ever important, and often I used to gloat over the beautiful buildings I could build if only it were unnecessary to cut holes in them; but the holes were managed at first frankly as in the Winslow house and later as elementary constituents of the structure grouped in rhythmical fashion, so that all the light and air and prospect the most rabid clinet could wish would not be too much from an artistic standpoint; and of this achievement I am proud. The groups are managed, too, whenever required, so that overhanging eaves do not shade them, although the walls are still protected from the weather. Soon the poetry-crushing characteristics of the guillotine window, which was then firmly rooted, became apparent and, single-handed I waged a determined battle for casements swinging out, although it was necessary to have special hardware made for them as there was none to be had this side of England. Clients would come ready to accept any

innovation but "those swinging windows," and when told that they were in the nature of the proposition and that they must take them or leave the rest, they frequently employed "the other fellow" to give them something "near," with the "practical" windows dear to their hearts.

With the grammar so far established, came an expression pure and simple, even classic in atmosphere, using that much-abused word in its best sense; implying, that is, a certain sweet reasonableness of form and outline naturally dignified.

I have observed that Nature usually perfects her forms; the individuality of the attribute is seldom sacrificed; that is, deformed or mutilated by co-operative parts. She rarely says a thing and tries to take it back at the same time. She would not sanction the "classic" proceeding of, say, establishing an "order," a colonnade, then building walls between the columns of the order reducing them to pilasters, thereafter cutting holes in the wall and pasting on cornices with more pilasters around them, with the result that every form is outraged, the whole an abominable mutilation, as is most of the the architecture of the Renaissance wherein style corrodes style and all the forms are stultified.

In laying out the ground plans for even the more insignificant of these buildings a simple axial law and order and the ordered spacing upon a system of certain structural units definitely established for each structure in accord with its scheme of practical construction and æsthetic proportion, is practiced as an expedient to simplify the technical difficulties of execution, and, although the symmetry may not be obvious always the balance is usually maintained. The plans are as a rule much more articulate than is the school product of the Beaux Arts. The individuality of the various functions of the various features is more highly developed; all the forms are complete in themselves and frequently do duty at the same time from within and without as decorative attributes of the whole. This tendency to greater individuality of the parts emphasized by more and more complete articulation will be seen in the plans

IN THE CAUSE OF ARCHITECTURE.

for Unity Church, the cottage for Elizabeth Stone at Glencoe and the Avery Coonly house in process of construction at Riverside, Illinois. Moreover, these ground plans are merely the actual projection of a carefully considered whole. The "architecture" is not "thrown up" as an artistic exercise, a matter of elevation from a preconceived ground plan. The schemes are conceived in three dimensions as organic entities, let the picturesque perspective fall how it will. While a sense of the incidental perspectives the design will develop is always present, I have great faith that if the thing is rightly put together in true organic sense with proportions actually right the picturesque will take care of itself. No man ever built a building worthy the name of architecture who fashioned it in perspective sketch to his taste and then fudged the plan to suit. Such methods produce mere scene-painting. A perspective may be a proof but it is no nurture.

As to the mass values of the buildings the æsthetic principles outlined in proposition III will account in a measure for their character.

In the matter of decoration the tendency has been to indulge it less and less, in many cases merely providing certain architectural preparation for natural foliage or flowers, as it is managed in say, the entrance to the Lawrence house at Springfield. This use of natural foliage and flowers for decoration is carried to quite an extent in all the designs and, although the buildings are complete without this effloresence, they may be said to blossom with the season. What architectural decoration the buildings carry is not only conventionalized to the point where it is quiet and stays as a sure foil for the nature forms from which it is derived and with which it must intimately associate, but it is always *of* the surface, never *on* it.

The windows usually are provided with characteristic straight line patterns absolutely in the flat and usually severe. The nature of the glass is taken into account in these designs as is also the metal bar used in their construction, and most of them are treated as metal "grilles" with glass inserted forming a simple rhythmic arrangement of straight lines and squares made as cunning as possible so long as the result is quiet. The aim is that the designs shall make the best of the technical contrivances that produce them.

In the main the ornamentation is wrought in the warp and woof of the structure. It is constitutional in the best sense and is felt in the conception of the ground plan. To elucidate this element in composition would mean a long story and perhaps a tedious one though to me it is the most fascinating phase of the work, involving the true poetry of conception.

The differentiation of a single, certain simple form characterizes the expression of one building. Quite a different form may serve for another, but from one basic idea all the formal elements of design are in each case derived and held well together in scale and character. The form chosen may flare outward, opening flower-like to the sky as in the Thomas house; another, droop to accentuate artistically the weight of the masses; another be non-committal or abruptly emphatic, or its grammar may be deduced from some plant form that has appealed to me, as certain properties in line and form of the sumach were used in the Lawrence house at Springfield; but in every case the motif is adhered to throughout so that it is not too much to say that each building æsthetically is cut from one piece of goods and consistently hangs together with an integrity impossible otherwise.

In a fine art sense these designs have grown as natural plants grow, the individuality of each is integral and as complete as skill, time, strength and circumstances would permit.

The method in itself does not of necessity produce a beautiful building, but it does provide a framework as a basis which has an organic integrity, susceptible to the architect's imagination and at once opening to him Nature's wealth of artistic suggestion, ensuring him a guiding principle within which he can never be wholly false, out of tune, or lacking in rational motif. The subtleties, the shifting blending harmonies, the cadences, the nuances are a matter of his own nature, his own susceptibilities and faculties.

But self denial is imposed upon the architect to a far greater extent than upon any other member of the fine art family. The temptation to sweeten work, to make each detail in itself lovable and expressive is always great; but that the whole may be truly eloquent of its ultimate function restraint is imperative. To let individual elements arise and shine at the expense of final repose is for the architect, a betrayal of trust for buildings are the background or framework for the human life within their walls and a foil for the nature efflorescence without. So architecture is the most complete of conventionalizations and of all the arts the most subjective except music.

Music may be for the architect ever and always a sympathetic friend whose counsels, precepts and patterns even are available to him and from which he need not fear to draw. But the arts are to-day all cursed by literature; artists attempt to make literature even of music, usually of painting and sculpture and doubtless would of architecture also, were the art not moribund; but whenever it is done the soul of the thing dies and we have not art but something far less for which the true artist can have neither affection nor respect. . . .

Contrary to the usual supposition this manner of working out a theme is more flexible than any working out in a fixed, historic style can ever be, and the individuality of those concerned may receive more adequate treatment within legitimate limitations. This matter of individuality puzzles many; they suspect that the individuality of the owner and occupant of a building is sacrificed to that of the architect who imposes his own upon Jones, Brown and Smith alike. An architect worthy of the name has an individuality, it is true; his work will and should reflect it, and his buildings will all bear a family resemblance one to another. The individuality of an owner is first manifest in his choice of his architect, the individual to whom he entrusts his characterization. He sympathizes with his work; its expression suits him

and this furnishes the common ground upon which client and architect may come together. Then, if the architect is what he ought to be, with his ready technique he conscientiously works for the client, idealizes his client's character and his client's tastes and makes him feel that the building is his as it really is to such an extent that he can truly say that he would rather have his own house than any other he has ever seen. Is a portrait, say by Sargent, any less a revelation of the character of the subject because it bears his stamp and is easily recognized by any one as a Sargent? Does one lose his individuality when it is interpreted sympathetically by one of his own race and time who can know him and his needs intimately and idealize them; or does he gain it only by having adopted or adapted to his condition a ready-made historic style which is the fruit of a seed-time other than his, whatever that style may be?

The present industrial condition is constantly studied in the practical application of these architectural ideals and the treatment simplified and arranged to fit modern processes and to utilize to the best advantage the work of the machine. The furniture takes the clean cut, straight-line forms that the machine can render far better than would be possible by hand. Certain facilities, too, of the machine, which it would be interesting to enlarge upon, are taken advantage of and the nature of the materials is usually revealed in the process.

Nor is the atmosphere of the result in its completeness new and hard. In most of the interiors there will be found a quiet, a simple dignity that we imagine is only to be found in the "old" and it is due to the underlying organic harmony, to the each in all and the all in each throughout. This is the modern opportunity—to make of a building, together with its equipment, appurtenances and environment, an entity which shall constitute a complete work of art, and a work of art more valuable to society as a whole than has before existed because discordant conditions endured for centuries are smoothed away; everyday life here finds an expression germane to its

IN THE CAUSE OF ARCHITECTURE.

daily existence; an idealization of the common need sure to be uplifting and helpful in the same sense that pure air to breathe is better than air poisoned with noxious gases.

An artist's limitations are his best friends. The machine is here to stay. It is the forerunner of the democracy that is our dearest hope. There is no more important work before the architect now that to use this normal tool of civilization to the best advantage instead of prostituting it as he has hitherto done in reproducing with murderous ubiquity forms born of other times and other conditions and which it can only serve to destroy.

* * * * * *

The exteriors of these structures will receive less ready recognition perhaps than the interiors and because they are the result of a radically different conception as to what should constitute a building. We have formed a habit of mind concerning architecture to which the expression of most of these exteriors must be a shock, at first more or less disagreeable, and the more so as the habit of mind is more narrowly fixed by so called classic training. Simplicity is not in itself an end; it is a means to an end. Our æsthetics are dyspeptic from incontinent indulgence in "Frenchite" pastry. We crave ornament for the sake of ornament; cover up our faults of design with ornamental sensualities that were a long time ago sensuous ornament. We will do well to distrust this unwholesome and unholy craving and look to the simple line; to the clean though living form and quiet color for a time, until the true significance of these things has dawned for us once more. The old structural forms which up to the present time, have spelled "architecture" are decayed. Their life went from them long ago and new conditions industrially, steel and concrete and terra cotta in particular, are prophesying a more plastic art wherein as the flesh is to our bones so will the covering be to the structure, but more truly and beautifully expressive than ever. But that is a long story. This reticence in the matter of ornamentation is characteristic of these structures and for at least two reasons; first, they are the expression of an idea that the ornamentation of a building should be constitutional, a matter of the nature of the structure beginning with the ground plan. In the buildings themselves, in the sense of the whole, there is lacking neither richness nor incident but their qualities are secured not by applied decoration, they are found in the fashioning of the whole, in which color, too, plays as significant a part as it does in an old Japanese wood block print. Second; because, as before stated, buildings perform their highest function in relation to human life within and the natural efflorescence without; and to develop and maintain the harmony of a true chord between them making of the building in this sense a sure foil for life, broad simple surfaces and highly conventionalized forms are inevitable. These ideals take the buildings out of school and marry them to the ground; make them intimate expressions or revelations of the exteriors; individualize them regardless of preconceived notions of style. I have tried to make their grammar perfect in its way and to give their forms and proportions an integrity that will bear study, although few of them can be intelligently studied apart from their environment. So, what might be termed the democratic character of the exteriors is their first undefined offence—the lack, wholly, of what the professional critic would deem architecture; in fact, most of the critic's architecture has been left out.

There is always a synthetic basis for the features of the various structures, and consequently a constantly accumulating residue of formulae, which becomes more and more useful; but I do not pretend to say that the perception or conception of them was not at first intuitive, or that those that lie yet beyond will not be grasped in the same intuitive way; but, after all, architecture is a scientific art, and the thinking basis will ever be for the architect his surety, the final court in which his imagination sifts his feelings. . . .

The few draughtsmen so far associated with this work have been taken into the draughting room, in every case almost wholly unformed, many of them with no particular previous training, and patiently nursed for years in the atmosphere of the work itself, until, saturated by intimate association, at an impressionable age, with its motifs and phases, they have become helpful. To develop the sympathetic grasp of detail that is necessary before this point is reached has proved usually a matter of years, with little advantage on the side of the college-trained understudy. These young people have found their way to me through natural sympathy with the work, and have become loyal assistants. The members, so far, all told here and elsewhere, of our little university of fourteen years' standing are: Marion Mahony, a capable assistant for eleven years; William Drummond, for seven years; Francis Byrne, five years; Isabel Roberts, five years; George Willis, four years; Walter Griffin, four years; Andrew Willatzen, three years; Harry Robinson, two years; Charles E. White, Jr., one year; Erwin Barglebaugh and Robert Hardin, each one year; Albert McArthur, entering.

Others have been attracted by what seemed to them to be the novelty of the work, staying only long enough to acquire a smattering of form, then departing to sell a superficial proficiency elsewhere. Still others shortly develop a mastery of the subject, discovering that it is all just as they would have done it, anyway, and, chafing at the unkind fate that forestalled them in its practice, resolve to blaze a trail for themselves without further loss of time. It is urged against the more loyal that they are sacrificing their individuality to that which has dominated this work; but it is too soon to impeach a single understudy on this basis, for, although they will inevitably repeat for years the methods, forms and habit of thought, even the mannerisms of the present work, if there is virtue in the principles behind it that virtue will stay with them through the preliminary stages of their own practice until their own individualities truly develop independently. I have noticed that those who have made the most fuss about their "individuality" in early stages, those who took themselves

most seriously in that regard, were inevitably those who had least.

Many elements of Mr. Sullivan's personality in his art—what might be called his mannerisms—naturally enough clung to my work in the early years, and may be readily traced by the casual observer; but for me one real proof of the virtue inherent in this work will lie in the fact that some of the young men and women who have given themselves up to me so faithfully these past years will some day contribute rounded individualities of their own, and forms of their own devising to the new school.

This year I assign to each a project that has been carefully conceived in my own mind, which he accepts as a specific work. He follows its subsequent development through all its phases in drawing room and field, meeting with the client himself on occasion, gaining an all-round development impossible otherwise, and insuring an enthusiasm and a grasp of detail decidedly to the best interest of the client. These privileges in the hands of selfishly ambitious or overconfident assistants would soon wreck such a system; but I can say that among my own boys it has already proved a moderate success, with every prospect of being continued as a settled policy in future.

Nevertheless, I believe that only when one individual forms the concept of the various projects and also determines the character of every detail in the sum total, even to the size and shape of the pieces of glass in the windows, the arrangement and profile of the most insignificant of the architectural members, will that unity be secured which is the soul of the individual work of art. This means that fewer buildings should be entrusted to one architect. His output will of necessity be relatively small— small, that is, as compared to the volume of work turned out in any one of fifty "successful offices" in America. I believe there is no middle course worth considering in the light of the best future of American architecture. With no more propriety can an architect leave the details touching the form of his concept to assistants, no matter how sym-

IN THE CAUSE OF ARCHITECTURE.

pathetic and capable they may be, than can a painter entrust the painting in of the details of his picture to a pupil; for an architect who would do individual work must have a technique well developed and peculiar to himself, which, if he is fertile, is still growing with his growth. To keep everything "in place" requires constant care and study in matters that the old-school practitioner would scorn to touch. . . .

As for the future—the work shall grow more truly simple; more expressive with fewer lines, fewer forms; more articulate with less labor; more plastic; more fluent, although more coherent; more organic. It shall grow not only to fit more perfectly the methods and processes that are called upon to produce it,

but shall further find whatever is lovely or of good repute in method or process, and idealize it with the cleanest, most virile stroke I can imagine. As understanding and appreciation of life matures and deepens, this work shall prophesy and idealize the character of the individual it is fashioned to serve more intimately, no matter how inexpensive the result must finally be. It shall become in its atmosphere as pure and elevating in its humble way as the trees and flowers are in their perfectly appointed way, for only so can architecture be worthy its high rank as a fine art, or the architect discharge the obligation he assumes to the public—imposed upon him by the nature of his own profession.

Frank Lloyd Wright.

EXHIBIT OF FRANK LLOYD WRIGHT AT THE CHICAGO ARCHITECTURAL CLUB, 1908.

Buffalo, N. Y.   THE LARKIN BUILDING.

The Larkin Building is one of a large group of factory buildings situated in the factory district of Buffalo. It was built to house the commercial engine of the Larkin Company in light, wholesome, well-ventilated quarters. The smoke, noise and dirt incident to the locality made it imperative that all exterior surfaces be self cleaning and the interior be created independently of this environment. The building is a simple working out of certain utilitarian conditions, its exterior a simple cliff of brick whose only "ornamental" feature is the exterior expression of the central aisle, fashioned by means of the sculptured piers at either end of the main block. The machinery of the various appurtenance systems, pipe shafts incidental thereto, the heating and ventilating air in-takes, and the stairways which serve also as fire escapes, are quartered in plan and placed outside the main building at the four outer corners, so that the entire area might be free for working purposes. These stair chambers are top-lighted. The interior of the main building thus forms a single large room in which the main floors are galleries open to a large central court, which is also lighted from above. All the windows of the various stories or "galleries" are seven feet above the floor, the space beneath being utilized for steel filing cabinets. The window sash are double, and the building practically sealed to dirt, odor and noise, fresh air being taken high above the ground in shafts extending above the roof surfaces. The interior is executed throughout in vitreous,

IN THE CAUSE OF ARCHITECTURE.

Buffalo, N. Y.   THE LARKIN BUILDING

cream-colored brick, with floor and trimmings of "magnesite" of the same color. The various features of this trim were all formed within the building itself by means of simple wooden molds, in most cases being worked directly in place. So the decorative forms were necessarily simple, particularly so as this material becomes very hot while setting and expands slightly in the process. The furnishings and fittings are all of steel and were designed with the structure. The entrance vestibules, from either street and the main lobby, together with the toilet accommodations and rest rooms for employees, are all located in an annex which intercepts the light from the main office as little as possible. The fifth floor is given to a restaurant for employees, with conservatories in mezzanines over kitchen and bakery at either end, opening in turn to the main roof, all of which together constitutes the only recreation ground available for employees. The structure, which is completely fireproof, together with its modern heating, ventilating and appurtenance system, but exclusive of metal fixtures and furnishings, cost but little more than the average high class fireproof factory building—18 cts. per cubic foot. Here again most of the critic's "architecture" has been left out. Therefore the work may have the same claim to consideration as a "work of art" as an ocean liner, a locomotive or a battleship.

66

LARKIN BUILDING—FOURTH STORY GALLERY.

LARKIN BUILDING—OFFICERS' DESKS—FLOOR OF MAIN COURT.
Buffalo, N. Y.

IN THE CAUSE OF ARCHITECTURE.

LARKIN BUILDING—CENTRAL COURT.

THE ARCHITECTURAL RECORD.

LARKIN BUILDING—METAL FURNITURE CLOSED TO ADMIT OF EASY CLEANING.

Buffalo, N. Y.   LARKIN BUILDING—METAL FURNITURE READY FOR USE.

IN THE CAUSE OF ARCHITECTURE.

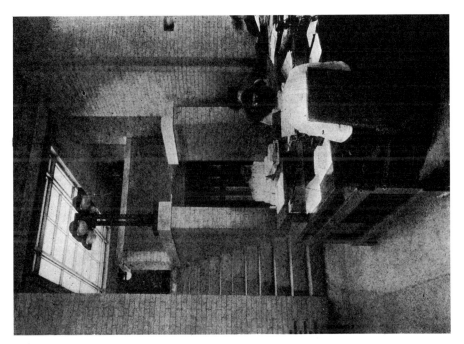

LARKIN BUILDING—TYPICAL GALLERY FLOOR.

LARKIN BUILDING—INFORMATION BUREAU AND TELEPHONE CENTRAL.
Buffalo, N. Y.

70

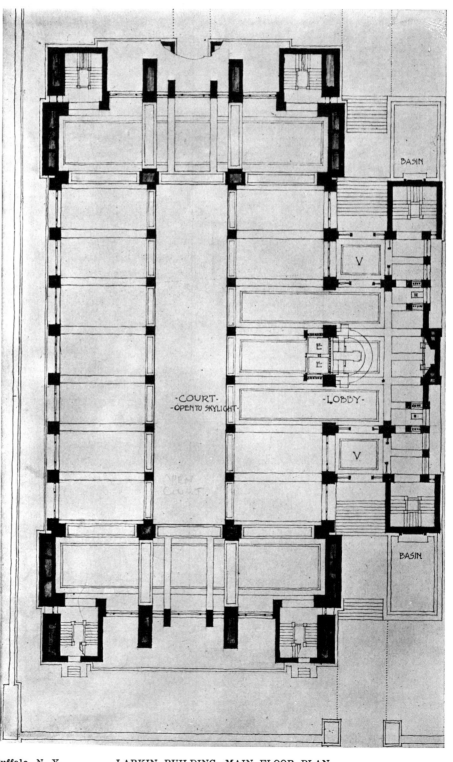

BASIN

V

LOBBY

COURT
OPEN TO SKYLIGHT

V

BASIN

Buffalo, N. Y.   LARKIN BUILDING—MAIN FLOOR PLAN.

Buffalo, N. Y.   THE LARKIN BUILDING—HOUSING AN INDUSTRY.

THE ARCHITECTURAL RECORD.

Springfield, Ill.   HOUSE OF MRS. S. L. DANA.
General exterior view shown above.   Interior of gallery, library beneath.
A house designed to accommodate the art collection of its owner and for entertaining extensively, somewhat elaborately worked out in detail. Fixtures and furnishings designed
with the structure.

IN THE CAUSE OF ARCHITECTURE.

HOUSE OF MRS. S. L. DANA—VIEW FROM FOURTH STREET.

DANA HOUSE—DETAIL OF MAIN ENTRANCE, SHOWING VISTA INTO LIVING HALL.

DANA HOUSE—GENERAL VIEW FROM CORNER.

DANA HOUSE—FIREPLACE ALCOVE AT END OF GALLERY. BALCONY ABOVE.

DANA HOUSE—DINING ROOM.

DANA HOUSE—GALLERY AND LIBRARY.

IN THE CAUSE OF ARCHITECTURE.

Kankakee, Ill.   HICKOX HOUSE.

BREAKFAST NOOK IN THE DANA HOUSE.

B. HARLEY BRADLEY HOUSE—LIVING ROOM.

Kankakee, Ill.

IN THE CAUSE OF ARCHITECTURE.

Kankakee, Ill.   B. HARLEY BRADLEY HOUSE—PLASTERED EXTERIOR.

B. HARLEY BRADLEY HOUSE—LIVING ROOM FIREPLACE.

THE ARCHITECTURAL RECORD.

P. A. BEACHEY HOUSE, OAK PARK, ILL.—BRICK, PLASTER AND TIMBER EXTERIOR.

DINING ROOM OF BRADLEY HOUSE.

IN THE CAUSE OF ARCHITECTURE.

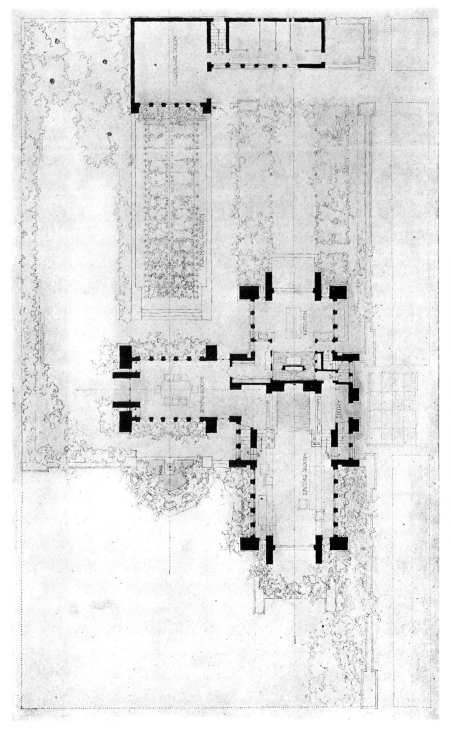

Oak Park, Ill.   H. J. ULLMAN HOUSE—GROUND PLAN OF PROPOSED RESIDENCE.
In this plan the dining room floor is at the garden level, with porch above the former; both dining room and porch being reached by steps from living room.

W. H. WINSLOW HOUSE—BRICK, STONE AND TILE EXTERIOR.

River Forest, Ill.

IN THE CAUSE OF ARCHITECTURE.

Oak Park, Ill.   THOMAS HOUSE.
    Basement entirely above ·ground.   Ground floor entrance to living rooms on first floor,
                                        bed rooms above.

ARTHUR HEURTLEY HOUSE.
Same type as Thomas House, with living rooms, kitchen and family bed rooms on main floor.
Two guest rooms and bath, children's playroom and servants' room on ground floor.

F. F. TOMEK HOUSE.   Plastered walls, tile roof.   Basement entirely above ground.   Ground floor entrance to living rooms on first floor.   Designed for low, damp prairie.   Bed rooms in upper story.

IN THE CAUSE OF ARCHITECTURE.

MRS. E. L. MARTIN'S HOUSE.

Oak Park, Ill.

A plastered house. The horizontal members utilized as protections for the plastered walls. The eaves, plastic in form, suited to the method of construction.

F. F. TOMEK HOUSE—SHOWING CANTILEVER ROOF OVER TERRACES.

Glencoe, Ill.   THE W. A. GLASNER HOUSE.

A characteristic type of wooden dwelling, of which a number have been build to meet various simple requirements. In this case all the rooms and the porch are on one floor, with servants' room and laundry below. The side walls beneath the windows are covered with undressed boards jointed with inserted battens. The frieze and underside of eaves are plastered. Total cost about $5,500. The whole fits its site on the edge of a picturesque ravine.

IN THE CAUSE OF ARCHITECTURE.

MRS. E. L. MARTIN'S HOUSE.

Oak Park, Ill.

Showing porch managed as a semi-detached pavilion. A practical solution of the "porch problem."

ROBERT CLARK HOUSE—HOUSE, STABLE AND ENCLOSED GARDEN.

Peoria, Ill.

IN THE CAUSE OF ARCHITECTURE.

General View.

Detail of exterior of assembly room.

THE HILLSIDE HOME SCHOOL—SANDSTONE AND SOLID OAK TIMBER CONSTRUCTION. Hillside, Wis.

MR. WALTER S. GERTS' SUMMER LODGE.

Birch Brook, Mich.

MR. CHARLES S. ROSS' SUMMER COTTAGE.

Lake Delavan, Wis.

IN THE CAUSE OF ARCHITECTURE.

HILLSIDE HOME SCHOOL—INTERIOR VIEW.

SUMMER COTTAGE—MRS. GEO. E. GERTS.
Birch Brook, Mich.

W. R. HEATH HOUSE.
Red brick with cement trimmings. Red tile roof.
Buffalo, N. Y.

IN THE CAUSE OF ARCHITECTURE.

MR. W. W. WILLITS' HOUSE—DETAIL.

Highland Park, Ill.　　　　MR. W. W. WILLITS' HOUSE.
Living rooms within the terrace. View from south.

THE ARCHITECTURAL RECORD.

MRS. HELEN W. HUSSER, BUENA PARK, CHICAGO.

S. M. B. Hunt House, La Grange, Ill. Plan and two views of a typical, moderate cost house of the ordinary basement and two-story type with plastered exterior and undressed wood trim. The main floor is treated as a single room with separate working department, and has been reduced to the simplest terms consistent with reasonable comfort and privacy. The house has a trunk room opening from the stair landing—four bed rooms and bath on the second story, store room and laundry in basement. Total cost about $6,000.00 complete.

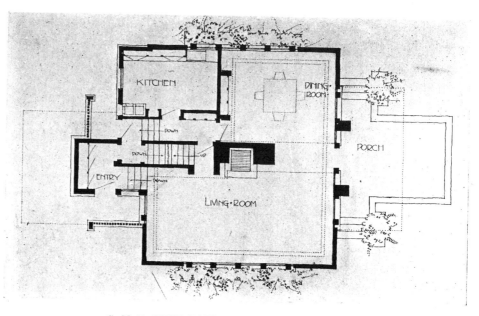

S. M. B. HUNT HOUSE—FIRST FLOOR PLAN.

La Grange, Ill.

IN THE CAUSE OF ARCHITECTURE.

LIVING ROOM SIDE.

S. M. B. HUNT HOUSE—PORCH SIDE.

La Grange, Ill.

THE ARCHITECTURAL RECORD.

D. D. MARTIN HOUSE—GENERAL VIEW.

Buffalo, N. Y.

IN THE CAUSE OF ARCHITECTURE.

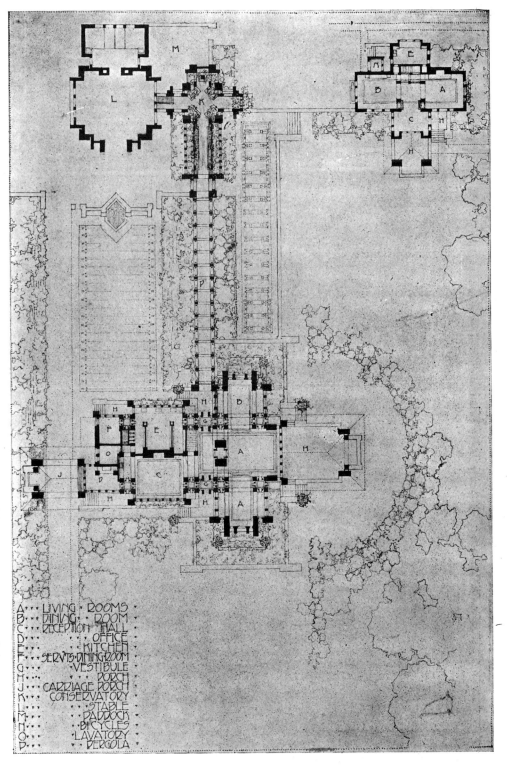

A...LIVING·ROOMS·
B...DINING·ROOM·
C...RECEPTION·HALL
D...........OFFICE·
E...........KITCHEN·
F...SERVTS·DINING ROOM·
G...........VESTIBULE·
H...........PORCH·
J...CARRIAGE·PORCH·
K...CONSERVATORY·
L...........STABLE·
M...........PADDOCK·
N...........BICYCLES·
O...........LAVATORY·
P...........PERGOLA·

D. D. MARTIN HOUSE—PLAN.

Buffalo, N. Y.

98

Details of conservatory.

Looking toward conservatory.

D. D. MARTIN HOUSE.

Buffalo, N. Y.

IN THE CAUSE OF ARCHITECTURE.

D. D. MARTIN HOUSE—HEAT AND LIGHT UNIT.

Reference to the general plan of the Martin house will show certain free standing groups of piers, of which the above is an illustration. In the central chamber formed by the piers the radiators are located, and the lighting fixtures are concentrated upon the piers themselves. Bookcases swinging outward are placed below between the piers; the open spaces above are utilized as cabinets, and from these the heat passes into the rooms. Fresh air is let into the central chamber through openings between the piers and the bookcases. The radiators and the appurtenance systems are thus made an artistic feature of the architecture.

(See page 45.) The Martin house is fireproof, the walls are of brick, floors of reinforced concrete overlaid with ceramic mosaic, roofs tiled. The vitreous brick used in the exterior walls is worked with bronzed joints into the walls and piers of the interior. The brick on these interior surfaces is used in a decorative sense as a mosaic. The woodwork throughout is of fumed white oak. A pergola connects the house with a conservatory, which in turn is connected by means of a covered way with the stable.

100

LIVING ROOM OF THE MARTIN HOUSE.

Fireplace opening with bronze doors to either hall or dining room or both. Facings of low toned gold mosaic; wistaria blossoms in bright gold.

IN THE CAUSE OF ARCHITECTURE.

D. D. MARTIN HOUSE—DINING ROOM.

102

Buffalo, N. Y.   D. D. MARTIN HOUSE.
                          Detail in conservatory.

IN THE CAUSE OF ARCHITECTURE.

Buffalo, N. Y.   D. D. MARTIN HOUSE.
                        Detail of library, bay and terrace.

THE BARTON HOUSE OF THE MARTIN GROUP.
Buffalo, N. Y.

This design is representative also of a type, total cost ranging from seven to ten thousand dollars. The main floor is treated as a single room, entered at the middle of the side. A central stair hall, with dining room and living room screened at either end, are formed within this room by architectural contrivances not extending to the ceiling. The kitchen and the porch balance each other as protruding wings on the minor axis. The second story contains four bed rooms, servants' room and bath. (See general plan, D. D. Martin House.)

IN THE CAUSE OF ARCHITECTURE.

Conservatory and stable.

D. D. MARTIN HOUSE.

Buffalo, N. Y.

Pergola and conservatory and entrance.   Stone bird houses.

106

BROWNE'S BOOK STORE—DETAIL OF INTERIOR.
Fine Arts Building, Chicago.

IN THE CAUSE OF ARCHITECTURE.

Entrance to office.

Oak Park, Ill.   OFFICE OF MR. FRANK LLOYD WRIGHT.
An alcove in the drafting room.

108

Oak Park, Ill.   RESIDENCE OF MR. H. H. CHENEY.
    A one-story brick house set within terraces and small gardens, enclosed by brick walls.

LIBRARY OF MR. WRIGHT'S OAK PARK OFFICE.

IN THE CAUSE OF ARCHITECTURE.

STUDY FOR DINING ROOM OF THE DANA HOUSE.
Springfield, Ill.

To avoid distortion in rendering, the side wall has been shown cut away. The decorative frieze around the room is treated with the Shumac, Golden Rod and Purple Aster that characterize our roadsides in September.

PLASTER MODEL—HOUSE AND TEMPLE FOR UNITY CHURCH—VIEW OF END OF AUDITORIUM.

Oak Park, Ill.

A concrete monolith cast in wooden molds or "forms" and now in process of construction. A photograph on another page shows the work so far completed. After removing the forms the exterior surfaces are washed clean to expose the small gravel aggregate, the finished result in texture and effect being not unlike a coarse granite. The columns, with their decoration, were cast and treated in the same way. The entrance to either building is common to both, and connects them at the center. Both buildings are lighted from above. The roofs are simple reinforced concrete slabs waterproofed. The auditorium is a frank revival of the old temple form, as better suited to the requirements of a modern congregation than the nave and transept of the cathedral type. The speaker is placed well out into the auditorium, his audience gathered about him in the fashion of a friendly gathering, rather than as fixed in deep ranks when it was imperative that the priest make himself the cynosure of all eyes. The audience enters independently of, and at the rear of the auditorium, by means of depressed passages on either side. After services the audience moves directly toward the pulpit and out at either side of the auditorium itself. Unity House is designed for the various social activities of the church and for the Sunday school.

IN THE CAUSE OF ARCHITECTURE.

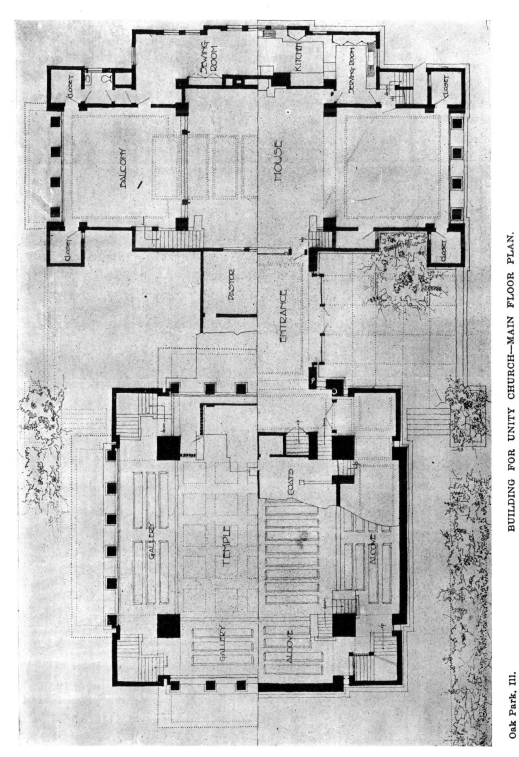

Oak Park, Ill.

BUILDING FOR UNITY CHURCH—MAIN FLOOR PLAN.

112

PERSPECTIVE STUDY—BUILDING FOR UNITY CHURCH.

Oak Park, Ill.

INEXPENSIVE CONCRETE HOUSE DESIGNED FOR THE LADIES' HOME JOURNAL—
PROCESS OF CONSTRUCTION SAME AS IN BUILDING FOR UNITY CHURCH.

BUILDING FOR UNITY CHURCH IN PROCESS OF CONSTRUCTION
Oak Park, Ill.

MR. RICHARD W. BOCK'S ATELIER.

This structure is designed for concrete construction similar to building for Unity Church.

IN THE CAUSE OF ARCHITECTURE.

MR. W. S. GERTS' HOUSE.

Glencoe, Ill.

Racine, Wis.   THE THOMAS P. HARDY HOUSE.

Situated on the bank of Lake Michigan. The street front is opposite to the view here given.

THE ELIZABETH STONE HOUSE.

Glencoe, Ill.

HOUSE FOR MR. B. J. WESTCOTT.

Springfield, Ohio.

A simple treatment of the same problem as the Coonley house at Riverside, Ill. Living room at center; dining room on one side and sleeping rooms on the other; service wing extending from the rear of the living room.

IN THE CAUSE OF ARCHITECTURE.

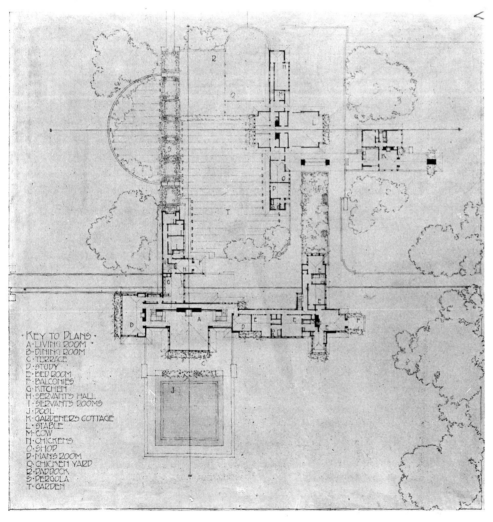

·KEY TO PLANS·
A·LIVING ROOM·
B·DINING ROOM
C·TERRACE
D·STUDY
E·BED ROOM
F·BALCONIES
G·KITCHEN
H·SERVANTS HALL
I·SERVANTS ROOMS
J·POOL
K·GARDENERS COTTAGE
L·STABLE
M·COW
N·CHICKENS
O·SHOP
P·MANS ROOM
Q·CHICKEN YARD
R·PADDOCK
S·PERGOLA
T·GARDEN

RESIDENCE OF MR. A. COONLEY.

Riverside, Ill.

A one-story house designed for the prairie, but with the basement entirely above ground, similar to Thomas, Heurtley and Tomek houses. All rooms, except entrance hall and play room, are on one floor. Each separate function in the house is treated for and by itself, with light and air on three sides, and grouped together as a harmonious whole. The living room is the pivot of the arrangement, with entrance, play room and terraces below, level with the ground, forming the main unit of the design. The dining room forms another unit. The kitchen and servants' quarters are in an independent wing. Family sleeping rooms form still another unit, and the guest rooms a pendant wing. Stable and gardener's cottage are grouped together and informally connected by a covered way which terminates in the gardener's verandah. An arbor crosses the garden to the rear, terminating in the service entrance. The stables, stable yards and gardens are enclosed by plastered walls.

RESIDENCE FOR MR. GEORGE M. MILLARD, HIGHLAND PARK, ILL.

Exterior of undressed wood throughout. The second story contains five bed rooms and two bath rooms. Man's room, laundry and store rooms in basement. This house is one of a type ranging in cost from seven to eight thousand dollars, complete.

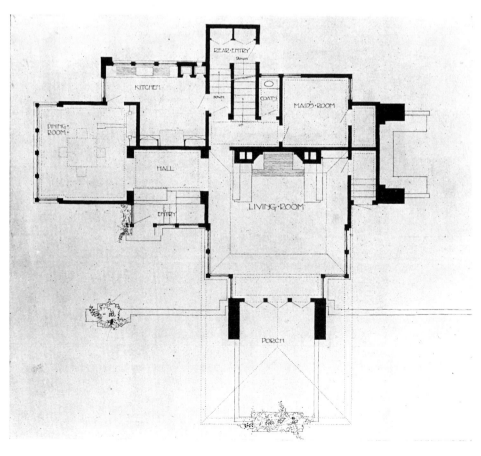

RESIDENCE OF MR. B. J. WESTCOTT.

Springfield, Ohio.

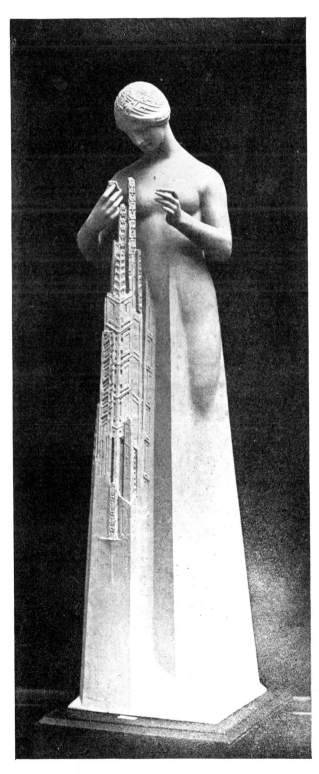

"FLOWER IN THE CRANNIED WALL."
A DECORATIVE FIGURE IN CREAM WHITE TERRA COTTA, DESIGNED FOR THE HALL-
WAY OF THE DANA HOUSE.

Richard W. Bock, Sculptor.

MAY 1914

IN THE CAVSE OF ~ ~ ARCHITECTVRE

SECOND PAPER

"STYLE, THEREFORE, WILL BE THE MAN, IT IS HIS. LET HIS FORMS ALONE"

BY FRANK LLOYD WRIGHT

NOTE.—In connection with the exhibition at the Chicago Art Institute of the Chicago Architectural Club during April and May, there will be an individual exhibit by Frank Lloyd Wright of the work done by him since his return from Europe. Some of the subjects shown will be the drawings of the New Imperial Hotel at Tokio, the Midway Gardens at Chicago, Lake Geneva Hotel, The Coonley Kindergartens, about fifteen residences, also models and plates of the twenty-five story building in San Francisco, The Coonley Play House and the Midway Gardens and details of furniture and special features of the building. The exhibit itself is to be in a separate room and installed in a characteristic manner. This second paper by Mr. Wright is a timely supplement to the very notable exposition of the artist motives actuating his work, which appeared in the Architectural Record in March, 1908.—Editor.

"NATURE has made creatures only; Art has made men." Nevertheless, or perhaps for that very reason, every struggle for truth in the arts and for the freedom that should go with the truth has always had its own peculiar load of disciples, neophytes and quacks. The young work in architecture here in the Middle West, owing to a measure of premature success, has for some time past been daily rediscovered, heralded and drowned in noise by this new characteristic feature of its struggle. The so-called "movement" threatens to explode soon in foolish exploitation of unripe performances or topple over in pretentious attempts to "speak the language." The broker, too, has made his appearance to deal in its slender stock in trade, not a wholly new form of artistic activity certainly, but one serving to indicate how profitable this intensive rush for a place in the "new school" has become.

Just at this time it may be well to remember that "every form of artistic activity is not Art."

Obviously this stage of development was to be expected and has its humorous side. It has also unexpected and dangerous effects, astonishingly in line with certain prophetic letters written by honest "conservatives" upon the publication of the former paper of 1908.

Although an utterance from me of a critical nature is painful, because it must be a personal matter, perhaps a seeming retraction on my part, still all that ever really happens is "personal matter" and the time has come when forbearance ceases to be either virtue or convenience. A promising garden seems to be rapidly overgrown with weeds, notwithstanding the fact that "all may raise the flowers now, for all have got the seed." But the seed has not been planted—transplanting is preferred, but it cannot raise the needed flowers.

To stultify or corrupt our architectural possibilities is to corrupt our aesthetic life at the fountain head. Her Architecture is the most precious of the susceptibilities of a young, constructive country in this constructive stage of development; and maintaining its integrity in this respect, therefore, distinctly a cause.

When, twenty-one years ago, I took my stand, alone in my field, the cause was unprofitable, seemingly impossible, almost unknown, or, if known, was, as a rule, unhonored and ridiculed—Montgomery Schuyler was- the one notable exception to the rule. So swiftly do things "come on" in this vigorous and invigorating age that although the cause itself has had little or no recognition, the work has more than its share of attention and has attracted to itself abuses seldom described—never openly attacked—but which a perspective of the past six years will enable me to describe, as I feel they must render the finer values in this work abortive for the time being, if they do not wholly defeat its aim. Many a similar work in the past has gone prematurely to ruin owing to similar abuses—to rise again, it is true, but retarded generations in time.

I still believe that the ideal of an organic* architecture forms the origin and source, the strength and, fundamentally, the significance of everything ever worthy the name of architecture.

And I know that the sense of an organic architecture, once grasped, carries with it in its very nature the discipline of an ideal at whatever cost to self interest or the established order.

It is itself a standard and an ideal.

And I maintain that only earnest artist integrity, both of instinct and of intelligence, can make any forward movement of this nature in architecture of lasting value.

The ideal of an organic architecture for America is no mere license for doing the thing that you please to do as you please to do it in order to hold up the strange thing when done with the "see-what-1-have-made" of childish pride. Nor is it achieved by speaking the fancied language of "form and function"—cant terms learned by rote—or prating foolishly of "Progress before Precedent"—that unthinking, unthinkable thing! In fact, it is precisely the total absence of any conception of this ideal standard that is made conspicuous by this folly and the practices that go with it. To reiterate the statement made in 1908:

This ideal of an organic architecture

---

*By organic architecture I mean an architecture that *develops* from within outward in harmony with the conditions of its being as distinguished from one that is *applied* from without.

for America was touched by Richardson and Root, and perhaps other men, but was developing consciously twenty-eight years ago in the practice of Adler & Sullivan, when I went to work in their office. This ideal combination of Adler & Sullivan was then working to produce what no other combination of architects nor any individual architect at that time dared even preach—a sentient, rational building that would owe its "style" to the integrity with which it was individually fashioned to serve its particular purpose—a "thinking" as well as "feeling" process, requiring the independent work of true artist imagination—an ideal that is dynamite, cap and fuse, in selfish, insensible hands—personal ambition, the lighted match.

At the expiration of a six year apprenticeship, during which time Louis Sullivan was my master and inspiration, twenty-one years ago, I entered a field he had not, in any new spirit, touched—the field of domestic architecture—and began to break ground and make the forms I needed, alone—absolutely alone.

These forms were the result of a conscientious study of materials and of the machine which is the real tool, whether we like it or not, that we must use to give shape to our ideals—a tool which at that time had received no such artistic consideration from artist or architect. And that my work now has individuality, the strength to stand by itself, honors Mr. Sullivan the more. The principles, however, underlying the fundamental ideal of an organic architecture, common to his work and to mine, are common to all work that ever rang true in the architecture of the world, and free as air to any pair of honest young lungs that will breathe deeply enough. But I have occasion to refer here only to that element in this so-called "new movement" which I have characterized by my own work and which should and, in a more advanced stage of culture, would be responsible to me for use or abuse of the forms and privileges of that work. Specifically, I speak only to that element within this element, now beyond private reach or control, ruthlessly characterizing and publicly exploiting the cause it does not comprehend or else that it cannot serve.

Some one for the sake of that cause must have some conscience in the matter and tell the truth. Since disciples, neophytes and brokers will not, critics do not, and the public cannot—I will. I will be suspected of the unbecoming motives usually ascribed to any man who comes to the front in behalf of an ideal, or his own; nevertheless, somehow, this incipient movement, which it has been my life work to help outfit and launch, must be protected or directed in its course. An enlightened public opinion would take care of this, but there is no such opinion. In time there will be; meantime good work is being wasted, opportunities destroyed or worse, architectural mortgages on future generations forged wholesale: and in architecture they must be paid with usurious interest.

The sins of the Architect are permanent sins.

To promote good work it is necessary to characterize bad work as bad.

Half-baked, imitative designs—fictitious semblances—pretentiously put forward in the name of a movement or a cause, particularly while novelty is the chief popular standard, endanger the cause, weaken the efficiency of genuine work, for the time being at least; lower the standard of artistic integrity permanently; demoralize all values artistically; until utter prostitution results. This prostitution has resulted in the new work partly, I have now to confess, as a by-product of an intimate, personal touch with the work, hitherto untried in the office of an American architect; and partly, too, perhaps, as one result of an ideal of individuality in architecture, administered in doses too strong, too soon, for architectural babes and sucklings; but chiefly, I believe, owing to almost total lack of any standard of artist integrity among architects, as a class, in this region at least. Of ethics we hear something occasionally, but only in regard to the relation of architects to each other when a client is in question— never in relation to sources of inspiration, the finer material the architect uses in shaping the thing he gives to his client. Ethics that promote integrity in this respect are as yet unformed and the young man in architecture is adrift in the most vitally important of his experiences, he cannot know where he stands in the absence of any well-defined principles on the part of his confreres or his elders.

If I had a right to project myself in the direction of an organic architecture twenty-one years ago, it entailed the right to my work and, so far as I am able, a right to defend my aim. Also —yet not so clearly—I am bound to do what I can to save the public from untoward effects that follow in the wake of my own break with traditions. I deliberately chose to break with traditions in order to be more true to Tradition than current conventions and ideals in architecture would permit. The more vital course is usually the rougher one and lies through conventions oftentimes settled into laws that must be broken, with consequent liberation of other forces that cannot stand freedom. So a break of this nature is a thing dangerous, nevertheless indispensable, to society. Society recognizes the danger and makes the break usually fatal to the man who makes it. It should not be made without reckoning the danger and sacrifice, without ability to stand severe punishment, nor without sincere faith that the end will justify the means; nor do I believe it can be effectively made without all these. But who can reckon with the folly bred by temporal success in a country that has as yet no artistic standards, no other god so potent as that same Success? For every thousand men nature enables to stand adversity, she, perhaps, makes one man capable of surviving success. An unenlightened public is at its mercy always—the "success" of the one thousand as well as of the one in a thousand; were it not for the resistance of honest enmity. society, nature herself even, would soon cycle madly to disaster. So reaction is essential to progress, and enemies as valuable an asset in any forward movement as friends, provided only they be honest; if intelligent as well as honest, they are invaluable. Some time ago this work reached the stage where it sorely needed honest enemies if it was to survive. It has had some honest enemies whose honest fears were expressed in the prophetic letters I have mentioned.

But the enemies of this work, with an exception or two, have not served it well. They have been either unintelligent or careless of the gist of the whole matter. It fact, its avowed enemies have generally been of the same superficial, time serving spirit as many of its present load of disciples and neophytes. Nowhere even now, save in Europe, with some few notable exceptions in this country, has the organic character of the work been fairly recognized and valued—the character that is perhaps the only feature of lasting vital consequence.

As for its peculiarities—if my own share in this work has a distinguished trait, it has individuality undefiled. It has gone forward unswerving from the beginning, unchanging, yet developing, in this quality of individuality, and stands, as it has stood for nineteen years at least, an individual entity, clearly defined. Such as it is, its "individuality" is as irrevocably mine as the work of any painter, sculptor or poet who ever lived was irrevocably his. The form of a work that has this quality of individuality is never the product of a composite. An artist knows this; but the general public, near-artist and perhaps "critic," too, may have to be reminded or informed. To grant a work this quality is to absolve it without further argument from anything like composite origin, and *to fix its limitations*.

There are enough types and forms in my work to characterize the work of an architect, but certainly not enough to characterize an architecture. Nothing to my mind could be worse imposition than to have some individual, even temporarily, deliberately fix the outward forms of his concept of beauty upon the future of a free people or even of a growing city. A tentative, advantageous forecast of probable future utilitarian development goes far enough in this direction. Any individual willing to undertake more would thereby only prove his unfitness for the task, assuming the task possible or desirable. A socialist might shut out the sunlight from a free and developing people with his own shadow, in this way. An artist is too true an individualist to suffer such an imposition, much less perpetrate it; his problems are quite other. The manner of any work (and all work of any quality has its manner) may be for the time being a strength, but finally it is a weakness; and as the returns come in, it seems as though not only the manner of this work or its "clothes," but also its strength in this very quality of individuality, which is a matter of its soul as well as of its forms, would soon prove its undoing, to be worn to shreds and tatters by foolish, conscienceless imitation. As for the vital principle of the work—the quality of an organic architecture—that has been lost to sight, even by pupils. But I still believe as firmly as ever that without artist integrity and this consequent individuality manifesting itself in multifarious forms, there can be no great architecture, no great artists, no great civilization, no worthy life. Is, then, the very strength of such a work as this is its weakness? Is it so because of a false democratic system naturally inimical to art? or is it so because the commercialization of art leaves no noble standards? Is it because architects have less personal honor than sculptors, painters or poets? Or is it because fine buildings are less important now than fine pictures and good books?

In any case, judging from what is exploited as such, most of what is beginning to be called the "New School of the Middle West" is not only far from the ideal of an organic architecture, but getting farther away from it every day.

A study of similar situations in the past will show that any departure from beaten paths must stand and grow in organic character or soon fall, leaving permanent waste and desolation in final ruin; *it dare not trade long on mere forms*, no matter how inevitable they seem. Trading in the letter has cursed art for centuries past, but in architecture it has usually been rather an impersonal letter of those decently cold in their graves for some time.

THE ARCHITECTURAL RECORD.

One may submit to the flattery of imitation or to caricature personally; every one who marches or strays from beaten paths must submit to one or to both, but never will one submit tamely to caricature of that which one loves. Personally, I, too, am heartily sick of being commercialized and traded in and upon; but most of all I dread to see the types I have worked with so long and patiently drifting toward speculative builders, cheapened or befooled by senseless changes, robbed of quality and distinction, dead forms or grinning originalities for the sake of originality, an endless string of hacked carcasses, to encumber democratic front yards for five decades or more. This, however, is only the personal side of the matter and to be endured in silence were there any profit in it to come to the future architecture of the "melting pot."

The more serious side and the occasion for this second paper is the fact that emboldened or befooled by its measure of "Success," the new work has been showing weaknesses instead of the character it might have shown some years hence were it more enlightened and discreet, more sincere and modest, prepared to wait, to wait to prepare.

The average American man or woman who wants to build a house wants something different—"something different" is what they say they want, and most of them want it in a hurry. That this is the fertile soil upon which an undisciplined "language speaking" neophyte may grow his crop to the top of his ambition is deplorable in one sense, but none the less hopeful in another and more vital sense. The average man of business in America has truer intuition, and so a more nearly just estimate of artistic values, when he has a chance to judge between good and bad, than a man of similar class in any other country. But he is prone to take that "something different" anyhow; if not good, then bad. He is rapidly outgrowing the provincialism that needs a foreign-made label upon "Art," and so, at the present moment, not only is he in danger of being swindled, but likely to find something peculiarly his own, in time, and valuable to

him, if he can last. I hope and believe he can last. At any rate, there is no way of preventing him from getting either swindled or something merely "different"; nor do I believe it would be desirable if he could be, until the inorganic thing he usually gets in the form of this "something different" is put forward and publicly advertised as of that character of the young work for which I must feel myself responsible.

I do not admit that my disciples or pupils, be they artists, neophytes or brokers, are responsible for worse buildings than nine-tenths of the work done by average architects who are "good school"—in fact, I think the worst of them do better—although they sometimes justify themselves in equivocal positions by reference to this fact. Were no more to come of my work than is evident at present, the architecture of the country would have received an impetus that will finally resolve itself into good. But to me the exasperating fact is that it might aid vitally the great things we all desire, if it were treated on its merits, used and not abused. Selling even good versions of an original at second hand is in the circumstances not good enough. It is cheap and bad—demoralizing in every sense. But, unhappily, I have to confess that the situation seems worse where originality, as such, has thus far been attempted, because it seems to have been attempted chiefly *for its own sake,* and the results bear about the same resemblance to an organic architecture as might be shown were one to take a classic column and, breaking it, let the upper half lie carelessly at the foot of the lower, then setting the capital picturesquely askew against the half thus prostrate, one were to settle the whole arrangement as some structural feature of street or garden.

For worker or broker to exhibit such "designs" as efforts of creative architects, before the ink is yet dry on either work or worker, is easily done under present standards with "success," but the exploit finally reflects a poor sort of credit upon the exploited architect and the cause. As for the cause, any growth that comes to it in a "spread" of this kind is unwholesome. I insist that this sort of thing is not "new school," nor this the way to develop one. This is piracy, lunacy, plunder, imitation, adulation, or what you will; it is not a developing architecture when worked in this fashion, nor will it ever become one until purged of this spirit; least of all is it an organic architecture. Its practices belie any such character.

"Disciples" aside, some fifteen young people, all entirely inexperienced and unformed—but few had even college educations—attracted by the character of my work, sought me as their employer. I am no teacher; I am a worker—but I gave to all, impartially, the freedom of my work room, my work and myself, to imbue them with the spirit of the performances for their own sakes, and with the letter for my sake, so that they might become useful to me; because the nature of my endeavor was such that I had to train my own help and pay current wages while I trained them.

The nature of the profession these young people were to make when they assumed to practice architecture entails much more careful preparation than that of the "good school" architect; theirs is a far more difficult thing to do technically and artistically, if they would do something of their own. To my chagrin, too many are content to take it "ready made," and with no further preparation hasten to compete for clients of their own. Now fifteen good, bad and indifferent are practicing architecture in the Middle West, South and Far West, and with considerable "success." In common with the work of numerous disciples (judging from such work as has been put forward publicly), there is a restless jockeying with members, one left off here, another added there, with varying intent—in some a vain endeavor to reindividualize the old types; in others an attempt to conceal their origin, but always—ad nauseam—the inevitable reiteration of the features that gave the original work its style and individuality. To find fault with this were unfair. It is not unexpected nor unpromising except in those unbearable cases where badly modified *inorganic* results seem to satisfy their authors' conception of originality; and banalities of form and proportion are accordingly advertised in haste as work of creative architects of a *"new school."* That some uniformity in performance should have obtained for some years is natural; it could not be otherwise, unless unaware I had harbored marked geniuses. But when the genius arrives nobody will take his work for mine—least of all will he mistake my work for his.

"The letter killeth." In this young work at this time, still it is the letter that killeth, and emulation of the "letter" that gives the illusion or delusion of "movement." There is no doubt, however, but that the sentiment is awakened which will mean progressive movement in time. And there are many working quietly who, I am sure, will give a good account of themselves.

Meanwhile, the spirit in which this use of the letter has its rise is important to any noble future still left to the cause. If the practices that disgrace and demoralize the soul of the young man in architecture could be made plain to him; if he could be shown that inevitably equivocation dwarfs and eventually destroys what creative faculty he may possess—that designing lies, in design to deceive himself or others, shuts him out absolutely from realizing upon his own gifts—no matter how flattering his opportunities may be—if he could realize that the artist heart is one uncompromising core of truth in seeking, in giving or in taking—a precious service could be rendered him. The young architect who is artist enough to know where he stands and man enough to use honestly his parent forms as such, conservatively, until he feels his own strength within him, is only exercising an artistic birthright in the interest of a good cause—he has the character at least from which great things may come. But the boy who steals his forms—"steals" them because he sells them as his own for the moment of superficial distinction he gains by trading on the results—is no artist, has not the sense of the first principles of the ideal that he poses and the forms that he abuses. He denies his birthright, an act characteristic and unimportant; but for a mess of pottage, he endangers the chances of a genuine forward movement, insults both cause and precedent with an astounding insolence quite peculiar to these matters in the United States, ruthlessly sucks what blood may be left in the tortured and abused forms he caricatures and exploits—like the parasite he is.

Another conditions as far removed from creative work is the state of mind of those who, having in the course of their day's labor put some stitches into the "clothes" of the work, assume, therefore, that style and pattern are rightfully theirs and wear them defiantly unregenerate. The gist of the whole matter artistically has entirely eluded them. This may be the so-called "democratic" point of view; at any rate it is the immemorial error of the rabble. No great artist nor work of art ever proceeded from that conception, nor ever will.

Then there is the soiled and soiling fringe of all creative effort, a type common to all work everywhere that meets with any degree of success, although it may be more virulent here because of low standards; those who benefit by the use of another's work and to justify themselves depreciate both the work and worker they took it from—the type that will declare, "In the first place, I never had your shovel; in the second place, I never broke your shovel; and in the third place, it was broken when I got it, anyway"—the type that with more crafty intelligence develops into the "coffin worm." One of Whistler's "coffin worms" has just wriggled in and out.

But underneath all, I am constrained to believe, lies the feverish ambition to get fame or fortune "quick," characteristic of the rush of commercial standards that rule in place of artist standards, and consequent unwillingness to wait to prepare thoroughly.

"Art to one is high as a heavenly goddess; to another only the thrifty cow that gives him his butter," said Schiller; and who will deny that our profession is prostitute to the cow, meager in ideals, cheap in performance, commercial in spirit; demoralized by ignoble ambition?

A foolish optimism regarding this only serves to perpetuate it. Foolish optimism and the vanity of fear of ridicule or "failure" are both friends of ignorance.

In no country in the world do disciples, neophytes or brokers pass artist counterfeit so easily as in these United States. Art is commercialized here rather more than anything else, although the arts should be as free from this taint as religion. But has religion escaped?

So the standard of criticism is not only low—it is often dishonest or faked somewhere between the two, largely manufactured to order for profit or bias. Criticism is worked as an advertising game, traders' instincts subject to the prevailing commercial taint. Therein lies a radically evil imposition that harms the public; that also further distorts, confuses and injures values and promotes bad work; that tends to render the integrity of artist and commerce alike a stale and unprofitable joke, and to make honest enemies even harder to find than honest friends. The spirit of fair play, the endeavor to preserve the integrity of values, intelligently, on a high plane in order to help in raising the level of the standard of achievement in the country, and to refrain from throwing the senseless weight of the mediocre and bad upon it—all this is unhappily too rare among editors. The average editor has a "constituency," not a standard. This constituency is largely the average architect who has bought the "artistic" in his architecture as one of its dubious and minor aspects, or the sophisticated neophyte, the broker and the quack, to whom printers' ink is ego-balm and fortune.

So until the standard is raised any plea for artist integrity is like a cry for water in the Painted Desert. As for competent criticism, the honest word of illuminating insight, where is it? Nothing is more precious or essential to progress. Where is the editor or critic not narrow or provincial? Or loose and ignorant? Or cleverly or superficially or cowardly commercial? Let him raise this standard! Friend or foe, there is still a demand for him even here; but if he did, he would fail—gloriously fail—of "success."

Is architecture, then, no longer to be practiced as an art? Has its practice permanently descended to a form of mere "artistic activity"?

The art of architecture has fallen from a high estate—lower steadily since the Men of Florence patched together fragments of the art of Greece and Rome and in vain endeavor to re-establish its eminence manufactured the Renaissance. It has fallen—from the heavenly Goddess of Antiquity and the Middle Ages to the thrifty cow of the present day. To touch upon these matters in this country is doubly unkind, for it is to touch upon the question of "bread and butter" chiefly. Aside from the conscienceless ambition of the near artist—more sordid than any greed of gold—and beneath this thin pretense of the ideal that veneers the curious compound of broker and neophyte there lurks, I know, for any young architect an ever present dread of the kind of "failure" that is the obverse of the kind of "success" that commercialized standards demand of him if he is to survive. Whosoever would worship his heavenly goddess has small choice—he must keep his eye on the thrifty cow or give up his dream of "success"; and the power of discrimination possessed by the cow promises ill for the future integrity of an organic architecture. The net result of present standards is likely to be a poor wretch, a coward who aspires pretentiously or theoretically, advertises cleverly and milks surreptitiously. There is no real connection between aspiration and practice except a tissue of lies and deceit; there never can be. The young architect before he ventures to practice architecture with an ideal, today, should first be sure of his goddess and then, somehow, be connected with a base of supplies from which he cannot be cut off, or else fall in with the rank and file of the "good school" of the hour. Any one who has tried it knows this; that is, if he is honest and is going to use his own material as soon as he is able. So the ever present economic question underlies this question of artist integrity, at this stage of our development, like quicksand beneath the footing of a needed foundation, and the structure itself seems doomed to shreds and cracks and shores and patches, the deadening compromises and pitiful makeshifts of the struggle to "*succeed!*" Even the cry for this integrity will bind the legion together, as one man, against the crier and the cry.

This is Art, then, in a sentimental Democracy, which seems to be only another form of self-same hypocrisy? Show me a man who prates of such "Democracy" as a basis for artist endeavor, and I will show you an inordinately foolish egotist or a quack. The "Democracy" of the man in the American street is no more than the Gospel of Mediocrity. When it is understood that a great Democracy is the highest form of Aristocracy conceivable, not of birth or place or wealth, but of those qualities that give distinction to the man as a man, and that as a social state it must be characterized by the honesty and responsibility of the absolute individualist as the unit of its structure, then only can we have an Art worthy the name. The rule of mankind by mankind is one thing; but false "Democracy"—the hypocritical sentimentality politically practiced and preached here, usually the sheep's clothing of the proverbial wolf, or the egotistic dream of self-constituted patron saints—is quite another thing. "The letter killeth"; yes, but more deadly still is the undertow of false democracy that poses the man as a creative artist and starves him to death unless he fakes his goddess or persuades himself, with "language," that the cow is really she. Is the lack of an artist-conscience, then, simply the helpless surrender of the would-be artist to this wherewithal Democracy with which a nation soothes itself into subjection? Is the integrity for which I plead here no part of this time and place? And is no young aspirant or hardened sinner to blame for lacking it? It may be so. If it is, we can at least be honest about that, too. But what aspiring artist could knowingly face such a condition? He would choose to dig in the ditch and trace his dreams by lamplight, on scrap paper, for the good of his own soul—a sweet and honorable, if commercially futile, occupation.

THE ARCHITECTURAL RECORD.

It has been my hope to have inspired among my pupils a personality or two to contribute to this work, some day, forms of their own devising, with an artistic integrity that will help to establish upon a firmer basis the efforts that have gone before them and enable them in more propitious times to carry on their practice with a personal gentleness, wisdom and reverence denied to the pioneers who broke rough ground for them, with a wistful eye to better conditions for their future.

And I believe that, cleared of the superficial pose and push that is the inevitable abuse of its opportunity and its nature, and against which I ungraciously urge myself here, there will be found good work in a cause that deserves honest friends and honest enemies among the better architects of the country. Let us have done with "language" and unfair use of borrowed forms; understand that such practices or products are not of the character of this young work. This work is a sincere endeavor to establish the ideal of an organic architecture in a new country; a type of endeavor that alone can give lasting value to any architecture and that is in line with the spirit of every great and noble precedent in the world of forms that has come to us as the heritage of the great life that has been lived, and in the spirit of which all great life to be will still be lived.

And this thing that eludes the disciple, remains in hiding from the neophyte, and in the name of which the broker seduces his client—what is it? This mystery requiring the catch phrases of a new language to abate the agonies of the convert and in the name of which ubiquitous atrocities have been and will continue to be committed, with the deadly enthusiasm of the ego-mania that is its plague? First, a study of the nature of materials you elect to use and the tools you must use with them, searching to find the characteristic qualities in both that are suited to your purpose. Second, with an ideal of organic nature as a guide, so to unite these qualities to serve that purpose, that the fashion of what you do has integrity or is *natively fit,* regardless of preconceived notions of style. *Style* is a by-product of the process and comes of the man or the mind in the process. The style of the thing, therefore, will be the man—it is his. *Let his forms alone.*

To adopt a "style" as a motive is to put the cart before the horse and get nowhere beyond the "Styles"—never to reach *Style.*

It is obvious that this is neither ideal nor work for fakirs or tyros; for unless this process is finally so imbued, informed, with a feeling for the beautiful that grace and proportion are inevitable, the result cannot get beyond good engineering.

A light matter this, altogether? And yet an organic architecture must take this course and belie nothing, shirk nothing. Discipline! The architect who undertakes his work seriously on these lines is emancipated and imprisoned at the same time. His work may be severe; it cannot be foolish. It may lack grace; it cannot lack fitness altogether. It may seem ugly; it will not be false. No wonder, however, that the practice of architecture in this sense is the height of ambition and the depth of poverty!

Nothing is more difficult to achieve than the integral simplicity of organic nature, amid the tangled confusions of the innumerable relics of form that encumber life for us. To achieve it in any degree means a serious devotion to the "underneath" in an attempt to grasp the *nature* of building a beautiful building beautifully, as organically true in itself, to itself and to its purpose, as any tree or flower.

That is the need, and the need is demoralized, not served, by the same superficial emulation of the letter in the new work that has heretofore characterized the performances of those who start out to practice architecture by selecting and electing to work in a ready-made "style."

MAY 1927

In the CAUSE OF ARCHITECTURE

By
Frank Lloyd Wright

1—THE ARCHITECT AND THE MACHINE

THE MACHINE is the architect's tool—whether he likes it or not. Unless he masters it, the Machine has mastered him.

The Machine? What is the machine?

It is a factor Man has created out of his brain, in his own image—to do highly specialized work, mechanically, automatically, tirelessly and cheaper than human beings could do it. Sometimes better.

Perfected machines are startlingly like the mechanism of ourselves—anyone may make the analogy. Take any complete mechanistic system and compare it with the human process. It is new in the world, not as a principle but as a means. New but already triumphant.

Its success has deprived Man of his old ideals because those ideals were related to the personal functions of hands and arms and legs and feet.

For feet, we have wheels; for hands, intricate substitutes; for motive power, mechanized things of brass and steel working like limited hearts and brains.

For vital energy, explosives, or expansives. A world of contrivance absorbs the inventive energy of the modern brain to a great extent and is gradually mastering the drudgery of the world.

The Machine is an engine of emancipation or enslavement, according to the human direction and control given it, for it is unable to control itself.

There is no initiative will in machinery. The man is still behind the monster he has created. The monster is helpless but for him—

I have said monster—why not savior?

Because the Machine is no better than the mind that drives it or puts it to work and stops it.

Greed may do with it what it did with slaves in "the glory that was Greece and the grandeur that was Rome"—only do it multiplied infinitely. Greed in human nature may now come near to enslaving all humanity by means of the Machine—so fast and far has progress gone with it.

This will be evident to anyone who stops to study the modern mechanistic Moloch and takes time to view it in its larger aspects.

Well—what of it! In all ages man has endured the impositions of power, has been enslaved, exploited and murdered by millions—by the initiative wills back of arms and legs, feet and hands!

But there is now this difference—the difference between a bow-and-arrow and gun-powder. A man with a machine may murder or enslave millions, whereas it used to take at least thousands to murder millions. And the man behind the machine has nothing on his conscience. He merely liberates an impersonal force.

What is true of the machine as a murderer is just as true of it as a servant.

Which shall it be? It is for the creative-artist to decide—For no one else. The matter is sociological and scientific only in its minor aspects. It is primarily a matter of using the machine to conserve life not destroy it. To enable human beings to have life more abundantly. The use of the machine can not conserve life in any true sense unless the mind that controls it understands life and its needs, as *life*—and understands the machine well enough to give it the work to do that it can do well and uses it to that end.

Every age and period has had its technique. The technique of the age or period was always a matter of its industrial system and tools, or the systems and tools were a matter of its technique. It doesn't matter which. And this is just as true to-day.

This age has its own peculiar—and,

unfortunately, unqualified technique. The system has changed. The Machine is our normal tool.

America (or let us say Usonia—meaning the United States—because Canada and Brazil are America too)—Usonia is committed to the machine and is machine-made to a terrifying degree. Now what has the mind behind and in control of the machine done with it to justify its existence, so far? What work suited to its nature has been given it to do? What, in the way of technique has been developed by its use that we can say really serves or conserves Life in our country outside mere acceleration of movement?

Quantity production?—Yes. We have ten for one of everything that earlier ages or periods had. And it is worth so far as the quality of life in it goes, less than one-tenth of one similar thing in those earlier days.

Outside graceless utility, creative life as reflected in "things" is dead. We are living on the past, irreverently mutilating it in attempting to modify it—creating nothing—except ten for one. Taking the soul of the thing in the process and trying to be content with the carcass, or shell or husk—or whatever it may be, that we have.

All Man-made things are worthy of life. They may live to the degree that they not only served utilitarian ends, in the life they served but expressed the nature of that service in the form they took as things. That was the beauty in them and the one proof of the quality of life in those who used them. To do this, love entered into the making of them. Only the joy of that love that gives life to the making of things proves or disproves the quality of the civilization that produced them.

See all the records of all the great civilizations that have risen and fallen in course of Time and you may see this evidence of love as joy in the making of their things. Creative artists—that is, workmen in love with what they were making for love of it—made them live. And they remain living after the human

beings whose love of life and their understanding of it was reflected in them, are thousands of years dead. We study them longingly and admire them lovingly and might learn from them—the secret of their beauty.

Do we?

What do we do with this sacred inheritance? We feed it remorselessly into the maw of the Machine to get a hundred or a thousand for one as well as it can do it—a matter of ubiquity and ignorance—lacking all feeling, and call it progress.

Our "technique" may therefore be said to consist in reproduction, imitation, ubiquity. A form of prostitution other ages were saved from, partly because it was foolish to imitate by hand the work of another hand. The hand was not content. The machine is quite content. So are the millions who now have as imitations bearing no intimate relation to their human understanding, things that were once the very physiognomy of the hearts and minds—say the souls of those whose love of life they reflected.

We love life, we Usonians as much as any people? Is it that we are now willing to take it in quantity too—regardless of inferior quality and take all as something canned—long ago?

One may live on canned food quite well—But can a nation live a canned life in all but the rudimentary animal expressions of that life? Indefinitely?

Canned Poetry, Canned Music, Canned Architecture, Canned Recreation. All canned by the Machine.

I doubt it, although I see it going on around me. It has its limits.

We must have the technique to put our love of life in our own way into the things of our life using for our tool the machine to our own best advantage—or we will have nothing living in it all—soon.

How to do it?

Well! How does any one master tools? By learning the nature of them and, by practice, finding out what and how they do what they do best—for one thing.

Let architects first do that with the Machine. Architects are or must be masters of the industrial means of their era. They are, or must be—interpreters of the love of life in their era.

They must learn to give it expression in the background for that life—little by little, or betray their office. Either that or their power as normal high-priests of civilization in a Democracy will never take its place where it is so badly needed. To be a mason, plasterer, carpenter, sculptor, or painter won't help architects much—now.

They may be passing from any integral relation to life as their architecture, a bad form of surface decoration superficially applied to engineering or buildings would seem to indicate and their function go to something other and else. An embarrassment of riches, in the antique, a deadly facility of the moment, a polyglot people—the necessity of "ready-made" architecture to clothe the nakedness of steel frames decently or fashionably, the poisonous taste of the period; these alibis have conspired with architects to land us where we all are at the mercy of the Machine. Architects point with pride to what has happened. I can not—I see in it nothing great—at least nothing noble. It is as sorry waste as riches ever knew. We have every reason to feel ashamed of what we have to show for our *"selves"* in any analysis that goes below the skin.

A kind of skin disease is what most architecture is now as we may view it today. At least it never is organic. It has no integrity except as a "composition." And modern artists, except architects, ceased to speak of "composition" long ago.

Fortunately, however, there is a growing conviction that architecture is something not in two dimensions—but with a third and that third dimension in a spiritual sense may be interpreted as the integral quality in the thing or that quality that makes it integral.

The quality of *life* in man-made "things" is as it is in trees and plants and animals, and the secret of character in them which is again "style" is the same. It is a materialization of spirit.

To put it baldly—Architecture shirks the machine to lie to itself about itself and in itself, and we have Architecture for Architecture's sake. A sentimental absurdity. Such "Architecture," being the buildings that were built when men were workmen—and materials and tools were otherwise—instead of recognizing Architecture as a great living Spirit behind all that—a living spirit that left those forms as noble records of a seed time and harvest other than ours, thrown up on the shores of Time, in passing. A Spirit living still only to be denied and belied by us by this academic assertion of ours that they are that spirit. Why make so foolish an assertion? I have asked the question in many forms of many architects in many places and always had to answer myself. For there is no philosophy back of the assertion other than a denial or a betrayal—that will hold together. Instead there is a doctrine of Expediency fit only for social opportunists and speculative builders or "schools." There is no other sense in it.

The Machine does not complain—It goes on eating it all up and crying continually for more.

Where is more coming from? We have already passed through nearly every discovered "period" several times forward and gone backward again, to please the "taste" of a shallow present.

It would seem, now, time to take the matter seriously as an organic matter and study its vitals—in a sensible way.

Why not find out what *Nature* is in this matter. And be guided by Principles rather than Expedients? It is the young man in architecture who will do this. It is too late for most successful practitioners of today to recover from their success. These essays are addressed to that young man.

JUNE 1927

In the CAUSE OF ARCHITECTURE

By
Frank Lloyd Wright

II—STANDARDIZATION, THE SOUL OF THE MACHINE

JOHN RUSKIN AND WILLIAM MORRIS turned away from the machine and all it represented in modern art and craft. They saw the deadly threat it was to all they loved as such—and eventually turned again to fight it, to the death—their death. They are memories now. Pleasant ones. They did not succeed in delaying destruction nor in constructing anything. They did, however, remind us of what we were losing by using the machine or, as they might have said, letting the machine use us.

Repetition carried beyond a certain point has always taken the life of anything addressed to the living spirit.

Monotony kills.

Human feeling loves the vigor of spontaneity, freshness, and the charm of the unexpected. In other words, it loves life and dreads death.

The Machine Ruskin and Morris believed to be the enemy of all life. It was and is so still, but only because the artist has shirked it as a tool while he damned it; until now he has been damned by it.

Standardization as a principle is at work in all things with greater activity than ever before.

It is the most basic element in civilization. To a degree it is civilization itself.

An oriental rug, lustrous, rich with color and light, gleaming with all the brilliant pattern opulent oriental imagination conceived, has a very definite basis of standardization in warp and woof. In the methodical stitches regularly taken with strands of woolen yarn, upon that regular basis of cotton strings, stretched tight, lies the primitive principle of standardization. Serving the imagination full well.

Standardization here serves the spirit well—its mechanics disappear in the glowing fabric of the mind—the poetic feeling of the artist weaver with love of beauty in his soul.

Standardization should have the same place in the fabric we are weaving which we call civilization—as it has in that more simple fabrication of the carpet. And the creative artist-mind must put it into the larger more comprehensive fabric.

How?

Not so simple.

This principle of standardization has now as its tool or body—the Machine. An ideal tool compared to which all that has gone before is as nothing.

Probably Gutenberg's invention of movable types was the first great advent of the machine in any sweeping form.

The blessing of that invention is obvious as is the curse that came with it.

The body of the book became volatile, almost infinite—and mind failed to keep up with it. Trash inundated the civilized world and streams of printed pages became wrapping paper to fill packing cases, light fires and blow unheeded about the gutters of the world.

A deluge. And yet the book lives. There are a thousand writers for one in earlier eras and mostly worth one-thousandth part as much. "Shifting type" was the principle of standardization at work. The machine is the "press," that we have to-day serving it. What happened here in printing has happened to nearly everything in our lives. Happened or is happening or soon to happen with similar but more disastrous results; quantity at expense of quality—with always the blessing that comes from it, making available to the poor and needy a cheap or debased form of what was once rare and precious. I am speaking of fine art from the architect's standpoint.

So we see in the Machine the fore-runner and ideal agent of Usonian Democracy such as it is. A Democracy sentimental and unsound, but that is another and longer story.

We see in this old force a new agency hard to control. A force once released into the world—never to be stopped until every thing in it once precious and valuable for its own sake in its intimate relation to former good or great life has been fed to the dogs, or swine, speaking bitterly. But meantime raising the opportunities for "having things" the world over with a chance of turning the dogs, or swine, into more human beings.

And, honestly let it be said, of putting all human beings perhaps at the mercy of swine and dogs.

This is where the creative artist steps in: to bring new life of the mind to this potent agency: new understanding that will make living more joyous and genuine by abolishing the makeshift, showing up imitation for the base thing it is—saving us from this inglorious rampage and rapine upon antiquity. There is no artist conscience, it seems, in all this. The artist is like a hungry orphan turned loose in a bake shop. The creative artist is not in it.

That ancient honor of the race, creative art, can not be dead. It needs only awakening. No wonder it lies all but moribund floating in the "deluge" at the mercy of the current of ubiquity, rushing toward—well, let us hope, toward the great peace of the great ocean.

This principle of standardization then, is no detriment to art or artist. It has always existed. And like any principle has its uses and its abuses.

How foolish therefore to take a prevalent abuse of any thing for the thing itself?

An artist is sentient. He is never fooled by brains or science or economics. He knows by feeling—say instinct—right or living, from wrong or dead.

He may not, however, have the technique to make his "knowing" effective and so remain inarticulate. But it is his duty to know, for his technique is what makes him serviceable to his fellows as artist. Acquiring the technique of the Machine as the tool of standardization,

mastering the nature of both, is the only thing now that will make him the living force necessary to salvage the flotsam and jetsam of the "deluge," or, let it all go and begin over again.

Begin another era: the modern era of the machine with all it implies, economically making life more joyous and abundant as a matter of quality as well as quantity.

Standardization apprehended as a principle of order has the danger of monotony in application.

Standardization can be murderer or beneficent factor as the life in the thing standardized is kept by imagination or destroyed by the lack of it.

By the "life" in the thing I mean the *integrity* of the thing (we are talking of the things of art and craft) in the sense of the third dimension—as I have already tried to explain it.

The "life" in the thing is that quality of it or in it which makes it perfectly *natural*—of course that means organic. And that simply means true to what made it, as it was made, and for what it was made. That would be the *body* of the "thing." A matter of good sense.

New opportunities have come, not to hand but to the mind.

This may not seem specific. But it is a point of view necessary to the understanding of the experiences which follow. For in that spirit the experiments were made and the results judged as good or bad that will appear as I write.

The first study of importance in this connection is of course, the nature of *materials*.

It is impossible to do anything intelligently to or with something you know nothing about. To know intimately the nature of wood, paper, glass, sheet metal, terra cotta, cement, steel, cast iron, wrought iron, concrete, is essential to knowing how to use the tools available to make use of those materials, sensibly or artfully.

So let us glance at these more staple materials. We will find certain properties in all, that standardization will serve well; and other properties, too, that standardization, carried too far, will kill.

The principle of standardization, applied, may be said to be a matter of knowing by a *study* of the nature of whatever we apply it to—when to quit.

Let us begin with a short study of wood.

What is wood?

A workable, fibrous material got from trees in almost any length, certain breadths and thicknesses, now standardized. It may be had in almost any color or texture, as trees are growing in great variety all over the world. Different woods vary in characteristics, made known by use in all ages. To it man has had recourse for nearly every need. He has made of it a part, or entirely, in one form or another, nearly everything he uses. It may be polished, or painted, or stained, to bring out its grain which is the great characteristic of its beauty. It may be sawed or cut to bring this beauty to the surface in various ways. It was once laborious to hand-saw and cut and smooth it. Machines now do all that better. Machines cut veneers so cheaply and so thin and so wide they may be applied like wall paper to broad surfaces. Machines cut rotary veneers from the curling surface of the log in any width, unwinding the surface with a cut of the grain unknown before. Really, this property of wood has been liberated and made available in beautiful sheets, so beautiful in surface that it is folly to mold it, and join it, and panel it painfully any more as before.

It may be used in broad simple plastic ways now even more cheaply than in laborious joinery with its tendency to go to pieces because it was all in pieces.

Much more could be said. Here is enough to indicate new possibilities of design in machined wood.

Inlaid lines are characteristic too,—slender inlaid decorative purflings or battens between wide, plain, broad, etc., etc.

Plastic treatment, now, you see, instead of *constructed* ones or "structuralities."

There are infinite possibilities here. And in making wood into furniture, clean straightline effects, as delicate as may be, are characteristic of the machine. A lim-

itation that makes the nature of wood very beautiful as it appears within these limitations of form.

Wood carving usually did violence to the nature of wood. It tended to mutilate and destroy it.

The machine can inlay, fret and bring up the beauty of wood in plastic treatments more true to the nature of the wood. Why not then, forget ancient models that are especially made to suit freedom of the hand? The nature of wood was overwrought and lost in three out of five of such models anyway. But here the beauty that is wood lives above standardization, if the architect sees it and uses it in this new " plastic " sense.

Let us take glass.

Glass was once a delightful substance in itself. It is now chiefly a perfect "clarity" or nothing very delightful.

Such clearness in polished glass as we have is new in the world. We may have great polished surfaces for reflections, leaving openings as though nothing closed them—limpid surfaces playing the same part in all interiors that water plays in the landscape. We have lost a substance but found a freedom infinitely precious to the designer of buildings. This is the mechanical plate glass of the machine. New opportunities here. Imagine a few.

There is electro glazing to introduce the element of pattern into the clear glass in delicate straight lines in bewildering delicacy and variety.

The mind must enter now to take the place of what, in the antique, was adorable as a natural quality of the glass itself. The scene has shifted, but we are still better off, in glass.

We can make colored glass for the painter to use as pigment in his hand, but it is now a lesser interest. We have limpid surfaces, true reflections and unobstructed vision due to the machine.

And there is steel.* A new thing under the sun. And the most significant material of this age. The one that has done most harm to the established order—or Pseudo-Classic.

*Steel is the next essay in this series.

AUGUST 1927

In the CAUSE OF ARCHITECTURE

By
Frank Lloyd Wright

PART III. STEEL

STEEL IS THE epic of this age.

Steel has entered our lives as a "material" to take upon itself the physical burden of our civilization.

This is the Age of Steel. And our "culture" has received it as ancient Roman culture received the great gift of the masonry arch. For centuries the Romans pasted the trabeated Greek forms of their "culture" on the arch in front as architecture, while the arch did the work behind.

Finally the noble virtue of the arch overcame the sham culture of the period and came forth and lived as a great and beautiful contribution to mankind.

Steel is still smothered in aesthetic gloom, insulted, denied and doomed by us as was the masonry arch by the Romans. Inherent virtue will triumph here, too, in course of time. So much wasted time!

This stupendous material—what has it not done for Man?

What may it not yet do for him with its derivatives and associates as the glare of the converters continues to mount into the sky, day and night.

Now, ductile, tensile, dense to any degree, uniform and calculable to any standard, steel is a known quantity to be dealt with mathematically to a certainty to the last pound; a miracle of strength to be counted upon!

Mathematics in the flesh—at work for man!

A mere plastic material, thin and yet an ultimate rigidity, rolled hot or rolled cold to any desired section of any strength unlimited in quantity; or, continuously night and day, drawn into thin strands of enormous strength and length as wire—enough to wind the world into a steel covered ball; or, rolled in any thickness into sheets like paper, cut by the shears into any size.

A rigidity condensed in any shape conceivable, to be as easily bored, punched, planed, cut, and polished, too, as wood once was. More easily and cheaply curved or bent or twisted or woven to any extent and the parts fastened together. A material that in the processes already devised not only takes any shape the human brain can reduce to a diagram but can go on producing it until the earth is covered with it—and there is no escape from it. No, none!

For it is cheap.

Cheaper in its strength and adaptability than anything man ever knew before—thousands of times over.

But it has it in its nature to change its volume with changes of temperature.

It has a fatal weakness.

Slowly it disintegrates in air and moisture and has an active enemy in electrolysis. It is recovering from this weakness. It is only fair to say that it may become, soon, immune. Then, what?

Meanwhile, owing to its nature it may be plated with other metals or protected by coverings of various sorts, or combined with them. In itself it has little beauty, neither grain, nor texture of surface. It has no more "quality" in this sense than mud. Not so much as sand. It is a creature wholly dependent upon imaginative influences for "life" in any aesthetic sense at the hand of a creator.

So is terra cotta. So is concrete, although both these friable materials have certain internal possibilities of texture and color.

So also relatives of steel have beautiful permanent surfaces—bronze, brass, silver, gold, aluminum, copper, tin and zinc and others. It would be interesting to write about them all.

But the weaknesses of steel are not fatal to beautiful use, nor is the lack of individuality in texture other than an opportunity for the imagination.

Yet, how or where is steel evident in our life as a thing of beauty in itself? In tools? Yes, in knives and saws and skates: in hardware. In engines, in the rails of the railroad, in the locomotive, the submarine, the torpedo boat, the aeroplane. In bridges? Yes, but only where the engineer was inspired and allowed his stresses and strains to come and go clean in the members, innocent of any desire or intent on his part to "ornament" them. Used honestly by engineers, steel has something of the beauty of mathematics.

Remember, however, that music is but sublimated mathematics. And the engineer is no more capable of giving steel structure the life of "beauty" it should have than a professor of mathematics is capable of a symphony in music.

The principles of construction which find in steel a medium that will serve with safety economically in various designs as support for enormous loads to span wide spaces, or supporting enormous loads to enormous height,' are, as long as they are really kept scientific and clean, showing as such, the best work we have to show.

And it is much.

But it is not the architect who can show it.

When the architect has dealt with it what has he done? The skyscraper and lied about it. The modern Cathedral, lifeless, dummy, supported from within to appear "life like" without. Anything you wish to name as architecture will be likewise.

Anything you may name as engineering where architects coöperated will be similar, probably.

An exception here and there is now manifest, already late. This era is fast and furious in movement. But all movement is not progress. Architecture has not progressed with steel. "Architecture" has all but died of it while architects were singing their favorite hymns and popular Christmas carols to the medieval antique.

Incredible folly! "Tower" Buildings, East River bridges, St. John the Divine's, States Capitols, and all. How all of them mock integrity! Wherein lies the artist grasp of the "masters" who design such structures?

Had Bach or Beethoven made music the mathematics of which would be like the principles of construction in such edifices, what would such music sound like? Pandemonium, requiring hideous grimaces and falsities of tone and absurdities of concatenation with no rhythm, obvious or occult, outrage to the mind. Inconceivable!

For the principles of construction now find in steel because it is a strictly calculable material of miraculous strength, ideal expression as the sinews and bones of structure.

The architect has been satisfied to leave the mathematical sinews and bones unbeautiful, although serviceable as such, and content to hang garments over them rented from some costumers or not even that—pawed from the scrap heap of antiquity.

It is superstition or plain ignorance to believe these sinews and bones incapable of beauty as such—if such, to be clothed with a flesh that will be living on them, *an expression of them!*

Is it reasonable too to go further and say "sinews and bones"? Yes, but not as in the human frame but as a new world of form in themselves capable of being beautiful in themselves in a new sense, so devised in construction that flesh is unnecessary.

Why should not the structural principle be expressed artistically as well as scientifically for its own sake in this ideal material? Expressed with a knowledge of rhythm and synthesis of form that a master musician would bring to his mathematics? Can we not imagine a building to be serviceably beautiful and beautifully serviceable as it is naturally made— in steel? Glass is all that is needed really after we have honestly insured the life of the steel.

And, added to this immense possibility, here enters a vital modern probability:

Steel is most economical in tension; the steel strand is a marvel, let us say, as compared with anything the ancients knew; a miracle of strength for its weight and cost. We have found now how to combine it with a mass material, concrete, which has great strength in compression. The co-efficient of expansion and contraction of both materials is the same in changes of temperature. The more bulky material protects the slighter material from its enemy, disintegration. The heavier material, or protector, strangely grows stronger as it grows older. Permanent "flesh" if we care to so regard it.

A valuable partnership in materials in any case more congenial to the architect than steel alone for he can do more richly with flesh and sinews than he can with sinews and bones, perhaps. Certainly, if regarded as such by him.

Here we have reinforced concrete, a new dispensation. A new medium for the new world of thought and feeling that seems ideal: a new world that must follow freedom from the imprisonment in the abstract in which tradition binds us. Democracy means liberation from those abstractions, and therefore life, more abundantly in the concrete. This is not intended as a pun. It happens to be so literally, for concrete combined with steel strands will probably become the physical body of the modern civilized world

Here again and especially has the machine liberated the creative architect.

And he prefers his bonds!

The old structural limitation that took form as masonry, lintels and arches, "natural" posts and beams, is all gone. There is in their place a science of mathematics applied to materials of marvelous new properties and strength, here to the architect's hand instead—"mathematics materialized at work for man."

What are we, as architects, going to do with it? For as yet, we have done nothing with it on principle. We have merely "made shift." Architects have avoided an open break with the powers that be, on the ground of impotence, only by psalm singing and caroling in the name of tradition. But, enough.

Here in addition to the possibility of steel alone, is a perfect wedding of two plastic materials. A wondrous freedom! Freedom worthy of ideal democracy. Astounding! That upon so simple a means such a vast consequence to human life depends. But so it does. And just so simple has the initiation of far reaching changes brought by evolution always been.

The limitation of the human imagination is all that ties the hands of the modern architect except the poison in his veins fostered by "good taste" for dead forms.

His imagination now must devise the new cross sections for the machine more suitable for use in harmoniously framing steel. Rivets have interesting effects as well as facts. Steel plates have possibilities combined with posts and beams. And now there is electric welding to make the work more simple and integral. Posts may become beautiful, beams too. The principle of the "gusset" has a life of its own, still, Strangely, here is plastic material delivered by the Machine in any rigid structural form to be fastened together as members in a structural design.

The design may emphasize the plastic as structural or the structural as plastic. What that means in detail is a liberal education in itself. It must be had by the young architect. He will have to go to work at it himself.

And again, easier to comprehend are the new forms brought to hand by reinforced concrete.

First among them is the slab—next the cantilever—then the splay.

To be able to make waterproof, weatherproof slabs of almost any size or continuity is a great simplification. A great means to a great end. To be able to make these slabs so they may be supported beneath as a waiter supports his tray on the fingers of his upraised arm, leads to another marvelous release, a new freedom.

This is the economic structural principle of the cantilever. A new stability as well as a new economy. The most romantic of all structural possibilities is here.

And last, there is the splay or sloping wall, used as a slide from wall into projections or from floors into walls or used in connection with the cantilever slab. It may be used as an expression of form in itself for protection or light. For economy it may be useful as support in both cases and enhance the plastic effect of the whole.

There is nothing in architecture ready made to meet these sweeping new "freedoms."

What a release is here! The machine brought it in the ubiquitous ductile steel strand with its miraculous strength and the fortunate wedding of that strength with poured concrete.

What a circumstance!

Here, "young men in architecture," is your palette. The "foyer" of your new world.

Let us of the former generation see you at work on it, in it for all you are worth.

And here again, the password is the word "plastic." "Structuralities" as such must be forgotten. If you will take paper and fold it and bend it, or cardboard sheets and cut them and fit and arrange them into models for buildings, you will see the sense of the new structure in its primitive aspect. And then, after this superficial external view, get inside and make the whole line as one plastic entity—however the slabs tend to separate or fall to themselves.

And never lose sight of the fact that all in this new world is no longer in two dimensions. That was the old world.

We are capable of a world now in three dimensions; the third, as I have said before, interpreted as a spiritual matter that makes all integral—"at one."

How life may be blessed by the release this simple development of its viewpoint will bring to mankind.

Paintings and sculpture for use to enrich and enhance the work, still live. They now live a detached life as things apart, for and by themselves. It is a pity, for they can never thrive in that separate life.

Unfortunately, there is a conviction in certain quarters—if it amounts to a "conviction," — chiefly European, — that ornamentation is untrue to the Machine in this, the Machine Age. That the use of ornamentation is a romanticism and therefore inappropriate.

The contrary is the case.

But it is true that ornamentation in the old sense as an "applied" thing, as something added to the thing superficially, however cleverly adapted or "composed" is dead to this new world.

Ornamentation in the plastic sense* is as characteristic of the thing we call the machine as ornamentation in the old sense was a characteristic feature of "The Renaissance"; more so, because it is the imagination living in the process and so woven into the life of the thing. A matter of the "constitution" of the thing. The trace of human imagination as the poetic language of line and color must now live *in* the thing so far as it is natural to it. And that is very far.

* * *

*This phase of the machine as the creative architect's tool will be treated next as *Fabrication and Imagination*.

OCTOBER 1927

In the CAUSE OF ARCHITECTURE

By
Frank Lloyd Wright

IV. FABRICATION AND IMAGINATION

TIME WAS WHEN the hand wrought. Time is here when the *process* fabricates instead.

Why make the fabrication a lie or allow it to become one when we try to make it "beautiful"? Any such lie is an abuse of Imagination.

All Man has above the brute, worth having, is his because of Imagination. Imagination made the Gods—all of them he knows—it is the Divine in him and differentiates him from a mere reasoning animal into a God himself. A creative being is a God. There will never be too many Gods.

Reason and Will have been exalted by Philosophy and Science. Let us now do homage to Imagination.

We have suspected it and punished it and feared it long enough.

Imagination is so intimately related to sentient perception—we can not separate the two. Nor need do so.

Let us call Creative-Imagination the Man-light in Mankind to distinguish it from intellectual brilliance. It is strongest in the creative-artist. A sentient quality. To a degree all developed individuals have this quality, and to the extent that it takes concrete form in the human fabrications necessary or desirable to human life, it makes the fabrication live as a reflection of that Life any true Man loves as such—Spirit materialized.

The Machine is an obedient, tireless fabricator of a non-sentient product. A shaper and drawer of steel, a weaver of fabrics—"casting" forms continually in every material solvent by fire or water.

So the study of the process is as important as the study of the Machine. It is another phase of the Machine and in the method of the process too lies the opportunity for the artist. Unless he understands it what can he do with it—to qualify its product—from within? To modify it externally is not enough. He has been on the surface, as intimately related to its nature as a decalcomania on a tin box-cover is to the Nature of the thing going on inside. He has been a decorative label when he has been at all.

Let us, then, get inside.

We will find all the magic of ancient times magnified—Aladdin with his wonderful lamp had a poor thing relatively in that cave of his. Aladdin's lamp was a symbol merely for Imagination. Let us take this lamp inside, in the Architect's world.

Where begin? With mechanistic processes like weaving? printing? stamping? Or with casting? Or with plastic, chemicalized materials like concrete, plastering, steel making, glass making, paper making, ceramics?

One must serve for all. Then let us take one that is both a chemical-process and casting—concrete.

Concrete is a plastic material but sets so slowly as yet that moulds or so called "forms" are used to give it *shape*. It must be held, until it hardens sufficiently, to hold the shape desired.

Ordinarily in itself it has no texture unless the mould leaves it on the surface. It is, however, possible to use fine colored-gravel or crushed-marble or granite in the mixture so the superficial-cement (retarded in setting by some substance like soap applied to the interior surfaces of the "forms") may be easily washed away, leaving the hard gleaming aggregate exposed in almost any color or texture.

All composite materials like concrete

have possibilities of bringing out the nature of the mixture in some kind of surface treatment, and the materials may be variously composed in the substances mixed to secure these effects of texture and color desired in the finished product.

But, mainly, concrete is still a mass material taking form from moulds, erroneously called "forms."

The materials of which the moulds themselves are made, will, therefore, modify the shape the concrete naturally takes, if indeed it does not wholly determine it.

Unity Temple at Oak Park was entirely cast in wooden boxes, ornamentation and all. The ornament was formed in the mass by taking blocks of wood of various shapes and sizes, combining them with strips of wood, and, where wanted, tacking them in position to the inside faces of the boxes.

The ornament partakes therefore of the nature of the whole, belongs to it. So the block and box is characteristic of the forms of this temple. The simple cubical masses are in themselves great concrete blocks.

The design makes a feature of this limitation as to form as they are grouped to express the great room within.

Here is a building, a monolith in mono-material, textured as described above, left complete as it came from the moulds—permanent architecture.

The whole is a great casting articulated in sections according to the masses of concrete that could safely be made to withstand changes of temperature in a severe climate.

It is a good record of this primitive period in the development of concrete building when it was necessary to pour the material into boxes to "set it" into shape.

It is a "natural" building therefore, in a transition-period of the development of the use of concrete.

I say a period of transition because concrete is essentially a plastic material, sometime to be used as such; used as a plastic material by plastering upon cores or upon steel fabrications. The resultant form may then take the shapes characteristic of drifted snow or sand or the smooth conformation of animals perhaps —as they become finished buildings.

But at the present time there comes a less cumbersome and a cheaper because less wasteful method than the moulds on a large scale that built Unity Temple. It was necessary then to build a rough building complete in wood as a "mould" into which the temple could be cast.

Now, in this easier more plastic method, standardization enters as the *unit-system*.

A unit-mass of concrete, size and shape determined by the work intended to be done and what weight a man can reasonably be expected to lift and set in a wall, is fixed upon. This in order to avoid the expensive larger moulds—say, the slab block we make 16-in. by 16-in. x 2½-in. thick.

Mechanical steel or aluminum moulds are made in which to precast the whole building in a small "unit" of that size. Grooves are provided in the edges of the slab-blocks so a lacing of continuous steel rods may be laid in the vertical and horizontal joints of the block slabs for tensile strength. The grooves are large as possible so they may be poured full of concrete after each course of blocks is set up, girding and locking the whole into one firm slab. Here ultimately we will have another monolith *fabricated* instead of *poured* into special wooden moulds. The moulds in this case are metal, good for many buildings, and take the impress of any detail in any scheme of pattern or texture imagination conceives. The whole building "precast" in a mould a man can lift.

Here the making of the structural-unit and the process of fabrication become complete synchronized standardizations. A building for the first time in the world may be lightly fabricated, complete, of mono-material—literally woven into a pattern or design as was the oriental rug earlier referred to in "Standardization": fabrication as infinite in color, texture and variety as in that rug. A certain simple technique larger in organization but no more complex in execution than that of the rug-weaving, *builds* the building. The diagrams and unit moulds are

THE ARCHITECTURAL RECORD

less *simple*. They have much study put on them, and organization becomes more than ever important.

When Machine-Standardizing enters, all must be accurate, precise, organized.

The Machine product can stand no slovenly administration for it can make good no mistakes.

The limitations of both process and material are here very severe, but when these are understood and accepted we may "weave" an architecture at will—unlimited in quality and quantity except by the limitation of imagination.

Several mechanical moulds may be thrown into a Ford and taken where gravel and sand abound. Cement is all else needed, except a few tons of ¼ in. commercial steel bars, to complete a beautiful building. This—and an organization of workmen trained to do one thing well.

The ground is soon covered with slab-blocks, the block-stuff curing in moisture. After that, it is all a matter of reading the architect's diagrams, which is what his plans now become. They are not tediously figured with haphazard dimensions any longer. They are laid out by counting blocks, corner blocks and half-blocks; so many blocks wide, so many high, and showing where specific blocks go is like counting stitches in the "woof" and threads in the "warp." Building is a matter of taking slab-block stitches on a steel warp.

So, a livable building may be made of mono-material in one operation!

There is an outer shell and an inner shell separated by a complete air space.

The inner walls, floors and ceilings which this inner shell becomes are the same as the outside walls, and, fabricated in the same way at the same time.

Windows? made in the shop, standardized to work with the block slab units. Made of sheet-metal finished complete and set in the walls as the work proceeds.

Piping? Cut to the standard unit-length in the shop and set into the hollow spaces. Plastering? None. Carpenter work? None. Masonry? None. "Form" work? None. Painting? None. Decorations? All integral, cast into the structure as de-

signed with all the play of imagery known to Persian or Moor.

The process of elimination which *standardization* becomes has left only essentials. Here is a process that makes of the mechanics of concrete building a mono-material and mono-method affair instead of the usual complex quarreling aggregation of processes and materials: *builds* a building permanent and safe, dry and cool in summer, dry and warm in winter. Standardization here effects economy of effort and material to the extreme, but brings with it a perfect freedom for the imagination of the designer who now has infinite variety as a possibility in ultimate effects after mastering a simple technique.

I give here only one instance of many possibilities in this one material.

What precisely has happened?

Well, one consistent economical imperishable whole instead of the usual confusion of complexities to be reduced to a heap of trash by time.

A quiet orderly simplicity and all the benefits to human beings that come with it.

A simple, cheap material everywhere available, the common stuff of the community—here made rare and exquisite by the Imagination.

Imagination conceives the "fabric" of the whole. The "unit" is absorbed as agreeable texture in the pattern of the whole. Here, too, is certainty of results as well as minimum of costs assured to the human being by free use of the Machine, in perfect control. The whole now in human scale and thoroughly humane. Here is true technique. The technique of a principle *at work*; at work in every minor operation with this material—concrete. Here the material is affected by a process suited to the result desired to such an extent that Architecture may live in our life again in our Machine-age as a free agent of Imagination.

Copper, glass—all materials are subject to similar treatment on similar terms according to their entirely different natures.

The forms and processes will change

as the material changes—but the principle will not. In the case of each different material treated the expression of the whole would become something quite different with new beauty. So comes a true variety in unity in this, the Machine Age.

Coition at last. The third dimension triumphant.

The sickening monotony achieved by a two-dimensional world in its attempts to be "different" mercifully ended, perhaps forever.

True variety now becomes a *natural consequence; a natural* thing. We can live again and more abundantly than ever before. Differently, yet the same.

Such harmony as we knew in the Gothic of "Le Moyen Age" is again ours —but infinitely expanded and related to the individual Imagination, intimately, and therefore to the human being as a unit of scale.

Is Machine-Standardization a hindrance? No, a release.

Boundless possibility, and with that comes increase of responsibility. Here, in the hand of the creative-artist, in *fabrication* in this sense, lies the whole expression, character and style, the *quality,* let us say, in any spiritual sense, of modern life.

The integrity of it all as an *expression* is now a matter of the creative-artist's Imagination *at work.*

Where is he? And if *he* is, may he be trusted with such power? Yes, if he has the Gift. If he is "God" in the sense that "man-light" lives in him in his work.

But should he fall short of that, if he is faithful, looking to principle for guidance, he is sufficiently disciplined by the honest technique of fabrication to be sure to produce steady quiet work.

Inspiration cannot be expected in any total fabric of civilization. It may only be expected to inspire the whole and lay bare the *sense of the thing* for others.

The whole is safe when discovered principle is allowed to work! Going *with* Nature in the use of Imagination may seem little different from going against Nature—but how different the destination and the reward!

It has been said that "Art is Art precisely in that it is not Nature," but in "obiter-dicta" of that kind the Nature referred to is nature in its limited sense of material appearances as they lie about us and lie to us.

Nature as I have used the word must be apprehended as the life-principle constructing and making appearances what they are, for what they are and in what they are. Nature inheres in all as *reality.* Appearances take form and character in infinite variety to our vision because of the natural inner working of this Nature-principle.

The slightest change in a minor feature of that "Nature" will work astounding changes of expression.

When the word Nature is understood and accepted in this sense, there is no longer any question of originality. It is natural to be "original" for we are at the fountain-head of all forms whatsoever.

The man who has divined the character of the ingrown sense-of-the-pine, say, can make other pine trees true to the species as any that may continually recur in the woods; make pine-tree forms just as true to the species as we see it and as we accept it as any growing out of doors rooted in the ground.

But, principles are not formulas. Formulas may be deduced from Principles, of course. But we must never forget that even in the things of the moment principles live and formulas are dead. A yardstick is a formula—Mathematics the principle. So, beware of formulas, they are dangerous. They become inhibitions of principle rather than expressions of them in non-sentient hands.

This principle understood and put to work, what would happen to our world? What would our world be like if the Nature-principle were allowed to work in the hands of Creative imagination and the *formulae* kept where it belongs?

Note.—The chemicalization of concrete or cement is too well-known to need any attention here.

THE ARCHITECTURAL RECORD.

V. The New World

The new world? A dangerous title.

But for a sense of humour in this old one there would be no new one. Length and breadth—with just enough thickness to hold them together for commercial purposes we have had in the old world, and all *that* implies in Art and Philosophy.

The new world begins to be when the little "thickness" we have had in the old one becomes *depth* and our sense of depth becomes that sense of the thing, or the quality in it that makes it *integral*— gives it integrity as such. With this "quality" the new world develops naturally in three dimensions out of the one which had but two.

The abstractions and aesthetic lies of a canned pictorial-culture crumble and fade away, worn out and useless.

"Institutions" founded upon those abstractions to serve that culture, crumble. And Architecture now belonging to, and refreshing as the forests or prairies or hills, the human spirit is free to blossom in structure as organic as that of plants and trees. Buildings, too, are children of Earth and Sun.

Naturally we have no more Gothic Cathedrals for the busy gainful-occupations. No more Roman or Greek Sarcophagi for the sacred Banking-business. No more French châteaux for Fire-Engine houses. No more Louis XIV, or Louis XV, or Louis XVI, or any Louis at all, for anything at all!

The Classics? A fond professorial dream.

The Periods? Inferior desecration.

Picture-Post-Card Homes? Museum relics affording much amusement.

The Skyscraper—vertical groove of the landlord? Laid down flat wise. A trap that was sprung.

Churches? We fail to recognize them.

Public Buildings? No longer monuments.

Monuments? Abolished as profane.

Industrial Buildings? Still recognizable—for they were allowed to be themselves in the old world.

Commercial Buildings, industrial, or official? Shimmering, iridescent cages of steel and copper and glass in which the principle of standardization becomes exquisite in all variety.

Homes? Growing from their site in native materials, no more "deciduous" than the native rock ledges of the hills, or the fir trees rooted in the ground, all taking on the character of the individual in perpetual bewildering variety.

The City? Gone to the surrounding country.

The landlords' exploitation of the herd-instinct seems to be exploded. That instinct is recognized as servile and is well in hand—but not in the landlord's hand.

A touch-stone now by way of the human-mind lies in reach of human-fingers everywhere to enable the human-being to distinguish and accept the quick and reject the dead!

It would seem after all, that this "new world" is simply a matter of being one's *self*.

Beech trees are welcome and allowed to be Beech trees because they are Beeches. Birches because they are Birches. Elms are not Oaks and no one would prefer them if they were, or get excited about making them so if they could.

Nor are Evergreens Christmas-trees.

Materials everywhere are most valuable for what they are—in themselves— no one wants to change their nature or try to make them like something else.

Men likewise—for the same reason: a reason everywhere working in everything.

So this new world is no longer a matter of seeming but of *being*.

Where then are we?

We are in a corner of the Twentieth Century emerging into the Twenty First —and the first Democracy of *being* not seeming.

The highest form of Aristocracy be it said the world has ever seen is this Democracy, for it is based upon the qualities that make the man a man.

We know, now, the tragedy of a civilization's lying to itself. We see the futility of expecting in hope, that a culture willing to deceive itself could or would know how to be sincere with others—or allow them happiness, or know happiness itself.

What an inglorious rubbish heap lies back there in the gloom of that duo-dimensional era! In that "Period" of superficial length and breadth with just enough "thickness" to make them hang together—for commercial purposes!

The "Period" of Fashion and Sham in which the "Picture" was the "cause" and not the consequence.

And the rubbish-heap gradually grew back there, useless, as the great simplicity of an Idea that was in itself an integrity rose to smite the Sham for what it was and proclaim, in fact, the Freedom we then professed.

SHAM and its brood—inbred by the ideals of "the classic" and its authority in education—fostered that duo-dimensional world beyond its ability to perform; educated it far and away beyond its capacity for life.

Character is Fate and invariably meets it. That old world was ripe for the rubbish heap and went to its destruction by the grinding of universal principles, grinding slow, nor yet so exceeding fine. For the awful simplicity of the Nazarene saw this "new world" at hand more than two thousand years ago. And here we are, two centuries later, only beginning to see it for ourselves.

Beginning to see it prepared by this simple enrichment of our *selves* in this sense of the "within" for our outlook. Beginning to understand and realize that the "Kingdom on Earth as it is in Heaven" of which He spoke was a Kingdom wherein each man was a King because Kingdom and King consisted of that quality of integrity of which, for lack of a better term, I have tritely spoken as the third-dimension. That all of the Beyond is within, is a truism.

And just so simple, although at the time less obvious, is the initiation of all great evolutionary changes whatsoever.

But this simple first principle of *being* that is now at work, for some strange reason came late and last.

Why?

We who have walked the Earth in eager search for the clear wine of Principle, tortured and denied or instead offered polluted water to quench an honest thirst, would like to know—why?

Were the Greeks poison? For us—yes. The Romans? More so.

Back there in the two-dimensional era we lived bewildered in a Roman-world—Romantic!

Not for nothing were we Romantic and did we speak a composite language corrupted from the Romance languages.

The honest Celt or Gaul or Teuton was corrupted by the Graeco-Roman corruption of the finer ancient culture of the Hellenes.

The Anglo-Saxon sanctified and re-corrupted the corruption, and polished sophistries, imprisoning abstractions, became recipes for good life in the name of the Good, the True and the Beautiful.

Hypocrisy for all cultivated men became as necessary as breathing and as "natural."

In order to be Beautiful—it became imperative to *lie!*

In order to *be* it became necessary to *seem.*

Art was a divorce from Nature.

"Nature" became the world of appearances round about us in our industrial life and all aspects of other individuals in relation to those appearances.

In the "Democracy" of the Nineteenth Century we witnessed the triumph of the insignificant as the fruit of the lie. A triumph by no means insignificant.

Some few unpopular individuals inhibited the "classic" in their education in that era, being afraid of it—seeing what it did to those who yielded to it, how it embalmed them in respectability and enshrined them in impotence. Seeing how it cut them off from Life and led them by the intellect into a falsified sense of living.

The precious quality in Man—Imagination—was shown the enticing objects man had made and shown them as so many "objectives." Therefore Imagination was offered patterns to the eye, not truths to the mind; offered abstractions to the Spirit not realities to the Soul. This was "Education."

To turn away from all that meant then,

owing to the supreme psychology of the herd, well—what it has meant.

Since one need no longer turn from reality to be respectable, all sacrifices in former worlds are made a privilege, something to have enjoyed.

For the scene has shifted. The burden—there is no burden like artificiality —has lifted.

Art having been *"artificiality"* for centuries has come through its terrible trial, hard put to it by the Machine—which stripped it to the bone—and lives.

It is living now because the Artifex survived the Artificer.

The Man has survived the Mime.

Be comforted—my young architect!

The "pictorial" still lives, for what it is, extended in this our new Usonian world, but as "consequence" not as "cause."

All we were given of love for the picturesque in gesture, form, color or sound —gifts to the five senses—is realized. Appearances are expanded into a synthesis of the five senses—we may call it a sixth if we please—and all become manifest materialization of Spirit.

Appearances are now a great assurance. A splendid enrichment of Life. The Pictorial is merely an incident, not an aim, nothing in itself or for itself or by itself; no longer an *end* sought for its own sake.

The picturesque? Therefore it is a by-product inevitably beautiful in all circumstances, from any and every point of view.

What wrought this miracle?

NATURE gradually apprehended as the principle of Life—the life-giving principle in making things with the mind, reacting in turn upon the makers.

Earth-dwellers that we are, we are become now sentient to the truth that living on Earth *is* a materialization of Spirit instead of trying to make our dwelling here a spiritualization of matter. Simplicity of Sense now honorably takes the lead.

To be good Gods of Earth *here* is all

the significance we have here. A God is a God on Earth as in Heaven. And there will never be too many Gods.

Just as a great master knows no masterpiece, and there are no "favourite" trees, nor color, nor flowers; no "greatest" master; so Gods are Gods, and all are GOD.

Be specific? I hear you—Young Man in Architecture.

Shall I too paint pictures for you to show to you this new world?

Show you "pictures" that I might make?

Would you not rather make them for yourself?

Because any picture I could make would not serve you well.

A specific "picture" might betray you. You might take it for the thing itself— and so miss its merely symbolic value, for it could have no other value.

This new world so far as it lives as such is conditioned upon your seeing it for yourself—out of your own love and understanding. It is that kind of world.

As another man sees it, it might entertain you. Why should you be "entertained?"

His specific picture, the better it might be the more it might forestall or bind you. You have had enough of that.

For yourself, by yourself, within yourself, then, visualize it and add your own faithful building to it, and you cannot fail.

We are punished for discipleship— and, as disciples, we punish the thing we love.

Who, then, can teach? Not I.

It too is a gift.

Already I have dared enough. Try to see—in work.

Idealism and Idealist are the same failure as Realism and Realistic. Both the same failure as Romance and Romantic.

Life is. We are.

Therefore we will loyally love, honestly work and enthusiastically seek, in all things—the one thing of Value—Life.

It is not found in pictorial shallows.

JANUARY 1928

IN THE CAUSE OF ARCHITECTURE

By Frank Lloyd Wright

1. THE LOGIC OF THE PLAN

Plan! There is something elemental in the word itself. A pregnant plan has logic—is the logic of the building squarely stated. Unless it is the plan for a foolish Fair.

A good plan is the beginning and the end, because every good plan is organic. That means that its development in all directions is inherent—inevitable.

Scientifically, artistically to foresee all is "to plan." There is more beauty in a fine ground plan than in almost any of its ultimate consequences.

In itself it will have the rhythms, masses and proportions of a good decoration if it is the organic plan for an organic building with individual style—consistent with materials.

All is there seen—purpose, materials, method, character, style. The plan? The prophetic soul of the building—a building that can live only because of the prophecy that is the plan. But it is a map, a chart, a mere diagram, a mathematical projection before the fact and, as we all have occasion to know, accessory to infinite crimes.

To judge the architect one need only look at his ground plan. He is master then and there, or never. Were all elevations of the genuine buildings of the world lost and the ground plans saved, each building would construct itself again. Because before the plan is a plan it is a concept in some creative mind. It is, after all, only a purposeful record of that dream which saw the destined building living in its appointed place. A dream—but precise and practical, the record to be read by the like-minded.

The original plan may be thrown away as the work proceeds—probably most of those for the most wonderful buildings in the world were, because the concept grows and matures during realization, if the master-mind is continually with the work. But that plan had, first, to be made. Ultimately it should be corrected and recorded.

But to throw the plans away is a luxury ill afforded by the organizations of our modern method. It has ruined owners and architects and enriched numberless contractors. Therefore conceive the building in the imagination, not on paper but in the mind, thoroughly—before touching paper. Let it live there—gradually taking more definite form before committing it to the draughting board. When the thing lives for you—start to plan it with tools. Not before. To draw during conception or "sketch," as we say, experimenting with practical adjustments to scale, is well enough if the concept is clear enough to be firmly held. It is best to cultivate the imagination to construct and complete the building before working upon it with T square and triangle. Working on it with triangle and T square should modify or extend or intensify or test the conception—complete the harmonious adjustment of its parts. But if the original concept is lost as the drawing proceeds, throw all away and begin afresh. To throw away a concept entirely to make way for a fresh one—that is a faculty of the mind not easily cultivated. Few have that capacity. It is perhaps a gift—but may be attained by practice. What I am trying to express is that the plan must start as a truly creative matter and mature as such. All is won or lost before anything more tangible begins

154

The several factors most important in making the plans—after general purpose or scheme or "project" are,.

2nd—Materials.
3rd—Building methods.
4th—Scale.
5th—Articulation.
6th—Expression or Style.

In the matter of scale, the human being is the logical norm because buildings are to be humanly inhabited and should be related to human proportions not only comfortably but agreeably. Human beings should look as well in the building or of it as flowers do.

People should belong to the building just as it should belong to them. This scale or unit-of-size of the various parts varies with the specific purpose of the building and the materials used to build it. The only sure way to hold all to scale is to adopt a unit-system, unit-lines crossing the paper both ways, spaced as pre-determined, say 4'-0" on centers—or 2'-8" or whatever seems to yield the proper scale for the proposed purpose. Divisions in spacing are thus brought into a certain texture in the result; ordered scale in detail is sure to follow.

A certain *standardization* is established here at the beginning, like the warp in the oriental rug. It has other and economic values in construction. I have found this valuable in practice even in small houses. Experience is needed to fix upon the proper size of the unit for any particular building. Trained imagination is necessary to differentiate or syncopate or emphasize, to weave or play upon it consistently.

Scale is really proportion. Who can teach proportion? Without a sense of proportion, no one should attempt to build. This gift of sense must be the diploma Nature gave to the architect.

Let the architect cling, always, to the normal human figure for his scale and he cannot go so far wrong as Michelangelo did in St. Peter's at Rome. St. Peter's is invariably disappointing as a great building, for not until the eye deliberately catches a human figure for purposes of comparison does one realize that the building is vast. All the details are likewise huge and the sense of grandeur it might have if the great masses were qualified by details kept to human scale—this effect of grandeur—is lost in the degradation of the human figure. A strange error for a sculptor to make.

The safest practice in proportion is not to attempt to allow for "perspective", stilting domes as he did, changing pitches of roofs as many do, and modifying natural lines and masses to meet certain views from certain vantage points as the Greeks are said to have done, but to make the constitution of the thing right in itself. Let the incidental perspectives fall when and how they will. Trust nature to give proper values to a proper whole. The modifications she may make are better than any other. There is something radically wrong with a scheme that requires distortion to appear correct.

In the matter of materials. These also affect scale. The logical material under the circumstances is the most natural material for the purpose. It is usually the most beautiful—and it is obvious that sticks will not space the same as stones nor allow the same proportions as steel. Nor will the spacing adjustable to these be natural to made-blocks or to slabs or to a plastic modeling of form.

Sticks of wood will have their own natural volume and spacing determined by standards of use and manufacture and the nature of both.

A wood plan is slender: light in texture, narrower spacing.

A stone or brick plan is heavy: black in masses, wider in spacing.

Combination of materials: lightness combined with massiveness.

A cast-block building: such massing as is felt to be adequate to the sense of block and box and slab; more freedom in spacing.

The purely or physically plastic structure: center line of thin webbing with a flesh-covering on either side; unit-system may be abandoned.

Then there are the double-wall constructions requiring great skill in spacing so that the interior shell will work simply with the outer shell. And there are as many others as there are combinations of all these.

But the more simple the materials used—the more the building tends toward a mono-material building—the more nearly will "perfect style" reward an organic plan and ease of execution economize results. The more logical will the whole become.

A wood plan is seen in the plan for the Coonley house at Riverside, see page 52, and in the plan for "D101 house"

A cast-block and slab building: the plan for Unity Temple at Oak Park, (page 54).

Brick plans: the plan for the D. D. Martin residence at Buffalo, (page 53) and the Ullman house at Oak Park, Illinois, (page 55).

A steel-and-glass plan for a skyscraper, concrete supports and floor slabs: this plan will be used later in this series to illustrate another article.

The purely "plastic" structure may be seen in the "Einstein Tower" by Mendelsohn and buildings by European Modernists.

A double-wall construction, in this case of pre-cast blocks, is seen in the Ennis house at Hollywood, (page 56).

A thin concrete slab-structure: the merchandise building at Los Angeles.

In the matter of building methods. These too are meantime shaping the plan. In the

D. 101 HOUSE, STANDARD WOODEN CON-STRUCTION WITH 2'-0" UNIT SPACING ADAPTED TO ECONOMIZE LUMBER

Coonley house—the 4'-0" unit works with 16" centers as established in carpenter practice for the length of lath, the economical spacing of studs and nailing-bearings, standard lumber lengths.

In Unity Temple—the only limit was the mass of concrete that could withstand the violent changes of climate and remain related to human scale and easy construction. The box and blocks, however, determine the shape of every feature and every detail of the features, as it was all cast in "boxes." So a unit suitable for timber construction was adopted as the false-work in which it was cast was made of lumber. Multiples of 16", syncopated, was the scale adopted.

In the Martin house, brick was used. Brick lends itself to articulation in plan and is an easy material to use architecturally. Bricks naturally make corners and the corners are easily used for play of light and shade. The Martin house is an organized brick-pier building. It is when assembling groups of piers in rhythmical relation to the whole that brick comes out best according to its nature. A 7'-9" unit reduced by minor mullions to 3'-9", was used, in the horizontal only. There are other views of brick as legitimate as this one, to be used according to the individual "taste" of the designer. The broken masses of textured walls, for instance.

In the steel-and-glass building there are no walls. The method yields best to suspended screens, shop-fabricated. A mechan-

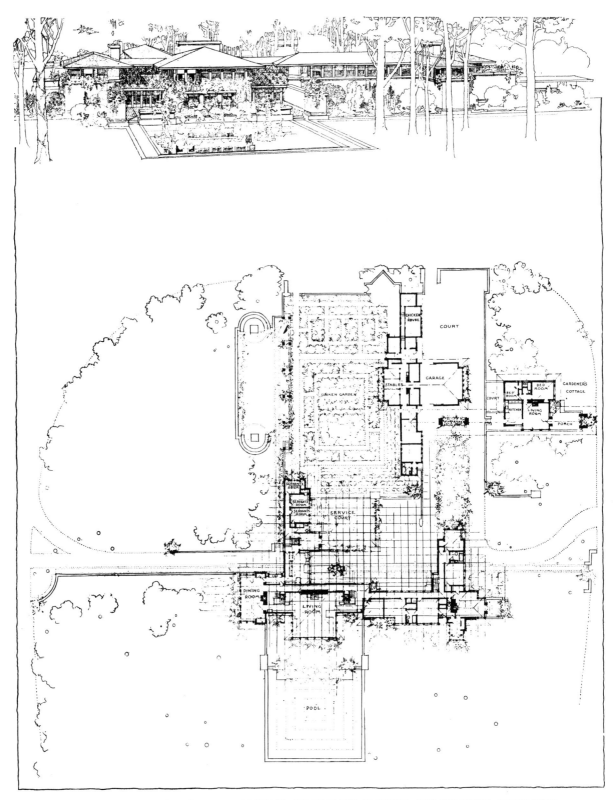

PLAN AND PERSPECTIVE, AVERY COONLEY HOUSE, RIVERSIDE, ILLINOIS
FRANK LLOYD WRIGHT, ARCHITECT
ILLUSTRATING THE WOOD PLAN

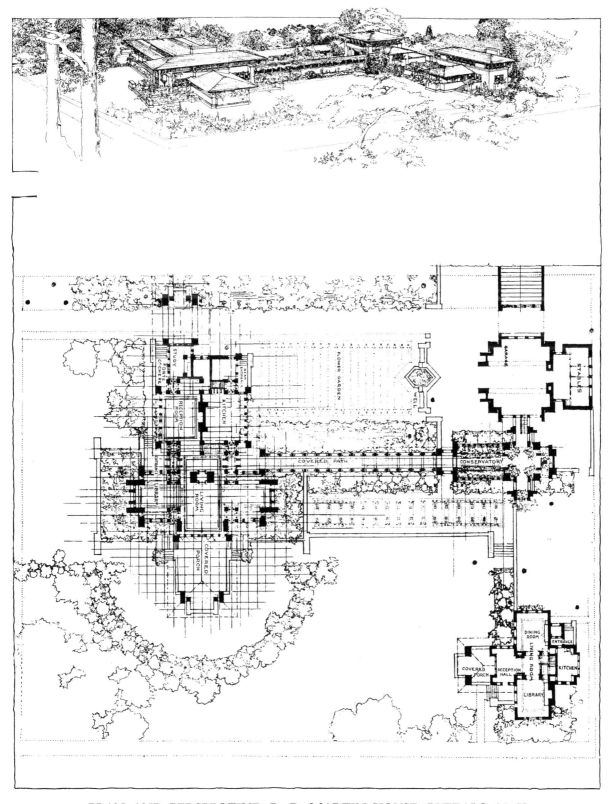

PLAN AND PERSPECTIVE, D. D. MARTIN HOUSE, BUFFALO, N. Y.
FRANK LLOYD WRIGHT, ARCHITECT
BRICK-PIER PLAN, 4′-6″ UNITS

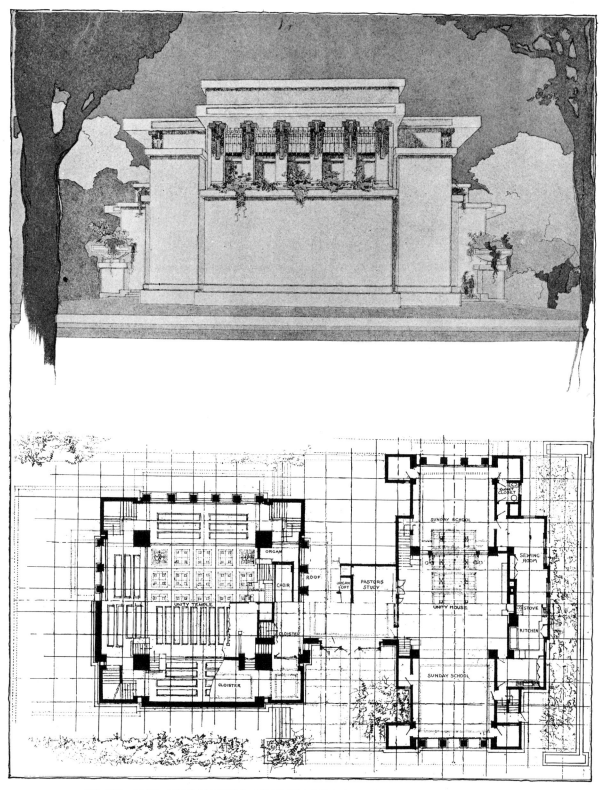

PLAN AND ELEVATION, UNITY TEMPLE, OAK PARK, ILLINOIS
FRANK LLOYD WRIGHT, ARCHITECT
PLAN ILLUSTRATING HORIZONTAL DIVISIONS, 7'·0"

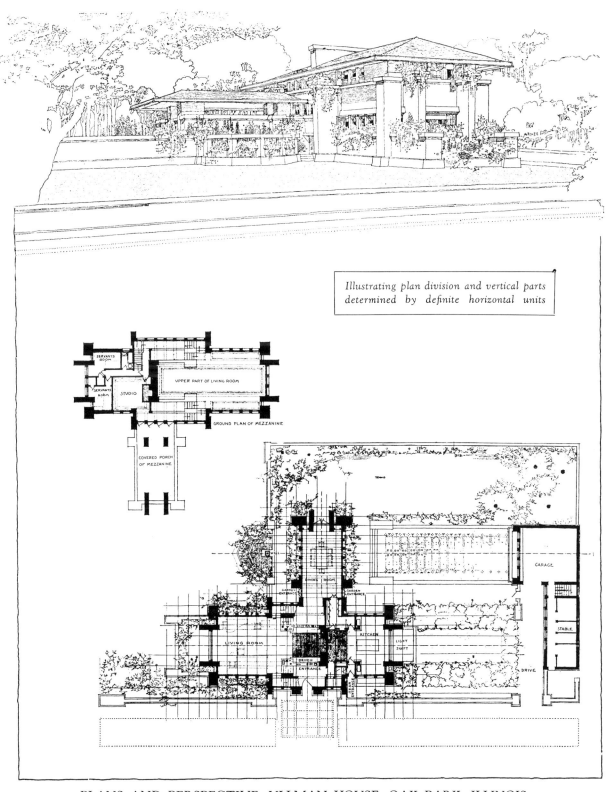

Illustrating plan division and vertical parts determined by definite horizontal units

PLANS AND PERSPECTIVE, ULLMAN HOUSE, OAK PARK, ILLINOIS
FRANK LLOYD WRIGHT, ARCHITECT
BRICK-PIER PLAN, 4'-6" UNITS

FLOOR PLAN, PLOT PLAN AND PERSPECTIVE, ENNIS HOUSE,
HOLLYWOOD, CALIFORNIA

FRANK LLOYD WRIGHT, ARCHITECT

ILLUSTRATING ARTICULATION EMPHASIZED BY TEXTURE

ized fabric enters here to give the form and style that is architecture. The structural supports and floor-slabs in this case happen to be concrete. They could be protected steel as well. Planned on a 4'–o" unit, emphasis on alternate verticals. No emphasis on horizontals.

In the pre-cast-block building, the method of building wholly determines the form and style. This is a mono-material structure planned on multiples of "16" inches square both horizontal and vertical. No emphasis.

The slab-building is an expression of another method. Cast-slabs, set sidewise and lengthwise, and flatwise, making everything, as may be seen in the result. Planned on multiples of 7'–o".

Concerning articulation. The Ennis house will serve to illustrate the principle which, once grasped, is simple.

In the building, each separate portion of the building devoted to a special purpose asserts itself as an individual factor in the whole.

The dining-room associated with terraces is one mass. The living-room with bedroom attached, another mass standing at the center on a terrace of its own—the dominating feature of the group.

Mr. Ennis's bedroom, semi-detached and used as a study or office, is another and terminal mass.

At the rear is the kitchen unit, a subordinate mass. All are connected by a gallery passing along the group at the rear. Finally the terrace-wall ends in a detached mass to the rear of the lot—the garage and chauffeur's quarters.

A little study will show how each separate room makes its own characteristic contribution to the whole mass.

The completed whole crowns the end of a high ridge in Hollywood and is a pre-cast slab-block building woven together with steel.

These articulations are as obvious in the plan as in the perspective. The Coonley house is similarly articulate.

Articulate buildings of this type have their parallel in the music of Bach particularly, but in any of the true form-masters in music.

It may be readily seen that in this particular direction lies infinite variety in expression. The sense of it is fundamental in any architectural release.

In the matter of expression and style.

As a matter of logic in the plan it is easy to see there can be none except as the result of scale, materials and building method. But with all that properly set, there is the important human equation at work in every move that is made. The architect weaves into it all his sense of the whole. He articulates—emphasizes what he loves.

No matter how technically faithful his logic may have been to his scale and materials and method—over and above all that, living in the atmosphere created by the orchestration of those matters, hovers the indefinable quality of style. Style emanating from the form, as seen by the man himself. And while it speaks to you of all those important matters, it leaves you imbued by dignity, grace, repose, gaiety, strength, severity, delicacy and of rhythmical order, in a musical sense, as the master wills—just as music does. Usually you hear music as you work. But not necessarily.

So every true building is of the quality of some man's soul, his sense of harmony and "fitness," which is another kind of harmony—more or less manifest in the fallible human process.

And his building will nobly stand, belonging to its site—breathing this message to the spirit quite naturally, so long as his work was well done or the course of human events does not inundate or human ignorance willfully destroy his building.

FEBRUARY 1928

IN THE CAUSE OF ARCHITECTURE

By Frank Lloyd Wright

II. WHAT "STYLES" MEAN TO THE ARCHITECT

In what is now to arise from the plan as conceived and held in the mind of the architect, the matter of style may be considered as of elemental importance.

In the logic of the plan what we call "standardization" is seen to be a fundamental principle at work in architecture. All things in Nature exhibit this tendency to crystallize—to form and then conform, as we may easily see. There is a fluid, elastic period of becoming, as in the plan, when possibilities are infinite. New effects may, then, originate from the idea or principle that conceives. Once form is achieved, that possibility is dead so far as it is a creative flux.

Styles in architecture are part and parcel of this standardization. During the process of formation, exciting, fruitful. So soon as accomplished—a prison house for the creative soul and mind.

"Styles" once accomplished soon become yard-sticks for the blind, crutches for the lame, the recourse of the impotent.

As humanity develops there will be less recourse to the "styles" and more style,—for the development of humanity is a matter of greater creative power for the individual—more of that quality in each that was once painfully achieved by the whole. A richer variety in unity is, therefore, a rational hope.

So this very useful tendency in the nature of the human mind, to standardize, is something to guard against as thought and feeling are about to take "form,"—something of which to beware,—something to be watched. For, over-night, it may "set" the form past redemption and the creative matter be found dead. Standardization is, then, a mere tool, though indispensable, to be used only to a certain extent in all other than purely commercial matters.

Used to the extent that it leaves the spirit free to destroy it at will,—on suspicion, maybe,—to the extent only that it does not become *a* style—or an inflexible rule—is it desirable to the architect.

It is desirable to him only to the extent that it is capable of new forms and remains the servant of those forms. Standardization should be allowed to work but never to master the process that yields the form.

In the logic of the plan we see the mechanics that is standardization, this dangerous tendency to crystallize into styles, at work and attempting to dispose of the whole matter. But if we are artists, no one can see it in the results of our use of it, which will be living and "personal," nevertheless.

There is a dictum abroad that "Great Art" is impersonal.

The Universal speaks by way of the Personal in our lives. And the more interesting as such the deliverer is, the more precious to us will that message from the Universal be. For we can only understand the message in terms of ourselves. Impersonal matter is no matter at all—in Art. This is not to say that the manner is more than the matter of the message—only to say that the man is the matter of the message, after all is said and done. This is dangerous truth for weak-headed egotists in architecture who may be in love with their own reflections as in a mirror.

But why take the abuse of the thing for the thing itself and condemn it to exalt the mediocre and fix the commonplace?

All truth of any consequence whatsoever, is dangerous and in the hands of the impotent—damned. Are we, therefore, to cling to "safe lies"? There is a soiled fringe hanging to every manful effort to realize anything in this world—even a square meal.

The Universal will take care of itself.

Let us tune up with it and it will sing through us, because of us, the song man desires most to hear. And that song is Man.

The question is now, how to achieve *style*, how to conserve that quality and profit to the fullest extent by standardization, the soul of the machine, in the work that is "Man." We have seen how standardization, as a method, serves as guide in the architect's plan, serves as a kind of warp on which to weave the woof of his building. So far, it is safe and may be used to any extent as a method while the "idea" lives. But the process has been at work in everything to our hand that we are to use with which to build. We can overcome that, even profit by it, as we shall see. The difficulty is that it has been at work upon the man for whom we are to build. He is already more or less mechanized in this the Machine-Age. To a considerable extent he is the victim of the thing we have been discussing—the victim, I say, because his ideas are committed to standards which he now wilfully standardizes and institutionalizes until there is very little fresh life left in him. To do so is now his habit and, he is coming to think, his virtue.

Here is the real difficulty and a serious one.

What fresh life the architect may have is regarded with distrust by him, suspected and perhaps condemned on suspicion, merely, by this habituate who standardizes for a living—now, and must defend himself in it. The plan-factory grew to meet his wants. Colleges cling to the "classic" to gratify him. His "means" are all tied up in various results of the process. He is bound hand and foot, economically, to his institutions and blindfolded by his "self-interest." He is the slave of the Expedient—and he calls it the Practical! He believes it.

What may be done with him?

Whatever was properly done would be to "undo" him, and that can't be done with his consent. He cannot be buried because it is a kind of living death he knows. But there are yet living among him those not so far gone. It is a matter of history that the few who are open to life have made it eventually what it is for the many. History repeats itself, as ever. The minority report is always right—John Bright pointed to history to prove it.

What we must work with is that minority—however small. It is enough hope, for it is all the hope there ever was in all the world since time began, and we believe in Progress.

These slaves to the Expedient are all beholden to certain ideas of certain individuals. They tend to accept, ready-made, from those individuals their views of matters like style and, although style is a simple matter, enough nonsense has been talked about it by architects and artists. So "Fashion" rules with inexorable hand. The simple unlettered American man of business, as yet untrained by "looted" culture, is most likely, in all this, to have fresh vision. And, albeit a little vulgar, there, in him, and in the minority of which we have just spoken, is the only hope for the architectural future of which we are going to speak.

The value of style as against standardized "styles" is what I shall try to make clear and, to illustrate, have chosen from my own work certain examples to show that it is a quality not depending at all upon "styles," but a quality inherent in every organic growth—as such. Not a self-conscious product at all. A natural one. I maintain that if this quality of style may be had in these things of mine, it may be had to any extent by Usonia, did her sons put into practice certain principles which are at work in these examples as they were once at work when the antique was "now." This may be done with no danger of forming a style—except among those whose

THE GRAMMAR OF A STYLE
FRANK LLOYD WRIGHT, ARCHITECT

characters and spiritual attainments are such that they would have to have recourse to one anyway.

The exhibition will become complete in the course of this series. The immediate burden of this paper is properly to evaluate this useful element of standardization with which the architect works for life, as in the "logic of the plan," and show how it may disastrously triumph over life as in the "styles" in this matter that confronts him now.

This antagonistic triumph is achieved as the consequence of man's tendency to fall in love with his tools, of which his intellect is one, and he soon mistakes the means for the end. This has happened most conspicuously in the architectural Renaissance. The "re-birth" of architecture. Unless a matter went wrong and died too soon there could be no occasion for "re-birth." But according to architects, architecture has been in this matter of getting itself continually re-born for several centuries until one might believe it never properly born, and now thoroughly dead from repeated "rebirth." As a matter of fact, architecture never needed to be born again—the architects who thought so did need to be; but never were.

A few examples may serve to show "architecture" a corpse, like sticking a pin into some member of a cadaver. Such architectural members for instance as the cornice—pilasters and architraves—the façade and a whole brain-load of other instances of the moribund.

But architecture has consisted of these things. And architecture before that had the misfortune to be a non-utilitarian affair—it was a matter of decorating construction or sculpturing, from the outside, a mass of building material. At its worst it became a mere matter of constructing decoration. This concept of architecture was peculiarly Greek. And the Greek concept became the architectural religion of the modern world and became so, strangely enough, just

when Christianity became its spiritual conviction. The architectural concept was barbaric, unspiritual—superficial. That did not matter. Architecture was "re-born" in Florence on that basis and never got anywhere below the surface afterward, owing to many inherent inconsistencies with interior life as life within, lived on. I am talking of "Academic" architecture.

Of the three instances we have chosen, the cornice would be enough to show—for as it was, the other two were, and so were all besides. We are now attacking the standard that became standardized.

It was a standard that, to the eye, had grace and charm but to the mind had, never, organic integrity. It was "exterior" as thought, however exquisite the refinement and refreshing the play of light and shadow, or enticing the form—or seductive the nuances of shade. It could live only on the surface—and thrive as a "cult." It was aristocratic as such. Sometimes an applied, studied elegance, it was often a studious refinement. But it had no interior vitality to inform new conditions and develop new forms for fresh life. The cornice, a constructed thing, constructed as a form for its own sake, became fixed as the characteristic architectural expression of this culture. The cornice was a gesture—a fine gesture, but an empty one. What original significance the cornice had was soon lost. It had come by way of the eaves of a projecting and visible roof. It stayed for "the look of the thing" centuries after its use and purpose had gone. It was said to be "a thing of beauty." It became the last word in the "language" of approved form, regardless of interior significance. And it hangs today in the eye of the sun, as dubious an excrescence as ever made shift. It has said the last word for "exterior" architecture. For the cornice has all but disappeared, and with it disappears a horde of artificialities no nearer truth.

Another concept of building enters in this coming era.

PARAPET DETAIL, BARNSDALL RESIDENCE
FRANK LLOYD WRIGHT, ARCHITECT

The building is no longer a block of building material dealt with, artistically, from the outside. The room within is the great fact about the building—*the room* to be expressed in the exterior as *space enclosed*. This sense of the *room* within, held as the great *motif* for enclosure, is the advanced thought of the era in architecture, and is now searching for exterior expression.

This is another conception of architecture entirely. It is probably new under the sun.

Here we have a compelling organic significance instead of seductive imposition-of-elegance.

Architecture so born needs no "re-birth." It will work out its own destiny at all times, in all places, under all conditions—naturally.

It will not fail of style.

This concept is a minority report in this democratic era. But it is the natural one for that era because it is consistent with the nature of the highest spiritual and ethical ideal of democracy.

To make clear to the young architect this "interior" initiative which is now his, is necessary to any comprehension on his part of the opportunity that is now to his hand in what may rise from his plan.

Once this interior viewpoint is grasped, his own nature will gather force from the idea and, with experience, become truly potent as a creative factor in modern life concerns.

"What significance?" This should be the question through which everything in the way of "form" should be sifted in imagination before it is accepted or rejected in his work.

Contrived elegancies the weary world has obediently borne and worn and regretfully cast aside in plenty, with undefined but inextinguishable hope.

But expressions of human life, rooted in that life, to grow and beneficently expand in human thought, compelled by our principle as great trees grow in their soil and expand in the air according to their interior

principle, beguiled by the sun—that is what the world needs and what democracy must have. This is the very meaning of democracy, if it is ever to have any meaning.

The word "democracy" is used far from any such interior significance as yet. But once born into the soul and mind of American youth, this sense of architecture will grow fast and become strong as only law is strong, however weak man-made laws may ever be and pusillanimous his "enforcements."

To show this ideal at work in concrete form it is unnecessary to arouse animosity or give pain by illustrations of the falsity of the old conception, or, to be fairer, let us say the superficial character of that concept.

If we show the principle at work in certain new buildings—and it may be seen there, clearly—we will have no occasion to molest tradition or dissect the forms that are now sacred. We may leave all decently in their shrouds where architects, urged by the idea of "re-birth" have, for centuries past, wantonly refused to leave them.

Beyond what has been said of architectural members we will not go. We will go forward and then whoever will, according to his disposition, at his leisure, may look backward.

Apropos of "style"—let us take—say—Unity Temple.

Style I have said was a quality of the form that character takes, and it becomes necessary to explain what character means.

Any consistent expression of an organic-entity, as such; any animal, tree or plant has "character" we may observe. In varying degree, this character may appeal to us as beautiful. It may even be what we call "ugly" and possess the *character* which is the secret of *style*.

Character is one of our strong words. It is loosely applied to any manifestation of force. Properly, it is used to signify "individual significance."

To be insignificant is to have no "character." Observe that we may use the word "character" for "style" and the word "style" for "character" with no great inconsistency. The words are not interchangeable, but applicable to either case. Character is the result of some inward force taking consistent outward shape, taking *form* consistent with its nature. The *exterior* any initial life-force naturally takes, reveals "character."

Character then is the significant expression of organic-entity. Yes but—

That sounds complicated—let's try again—

Character, like style, is the quality of "being" one's self—or itself—. That—too —but again incomplete.

Character is the result of nature-expression of the soul or life-principle of anything "organic" whatsoever—to the degree that the idea or life-impulse achieves consistent form to our senses—to that degree will "character" be evident.

Character then is not only fate—

As a final definition we may say that *"character" appears to be nature's "art."*

We may observe it in the smooth, dark-green water-melon, its swelling alchemy of pink flesh maturing in the sun, its multitude of black seeds, as we see its polished oval lifted above the surrounding tracery of grey-green vines,—or in the garter-snake darting its forked tongue from among the fretted leaves. How similar may be the markings, the "decoration" of both!

What, then, if all style must have character and all character has style—is the difference between character and style? Well—the difference is the difference between Truth and Beauty—both are forms of the same thing and inseparable from each other in any final analysis as the light ray is inseparable from its source. But we may enjoy the light, ignorant of its source, and speak of it—for that purpose we have the word style. Or we may look to the source, ignoring its consequences. To speak of that we have the word character.

Style is a consequence of character.

The serpent has "style." Bees as well as butterflies. So has the scarab that tumbles its ball of cow-manure in the hot sun of the dusty road. The white crane, the horse, the rat, every flower, any tree—even human beings, when they are natural—have it, because they are genuine. They have *character*. Buildings often have it when they too are genuine, not posing as "architecture." The rear of the New York Public Library has something of this quality of style, while the front has only "styles." The Woolworth Building would have had it to a degree but for professional Gothic prejudices and predilection. The Suspension Bridge from New York to Brooklyn has it. Some aeroplanes have it and some steamships: by no means all of them. Many grain elevators, steel plants, engines have it, and occasionally an automobile. The Wainwright building of Saint Louis by Adler & Sullivan, as a tall building, had it. There are many tall buildings, now, that are stylish to some degree but all more or less marred by "styles." Unity Temple, for a shameless instance, has style without prejudice or predilection. How did it get it? First by directly acknowledging the *nature* of the problem presented and expressing it with a sense of appropriate shape and proportion in terms of the *character* of the materials and the process of work that was to make the building. It does this consciously and sensibly, all in its own way, simply because there never is any other way.

Let us follow this building through the thought that built it, from the beginning—when Dr. Johonnot, the Universalist pastor, called and said he had always admired the little white church with a steeple as seen in the "East" and wanted something like that—follow its evolution to final *form*.

APRIL 1928

IN THE CAUSE OF ARCHITECTURE

By Frank Lloyd Wright

III. THE MEANING OF MATERIALS—STONE

THE country between Madison and Janesville, Wisconsin, is the old bed of an ancient glacier-drift. Vast, busy gravel-pits abound there, exposing heaps of yellow aggregate, once, and everywhere else, sleeping beneath the green fields. Great heaps, clean and golden, are always waiting there in the sun. And I never pass without emotion—without a vision of the long dust-whitened stretches of the cement-mills grinding to impalpable fineness the magic-powder that would "set" it all to shape and wish, both, endlessly subject to my will.

Nor do I come to a lumber-yard with its city-like, gradated masses of fresh shingles, boards and timbers, without taking a deep breath of its fragrance—seeing the forest that was laid low in it and the processes that cut and shaped it to the architect's scale of feet and inches—coveting it, *all*.

The rock-ledges of a stone-quarry are a story and a longing to me. There is suggestion in the strata and character in the formations. I like to sit and feel it, as it is. Often I have thought, were great monumental buildings ever given me to build, I would go to the Grand Canyon of Arizona to ponder them.

When, in early years, I looked south from the massive stone tower in the Auditorium Building where I was pencil in the hand of a master—the red glare of the Bessemer steel converters to the south of Chicago thrilled me as the pages of the Arabian Nights used to do—with a sense of terror and romance.

And the smothered incandescence of the kiln! In fabulous heat baking mineral and chemical treasure on mere clay—to issue in all the hues of the rainbow, all the shapes of Imagination and never yield to time—subject only to the violence or carelessness of man. These great ovens would cast a spell upon me as I listened to the subdued roar within them.

The potter's thumb and finger deftly pressing the soft mass whirling on his wheel, as it yielded to his touch; the bulbous glass at the end of slender pipe as the breath of the glass-blower and his deft turning, decided its shape—fascinated me. Something was being born.

With his "materials"—the architect can do whatever masters have done with pigments or with sound—in shadings as subtle, with combinations as expressive—perhaps out-lasting man himself.

Stone, wood, pottery, glass, pigments and *aggregates, metals, gems*—cast in the industrious maw of mill, kiln and machine to be worked to the architect's will by human-skill-in-labor. All this to his hand, as the pencil in it makes the marks that disposes of it as he dreams and wills. If he wills well—in use and beauty sympathetic to the creation of which he is creature. If he wills ill, in ugliness and waste as creature-insult to creation.

. . . .

These "*materials*" are human-riches.

They are Nature-gifts to the sensibilities that are, again, gifts of Nature.

By means of these gifts, the story and the song of *man* will be *wrought* as, once upon papyrus, and now, on paper it is written.

Each material has its own message and, to the creative artist, its own song.

Listening, he may learn to make two sing together in the service of man or separately as he may choose. A trio? Perhaps.

It is easier to use them solo or in duet than manifold.

CANTILEVER SLAB WITH CUT-LAVA EDGES OVER PASSAGE BETWEEN LOBBY AND GUEST WINGS
THE IMPERIAL HOTEL, TOKIO
FRANK LLOYD WRIGHT, ARCHITECT

The solo is more easily mastered than the orchestral score.

Therefore it is well to work with a limited palette and more imagination than it is to work with less imagination and more palette.

So—work wherever possible in mono-material, except where the use of sympathetic extra-materials may add the necessary grace or graceful necessity desirable—or unavoidable.

Each material *speaks a language* of its own just as line and color speak—or perhaps because they do speak.

Each has a story.

In most Architectures of the world stone

has suffered imitation of the stick. Even in oldest cultures like Chinese civilization, great constructions of stone imitate wood posts and beams in joinery—imitate literally great wood towering of poles and posts, beams, richly carved to imitate the carvings of the wooden ones that preceded them and could not endure. Undoubtedly the stick came first in architecture—came long before the stone. The ideas of forms that became associated with ideas of the beautiful in this use of wood took the more enduring material ignorant of its nature, and foolishly enslaved it to the idea of the ornamented stick.

Stone is the oldest of architectural materials on record, as to form, except as the stone itself embodies earlier wood-forms. So from Stonehenge to Maya masonry—the rude architecture of the Druid-Bards of whom Taliesin was one, down the ages to the intensely implicated and complicated tracery of the Goths—where stone-building may be said to have expired—stone comes first.

THE STORY OF STONE

Stone, as a building material, as human hands begin upon it—stonecraft—becomes a shapely block.

The block is necessarily true to square and level, so that one block may securely rest upon another block and great weight be carried to greater height.

We refer to such masses, so made, as masonry.

The stone may show a natural face in the wall, or a face characteristic of the tool used to shape it—or be flatly smoothed. Sometimes honed or polished.

The walls take on the character of the surface left by the mason's use of his tools.

The character of the wall-surface will be determined also by the kind of stone, by the kind of mason, the kind of architect. Probably by the kind of building. But, most of all, by the nature of the stone itself if the work is good stone-work.

Stone has every texture, every color and

—as in marble—also exquisite line combined with both—intensified clear down the scale until we arrive at what we call "precious" stone—and then on to jewels.

But most building stone—as Caen-stone, say—is a clear negative substance, like a sheet of soft beautiful paper, on which it is appropriate to cut images, by wasting away the surfaces to sink or raise traces of the imagination like a kind of human writing, carrying the ideology of the human-race down the ages from the primitive to the decadent.

Other stone is hard and glittering, hard to cut. By rubbing away at it with other stones the surface may be made to yield a brilliant surface, finally polished until its inner nature may be seen as though looked into, as in a glass—transparent.

Most marble is of this character. And granite. The very nature of the material itself becomes its own decoration.

To carve or break its surface, then, is a pity—if no crime.

Stones themselves have special picturesque qualities and were much cherished for their "qualities" in China and Japan. Perhaps these Orientals love stones for their own sake more than any other people. They seem to see in them the universe—at least the earth-creation, in little—and they study them with real pleasure and true appreciation.

The Byzantine mosaics of colored stone are a cherishing of these qualities, too. These mosaics on a large scale gave beautiful stone results—fine stone-work—good masonry.

But stone is a solid material, heavy, durable and most grateful for masses. A "massive" material we say, so most appropriate and effective in simple architectural masses, the nobler the better.

The Mayas used stone most sympathetically with its nature and the character of their environment. Their decoration was mostly *stone-built*. And when they carved it the effect resembled naturally enriched

LAVA-CUTTING TEN FEET SQUARE, SHOWING TEXTURE OF MATERIAL MODIFYING THE SEVERE CARVING
THE IMPERIAL HOTEL, TOKIO
FRANK LLOYD WRIGHT, ARCHITECT

stone surfaces such as are often seen in the landscape.

The Egyptians used stone—as the Chinese used stones—with real love and understanding.

The Greeks abused stone shamefully—did not understand its nature at all except as something to be painted or gilded out of existence. Before they painted it, they fluted and rolled and molded it as though it were wood—or degraded it far lower.

Polished sophistication is not at home with stone.

The Roman architects had no feeling about stone whatever. Their engineers did have—but there were few large stones.

LOCAL STONE—IN KEEPING WITH LOCALITY
TALIESIN, SPRING GREEN, WISCONSIN
FRANK LLOYD WRIGHT, ARCHITECT

They cut these prizes into wooden cornices to please the architects, and invented the arch to get along with small stones for construction.

The Goths made most of stone. But stone became for the Gothic imagination a mere negative material which they employed supremely well in a structural sense.

Stonecraft rose highest in the Gothic era.

But they, then, set to work and carved the beautiful construction elaborately and constructed carving in the spirit of the construction to an extent never before seen in the world. No arris was left without its moulding. It was as though stone blossomed into a thing of the human-spirit.

As though a wave of creative-impulse had seized stone and, mutable as the sea, it had heaved and swelled and broken into lines of surge, peaks of foam—human-symbols, images of organic life caught and held in its cosmic urge—a splendid song!

The song of *stone*?

No—because stone was used as a negative material neither limitations respected nor stone nature interpreted. In wood the result was pretty much the same as in iron or in plaster, in the hands of the Goths.

But as a building-material it was *scientifically* used. And such stone was usually chosen as had little to say for itself and so not outraged much by such cutting to the

WHEN STONE IS CONCRETE
BARNSDALL RESIDENCE, HOLLYWOOD, CALIFORNIA
FRANK LLOYD WRIGHT, ARCHITECT

shapes of organic life—as it was subjected to, by them.

We may say the stone was not outraged—but neither was it allowed to sing its own song—to be *itself*. Always nearer that, by them, than anywhere else since archaic times.

But it was not the *stone* that inspired the Cathedrals of the Middle Ages nor invited them. It limited them.

Had it not been so—what would they have been like? Was Gothic Architecture because of stone or regardless of it?

But that is going far afield for subtle matter, and casting the shadow of doubt upon one of the most beautiful spectacles of the triumph of the human spirit over matter.

A greater triumph will be man's when he triumphs through the nature of matter over the superstition that separates him from its spirit.

And that is where he is now in his industrial world as he faces stone, as an architect. As he sees stone in the story recorded by the buildings on the earth—there is not so much to help him now.

To "imitate" would be easy but no man's way.

His present tool the Machine can clumsily imitate, but without joy or creative impulse behind it when imitation is its menial office. As a mass-material he can now handle stone better and cheaper than ever before, if he allows it to be itself—if he lets it alone for what it is.

Or if—sympathetically—he brings out its nature in his use of it. The Chinese did this in the way they cherished and developed the natural beauties of jade—lapis-lazuli—crystal—malachite and cornelian, quartz—and great-stones as well.

Man has done this with his machine when he has sawed the blocks of marble and, opening them into thin slabs, spread them, edge to edge, upon walls as facings revealing and accenting its own pattern and color.

He has done this when he planes it and lays it up in a straight-line mass for its own sake, with the texture characteristic of his tools.

He has done this when he takes the strata of the quarry and lays it in like strata, natural edges out—in his walls. He has done this when he makes mosaic of stones and lays them in simple stone-patterns in color, for whole buildings—stone brocade.

He does this, when, inspired by the hardness and brilliance of the granite his Machine can now render so well, he makes his ultimate form as simple and clearly hard in mass and noble in outline when finished.

He may even introduce alternate and contrasting materials qualifying broad masses harmonious with stone qualities in horizontal bands or rich masses. Whenever, in his designs, he allows the natural beauty of the stone, as stone, to speak its own material-language, he has justified his machine as an artist's tool. And the nobility of his work will compensate for the loss of the imitations of organic-forms-of-life in the material itself—an imitation that used to be architecture.

Interpretation is still his.

So it will be seen again, as always, that if he now works *with* stone in this sense, using the new power which the machine has given him over it, he will gain a spiritual integrity and physical health to compensate him for the losses of the storyful beauties of that period, since passed, when a building, so far as its *architecture* was concerned, was a block of ornamentally sculptured stone.

It would take a volume to fully illustrate the story that is here written—a mere sketch in bare outline.

In each of the materials we have named there is treasure enough to make Aladdin's cave a mean symbol of an architect's riches, were each architect confined to only *one*.

Aladdin's lamp was a symbol for Imagination.

With this lamp the architect may explore the riches of the deep caves where treasure is waiting for him. And, through him, the human race waits too; for the key that unlocks the man-made door is hanging at his belt—still—though rusty with disuse and the lock itself now stiff with rust and lack of proper oiling.

Let him take his microscope and see the principle that "builds", in nature, at work in stone. Geometry the principle, busy with materials — producing marvels of beauty to inspire him. Read the grammar of the Earth in a particle of stone! Stone is the frame on which his Earth is modeled, and wherever it crops out—there the architect may sit and learn.

As he takes the trail across the great Western Deserts—he may see his buildings —rising in simplicity and majesty from their floors of gleaming sand—where organic life is still struggling for a bare existence: see them still, as the Egyptians saw and were taught by those they knew.

For in the stony bone-work of the Earth, the principles that shaped stone as it lies, or as it rises and remains to be sculptured by winds and tide—there sleep forms and styles enough for all the ages for all of Man.

NOTE:—See issue of Wendingen, Number 11 in 6th Series of 1924. Architect Widjeveldt Vossuistraat—Amsterdam—for a marvelous exposition of geometry at work in materials.—Called the *Architectonishe Phantasieen in de Wereld Der Kristallen*.

MAY 1928

IN THE CAUSE OF ARCHITECTURE

BY FRANK LLOYD WRIGHT

IV. THE MEANING OF MATERIALS—WOOD

FROM THE fantastic totem of the Alaskan —erected for its own sake as a great sculptured pole, seen in its primitive colors far above the snows—to the resilient bow of the American Indian, and from the enormous solid polished tree-trunks upholding the famous great temple-roofs of Japan to the delicate spreading veneers of rare, exotic woods on the surfaces of continental furniture, wood is allowed to be wood.

It is the most humanly intimate of all materials. Man loves his association with it, likes to feel it under his hand, sympathetic to his touch and to his eye. Wood is universally beautiful to Man. And yet, among higher civilizations, the Japanese understood it best.

They have never outraged wood in their art or in their craft. Japan's primitive religion, "Shinto," with its "be clean" ideal, found in wood ideal material and gave it ideal use in that masterpiece of architecture, the Japanese dwelling as well as in all, that pertained to living in it.

In that architecture may be seen what a sensitive material, let alone for its own sake, can do for human sensibilities.

Whether pole, beam, plank, board, slat or rod, the Japanese architect got the forms and treatments of his architecture out of tree-nature, wood-wise, and heightened the natural beauty of the material by cunning peculiar to himself.

The possibilities of the properties of wood came out richly as he rubbed into it the natural oil of the palm of his hand, ground out the soft parts of the grain to leave the hard fibre standing—an "erosion" like that of the plain where flowing water washes away the sand from the ribs of stone.

No western peoples ever used wood with such understanding as the Japanese did in their construction—where wood always came up and came out as nobly beautiful.

And when we see the bamboo rod in their hands—seeing a whole industrial world interpreting it into articles of use and art that ask only to be *bamboo*—we reverence the scientific art that makes wood *theirs*.

The simple Japanese dwelling with its fences and utensils is the *revelation* of wood.

Nowhere else may wood be so profitably studied for its natural possibilities as a major architectural material.

Material here fell into artistic hands—a religious sentiment protecting it, in all reverence for simplicity.

Sometimes in the oak-beamed and panelled rooms of Old England, when "carpentry" was restrained, oak was allowed to be something similar as is seen in oak-timbering of the Middle Ages. In the veneering of later periods the beauty of wood came out —but the carpenter-forms of the work invariably did violence to the nature of wood. The "cabinet-maker" had his way with it.

Woodwork soon became what we learned to call carpentry; more or less a make-shift. Panelling was its sum and substance where the pilaster would not stick nor the cornice hang.

All wooden joinery of the periods, soon or late, fell to pieces, and interruption by too many ingenious "members" frittered away wood-nature in confusion or in contortions of an ingenious but false or inferior "taste."

Outside primitive architectures, sympathetic use of wood in beautiful construction would be found far north or far south—

among the Norsemen, or among the South Sea Islanders.

Because of wood we have—the carpenter.

The carpenter loved wood in feeble ways—but he loved his tools with strength and determination. He loved his tools more. Good wood is willing to do what its designer never meant it to do—another of its lovable qualities—but therefore it is soon prostitute to human ingenuity in the makeshift of the carpenter. Wood, therefore, has more human outrage done upon it than man has done, even upon himself.

It has suffered more—far more than any of the materials in our category.

Where and when it is cheap and, so, become too familiar as it nearly always does in a new country, it soon falls into contempt. Man's longing for novelty tries to make it something else. To the degree that the carpenter-artist has succeeded in doing this—one might think—is he the artist-carpenter.

In his search for novelty, wood in his hands has been joined and glued, braced and screwed, boxed and nailed, turned and tortured, scroll sawed, beaded, fluted, suitably furbelowed and flounced at the carpenter's party—enough to please even him. By the aid of "modern" machines the carpenter-artist got it into Eastlake composites of trim and furniture, into Usonian jigger porches and corner-towers eventuating into candle snuffer domes or what would you have?; got it all over Queen Anne houses outside and inside—the triumph of his industrious ingenuity—until carpentry and millwork became synonymous with butchery and botchwork.

Queen Anne! What murder !

And even now—especially now—in the passing procession of the "periods" I never see orderly piles of freshly cut and dried timber disappearing into the mills to be gored and ground and torn and hacked into millwork without a sense of utter weariness in the face of the overwhelming outrage of something precious just because it

is by nature so kind, beneficent and lovely.

Man has glorified the Tree in the use he made of the Stick—but that he did long before the Louis, or the Renaissance got by way of Colonial and Eastlake—or was it Westlake—to Queen Anne; and then by way of the triumphant Machine to General-Grant-Gothic and the depths of degradation that soon came in the cut-and-butt of the fluted "trim," with turned corner-block and molded plinth-block.

This latter was the fashion in woodwork when I found the uses of wood I shall describe.

Machinery in that era was well under way and ploughed and tore and whirled and gouged in the name of Art and Architecture.

And all this was so effectually and busily done that the devastation began to be felt in the "boundless" Usonian forests. Conservative lumber-men took alarm and made the native supply go a little further by shrinking all the standard timber-sizes first, one-eighth of an inch both ways—then a little further on one-eighth inch more both ways—now still a little further—until a stud is become a bed-slat, a board kin to a curling veneer.

All standardized sticks great and small are shrinking by a changing standard to meet the deadly facility which the Machine has given to man's appetite for useless *things*.

Usonian forests show all too plainly terrible destruction and—bitter thought—nothing of genuine beauty has Usonia to show for it.

The darkness of death is descending on wood by way of unenlightened architecture.

The life of the tree has been taken in vain as the stick, the substance of the shapely stick to become imitation-a-la-mode; the precious efflorescent patterns of wood, to be painted out of sight; its silken textures vulgarized by varnish in the misshapen monstrosities of a monstrous "taste."

TAHOE CABIN, "SHORE TYPE"
FRANK LLOYD WRIGHT, ARCHITECT

The noble forest is become an ignominious scrap-heap in the name of Culture.

The Machine, then—was it—that placed this curse on so beautiful a gift to man? so friendly a material—this brother to the man —laid thus low in murder.

No.

Unless the sword in the hand of the swordsman murdered the man whose heart it ran through.

released upon the forest, for its devastation. Blame the lack of imaginative insight for the scrap-heap we have now to show for the lost trees of a continent—a scrap-heap instead of a noble architecture.

What should we have had to show were it otherwise? Vain speculation. What may we have to show for what is left—if base appetite becomes enlightened desire and imagination awakes and sees?

WALLS OF WOOD, UNPAINTED, "LET ALONE AS WOOD"

The Machine is only a tool. Before all, the man is responsible for its use.

His ignorance became devastation because his tool in callous hands became a weapon effective beyond any efficiency such hands had known before, or any sensibilities he ever had. His performance with his Machine outran not only his imagination which, long since, it vanquished, but the endurance of his own sensibilities as human.

No. Blame the base appetite the Machine

Well—we may have the nobility of the *material* if nothing else.

We may have simple timber construction, at least over-head, as a scientific art, free of affectation. The wood let alone as wood or as richly ornamented by hand in color or carving.

We may have satin-boarded wainscots— polished board above polished board, the joints interlocked by beaded insertion, so that shrinkage is allowed and the joint ornaments the whole in harmony with its nature, individualizing each board.

We may have plaster-covered walls banded into significant color-surfaces by plain wood-strips, thick or thin, or cubical insertion, wide or narrow in surface.

We may have ceilings rib-banded in rhythmical arrangements of line to give the charm of timbering without the waste.

We may use flat wood-strips with silken surfaces contrasting as ribbons might be contrasted with stuffs, to show what we meant in arranging our surfaces, marking them by bands of sympathetic flat-wood.

We may use a plastic system of varying widths, weights of finely-marked wood rib-bands to articulate the new plastic effects in construction never dreamed of before. The flat-strip came so easily into our hands, by way of the machine, to give us—the "backband" that follows all outlines even in an ordinary dwelling, by the mile, for a few cents per foot.

WOOD ENCASED IN AN ARMOR OF PAINT

We may compound composite-slabs of refuse lumber glued together under high pressure and press into the glue, facings of purest flowered wood veneer on both sides —making slabs of any thickness or width or length, slabs to be cut into doors, great and small, tops thin or thick—preserving the same flower of the grain over entire series or groups of doors as a unit, (see page 488).

We may mitre the flowered slabs across the grain at the edges of the breaks to turn the flowering grain around corners or down the sides and thus gain another plastic effect from the continuity of the flowering.

We may economically split a precious log into thin wide veneers and, suitably "backed," lay each to each, opening one sheet to lay it edge to edge with the sheet beneath it, like the leaves of a book so the pattern of the one becomes another greater pattern when doubled by the next.

We may cross-veneer the edges of top-surfaces so that the grain of the top carries the flower unbroken down over the ends as it does on the sides.

There is the flat fillet (it happens to be true to wood) to "talk" with—if one must "explain."

We may use the plain-spindle alternating with the thin flat-slat or square or round ones in definite rhythms of light and shade— allowing the natural color and marking of the wood to enrich and soften the surface made by them as a whole. With this we may bring in the accent block.

We have the edgewise and flatwise-strip or cubical stick and accent-block to "ingeniously" combine into screens for light-filters or for furniture.

TIMBER, ROUGH HEWN FROM THE LOG AND USED STRUCTURALLY

These treatments all allow wood to be wood at its best and the machine can do them all surpassingly better than they could be done by hand—a thousand times cheaper.

Thanks to the machine we may now use great slabs compounded under heat and pressure, where rotary-cut veneers unrolled from a log in sheets ten feet long and as wide as the circumference of the log will yield, in thicknesses of one-thirty-second of an inch, wood wall-paper. And we may lay these sheets, against various compounds, on ceilings—with any manipulation of the efflorescence, now exaggerated by the rotary cut, but still true to wood, and do this to any extent.

The finer properties of wood have been emancipated by the machine.

Observe that, naturally, all these are *plastic* effects. That is, used for the sake of the surfaces and lines of their "wood-quality" in contrast to other materials. Carving has a small place in the grammar of these effects, except as an "insert."

There is always the limiting frame or border, constricting surfaces — the most obvious of all uses to which wood is put. And there is always a use of the solid wood stick to be made into honest furniture. There is the wooden frame to be over-stuffed for deep comfort—wood showing only at extremities. In light stick-furniture wood combines well with plaited rattan or raffia.

In other words the beauty of wood as silken-texture or satin-surfaces upon which nature has marked the lines of its character in exquisite drawing and color qualifying flat-surfaces and rib-bands of infinite delicacy, in all variety—because we work *with* the machine, understanding wood, is more liberally ours.

Another opportunity is wood-inlay. There is the chequered turning of the grain to crossgrain in the same wood.

There are the patterns of inlay in contrasting woods.

There are the cunningly cut, denticulated or machined strips to be inlaid between boards or used as edging flat surfaces of veneer: the denticulations to be picked out by polychrome in transparent bright stains, perhaps.

There is the whole gamut of transparent color stains from brilliant red, green, yellow and blue, to all hues in between, to aid and intensify or differentiate these uses of wood.

And for exterior work there are characteristic board-and-batten effects—horizontal, vertical, diagonal or checkered, got out of planks or boards with surfaces rough from the saw to be color-stained or allowed to weather.

There are roofs boarded lengthwise of the slope, likewise inlaid between the joints but with properly devised ornamental copper flashing to come up over the edges and the ends.

There are brilliantly decorative treatments of poles, free standing as the Alaskan totem stood, or in rows, horizontal or vertical. Palisaded walls.

There are combinations of the slender pole and square-stick and the spindle-rod, alternating with the slat or the board in endless rhythmic variety.

All these undressed-wood, plastic treatments, are much the same as for inside work, allowing wood to be wood but coarser in scale with an eye to weathering in the joinery.

And finally after we have exhausted the board and machined inlaid-batten, and the spread of the figure of the wood-flowering over flat surfaces, and the combinations of the following back-band and the varying rib-band—the spindle-stick, the flat-slab and the rod, the marking-strip and the accent-block, the ornamental-pole—rectangular timbering ornamentally planked, the undressed, interlocking boards on walls and roof slopes—then—

We have combinations of all these. A variety sufficient to intrigue the liveliest imagination for as long as life lasts—without once missing the old curvatures and im-

aging of organic-forms; the morbid twists and curious turns, the contortions imposed on wood in the name of the "Styles" *mostly* using wood as a makeshift—or, if not, as something other than wood.

A most proper use of wood, now that we must economize, are these treatments using marking-bands or plastic-ribbons, defining, explaining, indicating, dividing, and relating plaster surfaces. It is economy in the material, while keeping the feeling of its beauty. Architectural-articulation is assisted and sometimes had alone by means of the dividing lines of wood.

In these plastic treatments—using wood gently banded or in the flat allowing its grain and silken surface even in the spindle-screens to assert itself and wood-quality to enter into effect of the whole, we have found the Machine a willing means to a simple end. But for the Machine this free plastic use of wood either in rib-bands or extended flowered surfaces would be difficult, uncharacteristic and prohibitive in cost.

Moreover this is true conservation of wood because in these effects it is used only for its qualities as a beautiful material. The tree need no longer be lost.

In these papers we are not speaking of "building" as a makeshift, but of building as the Art of Architecture. And while all building, as things are, cannot be architecture but must make shift—architecture should hold forth such natural ways and means for the true use of good materials that, from any standpoint of economical realization of the best the material can give to structure, architecture would put mere building to shame. Stupid waste characterizes most of the efforts of mere builders, always—even or especially when, building for profit.

Wood grows more precious as our country grows older. To save it from destruction by the man with the machine it is only necessary to use the machine to emancipate its qualities, in simple ways such as I have indicated, and satisfy the man.

There is no waste of material whatever in such uses, either in cutting up the tree or adapting the cutting to the work done when it is of the character described. The machine easily divides, subdivides, sands and polishes the manifold surfaces which any single good stick may be made to yield by good machine methods.

Wood can never be wrought by the machine as it was lovingly wrought by hand into a violin for instance, except as a lifeless imitation. But the beautiful properties of wood may be released by the machine to the hand of the architect. His imagination must use it in true ways—worthy of its beauty. His *plastic* effects will refresh the life of wood, as well as the human-spirit that lost it—as inspiration—long since.

THE FIVE DOORS OF THE CUPBOARD ABOVE THE TABLE WERE CUT FROM A SINGLE
CYPRESS VENEERED SLAB
LIVING ROOM, TALIESIN
FRANK LLOYD WRIGHT, ARCHITECT

JUNE 1928

IN THE CAUSE OF ARCHITECTURE

BY FRANK LLOYD WRIGHT

V. THE MEANING OF MATERIALS—THE KILN

I SEE TANG glazes and Sung soft-clay figures from Chinese tombs in my studio as I write,—a few of the noble Tang glazed horses that show Greek influence,—and Han pottery. Some fragments of the Racca blue-glazed pots and the colored tiles of the Persians in Asia Minor—"the cradle of the race,"—Egyptian vessels and scarabs.

It appears from a glance the oven is as old as civilization at least—which is old enough for us.

Our interest is not archaeological but architectural and begins with a lump of peculiarly pliable clay in the hand of the man who wants to make something useful and at the same time beautiful out of it,— at the time when he knows he can bake it hard enough to make it serviceable. Then it all begins to grow rapidly in the experimental search for different clays. The grinding of minerals, to make paste for a flux to pour over the vessels to make them impervious and beautiful—and the legion of earnest chemical experiments that followed. The research of devoted craftsmen for several hundred centuries have laid up treasure and all but lost it but for a specimen or two—times without number.

The remains are a fascinating record of man's creative endeavor on his earth. A record that tells more of him probably than any other—for in it we find not only pottery and building but painting, sculpture and script intimately related to the life of all the peoples who have inhabited the earth—since cave-dwellers built their fires.

All the materials we know, seem at one time or another in a state of flux. Fire is father-creator to them all—below ground. Light is mother-creator to all that rise in air out of the ground. Back to Fire again goes that which Fire made to be fused with man's creative power into another creation —that of his use and beauty.

Anything permanent as a constructive material comes into man's hands by way of Fire, as he has slowly learned to approach in "degrees" the heat in which his globe of earth was formed—and courage to set what he has himself made, again at its beneficent mercy. He knows much. But fire knows more and has constant surprises for him.

He will never exhaust them all—nor need to.

He has the Brick.

He has the Tile.

He has the Pot and Bowl.

He has the Vase.

He has the Image.

He may color them all—forever so far as he knows—with the hues of nature and qualify each according to any or all the sensibilities he has—taught by the qualities he loves in the work of Nature all about him.

We have hitherto been speaking of "natural" materials. The natural material here is of earth itself. But to produce this material known as Ceramics, another element, that of the artificer, has entered with Fire.

This product should therefore be nearer man's desire—molded, as it is, by himself. His creation is seen in it. What he has sensed of the story of his creation, he has put into it.

He sees as he is and this record will tell us what he sees, how he sees—as he sees it.

He has seen nothing he is not himself. He is the imaginative geometrical tracery of the Persian and Moor and the noblest brick buildings man has ever erected. He is the noble sculpture and pottery of the Han Dynasty in China, as well as the Satsuma and Nabeshima of Japan. His is the story painted on the pots and bowls of Greece no less than the flowered plaques of Byzantium, or upon the utensils of the Indian cliff dweller.

His sense of form he took from those forms already made as his natural environment. In his striving for excellence in quality he was taught what to love by stone, leaf and mold and flower—the book of "trees," the mosses and mists and the mosaics of foliage in the sun. Especially in China where his sense of Nature was profound did he learn from them. When he was at his best, he interpreted what he saw.

When he was inferior, he imitated it.

But always, superior or inferior, he was its reflection in his Ceramics as in a mirror.

And in spirit looking away from himself, his eyes fixed on Gods as God or God as Gods—fashioning and firing and building as he himself was burning, all the while, better than he *knew*.

What has Man to show for the Brick? I should offer the brick buildings of Asia Minor—Persia.

What he has to show for his Tile? Wherever Persian or Mohammedan influence was supreme.

What he has to show for the Pot and Bowl? Chinese pottery.

What he has to show for his Vase? The Grecian urn.

To show for his Image? Those of Egypt, Greece and China.

The modern contribution to Ceramics as building material is "Terra Cotta." A poor name for an important material—but so it is named. I suppose "earthen-ware" seemed inadequate or not specific.

And it is the greatest opportunity for the creative artist of all the materials he may choose. It is, of course, burned clay in any color or glaze for entire buildings—pottery buildings! Earthenware on a great scale.

Modern terra-cotta has known but one creative master—only one—Louis H. Sullivan.

He is dead. His work in terra-cotta will live long after him. His was the temperament and the imagination that naturally found in this impressionable material the ideal medium for his genius. Terra-cotta lives only as it takes the impression of human imagination. It is a material for the modeler. It is in the architect's hand what wax is in the sculptor's hand.

After the material takes shape, the surface treatments are all a matter of taste. They are limitless in quality and style.

And the chief business of terra-cotta has been to imitate stone. It would imitate anything else as readily—with gratitude—it seems. It is the misfortune of anything impressionable to be called upon to give imitations. Mimicry is all too human. To imitate is the natural tendency of men. Not Man.

But Louis H. Sullivan's exuberant, sensuous nature and brilliant imagination took terra-cotta—and it lived. It no longer asked permission of the Styles. It was *itself* because it was Louis H. Sullivan. In it this master created a grammar of ornament all his own. And notwithstanding certain realistic tendencies, an original style of ornamentation out of the man, astonishing in range, never lacking virility.

Into the living intricacy of his loving modulations of surface, "background"—the curse of all stupid ornament—ceased to exist. None might see where terra-cotta left off and ornamentation came to life. A fragment of Sullivanian Terra-cotta—were we at some remote period of time to be excavated—would be found with a thrill. It would mean that a man lived among us at a dead time in Art.

The Sullivanian motif was efflorescent, exvolute, supported by tracery of geometric motives—bringing up the clay in forms so delicate and varied and lively

BRICK MASSES
THE LARKIN BUILDING, BUFFALO, N. Y.
FRANK LLOYD WRIGHT, ARCHITECT

DETAIL OF BRICK WORK
THE ROBIE HOME, WOODLAWN AVENUE, CHICAGO
FRANK LLOYD WRIGHT, ARCHITECT

that no parallel in these respects exists.

We may see, for once, how completely a negative material can be appropriately brought to life by the creative artist. It is reassuring.

Is there in Architectural history another man who out of himself not only created an exuberant type of beautiful architectural relief but furnished it forth, always consistent in style, in amazing variety that could not have ended but with his death? Even toward the last of his life, enfeebled, disillusioned but indomitable, he drew with all his old-time freshness of touch a series of beautiful designs that show no falling off in power whatever—even in spontaneity.

His ornamentation was the breath of his life. Clay came into his hand, that both might live on forever.

Because, now that we know what terra-cotta can be, and how it can be, we shall never be satisfied to see it degraded to imitation again—nor satisfied to see it imitating him.

Taught by him we should learn how to use it. If not so well as he, at least on principle for its own sake as he did. His sense of Architecture found a fulness of expression in the plastic clay. Few architects ever find any such expression in any medium whatsoever.

Terra-cotta should revere him as its God, sing his praises, but, better than that, be true to his teaching which would mean more to him than psalms in his praise and his statue in the hills.

In the terra-cotta or pottery of Earthenware building we may have, today, the sum and substance of all the kiln ever gave to architecture.

Modern methods have made the complete terra-cotta building, inside and outside, as definite a possibility as was the Han vessel in its time or the Greek vase. But—who

A COTTAGE OF SAND-MOLD BRICK
THE CHENEY HOME, OAK PARK, ILLINOIS
FRANK LLOYD WRIGHT, ARCHITECT

would look upon it in its present state after Sullivan left it, as a work of Art?

It cannot live either on its own texture or color—to any great extent. And as for its design? It is a mendicant feeding on crumbs from the table of the styles.

Why? Is it because Sullivan is dead? Did this most valuable of modern achievements in "material" die with him, as it never really lived until he came?

No. Materials never die. This material is only asleep, waiting for some master to waken it to life.

Here, young man in architecture, is a golden opportunity quite boundless so far as imagination goes. Rescue the royal beggar from penury and slavery.

Where is the pottery-building beautiful in form and texture and color—as such?

Why are there not thousands cleaning themselves in the rain—warming themselves in the sun—growing richer with age instead of dingy and sad and old? Why do they look cheap and soon stale?

Just because there are no good pottery designs for good pottery buildings—so how can the pottery be good with no more inspiration than that?

A neglected minion of the Machine!

By way of terra-cotta we are here arrived at the matter of Ornament. Because terra-cotta chiefly lives by virtue of the human imagination in ornamentation.

As we intend to discuss ornament by itself on its merits, later, let us say now that true ornament is of the thing, never on it. The Material develops into its own ornamentation by will of the master. He does not impose forms upon it. He develops it into forms from the within which is characteristic of its nature—if he is "the master."

We may see this in Sullivanian Terra Cotta. The only limit to Sullivan's treatment was the degree to which the substance of the pliable clay would stay up between the thumb and finger and come through the fire. Background disappeared but surface was preserved. There was no sense of background, as such, anywhere. All was of the surface, out of the material. So no sense of ornament as *applied* to Terra-Cotta, because Terra-cotta became ornament and ornamented itself.

Terra-Cotta was this master's natural medium because his sense of beautiful form was the subtle fluctuation of flowering surface, song-like, as found in organic plant-life—the music of the crystal is seen as a minor accompaniment only.

The tones of the main theme are those of organic efflorescence—*growth* as it is performed by plant species. This idea of growth was the theme—invariably—which he glorified.

He created a "species" himself—and kept on creating others.

This procedure of Growth intrigued his imagination—inspired him. "Organic" was his God-word, as he traced Form to Function.

When, I suggested, as I once did, that quite as likely the function might be traced to the form, he disposed of the heresy—by putting it on a par with the old debating-school argument as to which came first, the Hen or the Egg. His interpretation was to him the Song-of-creation and he never tired of singing it. As it was visible to him in the growth of the plant he saw it in all—as indeed it may be.

Think of this when you see his synthetic motifs in his sentient Terra-Cotta.

And realize that there are ways of making a pottery building, the joints of the material becoming unit-lines in the pattern of the whole—which he, the pioneer, touches upon but was called away before realization or called away *to* realization—who knows? —and imagine the glorious marvel of beauty it might be.

I remember going to Palermo some years ago to see the mosaics of Monreale.

I had just got into the Cathedral-square and lifted my eyes to that great work when to the left I saw—or did I see it—for some moments I thought I dreamed—there against the sky—no not against it, of it, literally of the sky was a great dome of pure Racca blue.

I forgot the Cathedral for quite some time in the wonderful blue dome so simple in form—a heavenly thing. I have never recovered from it. And that effect was "Ceramic." Why not Terra Cotta? The old qualities in color firing can not be dead!

* * * *

To illustrate a simple use of brick I refer for noble examples to Ispahan, Sari, Veramin, Amol, Samarkand, Bokhara, and, of course, tile and pottery as well. Unfortunately I have little brickwork to my credit. I have chosen a few examples that show the walls solidified by emphasis of the horizontal joint, and examples showing the brick-pier and mass as I feel it to be natural in brick construction today. Brick is the material we in Usonia know and love best. We probably have brought brick-making to a pitch of perfection never existing in the world before at any time. And we use it, on the whole very well. Not only is the range inexhaustible in texture and color and shape, but the material itself is admirable in quality.

Together with it go all those baked-clay vitreous hollow bricks and hollow tiles which are probably the most useful of all materials in building in our climate.

* * * *

Usonian tiles and mosaics do not reach the quality of ancient or even contemporary materials of this nature. There is enough good material, however, to warrant a more general use which would inevitably cause it to grow better—and our day needs this development.

The nature of the mosaic either of stone, glass or ceramics is a truly architectural medium—useful in this era of the Machine and lending itself to plastic treatment with no insult to its nature. I should like to see whole buildings clothed in this medium.

Our pottery is imitative. We have had Teco, Rookwood and other types—all deserving experiments with something of originality in most of them. But none proceeding on principle to develop style, but of the nature and character of the process.

The "vessel" does not inspire us, it seems, as it did earlier people. Perhaps because we know no such need of it as they knew. I have chosen some natural "vessels" to show the help nature generously offers in the matter, to mention only one humble resource.

* * * *

The Usonian Image, likewise the Vase, is tentative when not openly imitative.

We seem to have little or nothing to say in the clay figure or pottery vase as concrete expression of the ideal of beauty that is our own. No sense of form has developed among us that can be called creative—adapted to that material. And it may never come. The life that flowed into this channel in ancient times apparently now goes somewhere else.

A few natural forms found in the Champlain clays seem interesting to me in this connection.

* * * *

Again our subject remains in barest outline—for to go adequately into this most human and important feature of all Man's endeavor to be and to remain beautiful the "kiln" would exhaust interesting volumes.

BRICK AND LAVA. CANTILEVER BALCONY OVER PROMENADE ENTRANCE SHOWING
PERFORATED BRICK SCREENS AND LIGHTING FIXTURES BUILT IN AS PART OF
THE ARCHITECTURE
HOTEL IMPERIAL, TOKIO
FRANK LLOYD WRIGHT, ARCHITECT

JULY 1928

IN THE CAUSE OF ARCHITECTURE

BY FRANK LLOYD WRIGHT

VI. THE MEANING OF MATERIALS—GLASS

Perhaps the greatest difference eventually between ancient and modern buildings will be due to our modern machine-made glass. Glass, in any wide utilitarian sense, is new.

Once a precious substance limited in quantity and size, glass and its making have grown so that a perfect clarity of any thickness, quality or dimension is so cheap and desirable that our modern world is drifting toward structures of glass and steel. Had the ancients been able to enclose interior space with the facility we enjoy because of glass, I suppose the history of architecture would have been radically different, although it is surprising how little this material has yet modified our sense of architecture beyond the show-windows the shop keeper demands and gets.

How that show-window plagued the architect at first and still teases the classicist! It has probably done more to show the classicist up as ridiculous than any other single factor.

The demand for visibility makes walls and even posts an intrusion to be got rid of at any cost. Architecture gave up the first story but started bravely above the glass at the second, nothing daunted and nothing changed. The building apparently stood in mid-air. Glass did it.

Crystal plates have generally taken the place of fundamental wall and piers in almost all commercial buildings; and glass, the curse of the classic, as an opportunity for the use of delicate construction of sheet metal and steel, is a tempting material not yet much explored. As glass has become clearer and clearer and cheaper and cheaper from age to age, about all that has been done with it architecturally is to fill the same opening that opaque glass screened before, with a perfect visibility now, except for the use to which the shop-man demands that it be put. The shop! That is where glass has almost come into its own. We have yet to give glass proper architectural recognition.

What is this magic material, there but not seen if you are looking through it? You may look at it, too, as a brilliance, catching reflections and giving back limpid light.

But it is what it is to-day because it may be seen through perfectly while it is an impenetrable stop for air currents, when due allowance is made for its fragility. When violence is done to it, it may be shattered, but a precious feature of the material is that it does not disintegrate.

I suppose as a material we may regard it as crystal—thin sheets of air in air to keep air out or keep it in. And with this sense of it, we can think of uses to which it might be put as various and beautiful as the frost-designs upon the pane of glass itself.

Glass has been servile in architecture beyond the painting done with it in cathedral windows. It has been a utilitarian affair except when used for candelabra, chandeliers or knobs—excepting only the mirror.

The sense of glass as the crystal has not yet to any extent entered into the poetry of architecture. It is too new, for one thing. For another thing, tradition did not leave any orders concerning it. It is strictly modern. Therefore, let us try to understand what it is. The machine has given to architects, in glass, a new material with which to work. Were glass eliminated now from buildings, it would be, so far as our buildings have gone, only like putting our eyes out. We could not see out or see into the building. We have gone so far with it as to make it the eyes of the building. Why not now combine it with steel, the spider's web, spin the building frame as an integument for crystal clearness—the crystal held by the steel as the diamond is held in its setting of gold—and make it the building itself?

All the diversity of color and texture available in any material is not only available but imperishable, in glass. So far as deterioration or decay is concerned, it is possible now to preserve the metal setting for an indefinite period. And it is the life of this setting alone that would determine the life of the building. It is time to give attention to that setting.

Shadows have been the brush-work of the architect when he modeled his architectural forms. Let him work, now, with light diffused, light refracted, light reflected—use light for its own sake—shadows aside. The prism has always delighted and fascinated man. The Machine gives him his opportunity in glass. The machine can do any kind of glass—thick, thin, colored, textured to order—and cheap. A new experience is awaiting him.

Then why are modern cities still sodden imitations of mediaeval strongholds? Black or white slabs of thick glass have already gone far as substitutes for marble slabs. They could easily go farther for their own

CORNER OF THE BARNSDALL RESIDENCE
HOLLYWOOD, CALIFORNIA
FRANK LLOYD WRIGHT, ARCHITECT

sake, in walls of buildings. Glass tiles, too, are not uncommon. Nor are glass mosaics an unusual sight.

All these uses together would form an incomparable palette for an architect. The difficulty is, architects are bound by traditional ideas of what a building must look like or be like. And when they undertake to use new materials, it is only to make them conform to those preconceived ideas.

Every new material means a new form, a new use if used according to its nature. The free mind of the natural architect would use them so, were the unnatural inhibition of that freedom not imposed upon all by a false propriety due to the timidity of ignorance.

The Persian, the Egyptian and the Moor had most insight concerning the mathematics of the principle at work in the crystal. The Persian and the Moor were most abstract; the Egyptian was most human. All knew more of the secrets of glass than we do—we who may revel in it unrestrained by economic considerations of any kind, and who understand it not at all, except as a mirror.

As a mirror, the vanity and elegance of the French brought glass into architectural use. Their brilliant salons, glittering with cut-glass pendants and floral forms blown in clear and colored glass, were something in themselves new in architecture. The very limitation of the size of the sheet available gave a feature in the joint that adds rather than detracts from the charm of the whole effect of their work.

But now the walls might disappear, the ceilings, too, and—yes—the floors as well. A mirror floor? Why not? In certain cases. Nicely calculated effects of this sort might

ture, if *architecturally* used. To use it so is not easy, for the tendency toward the tawdry is ever present in any use of the mirror.

But to extend the vista, complete the form, multiply a unit where repetition would be a pleasure, lend illusion and brilliance in connection with light-effects

WINDOW OF A RESIDENCE IN HOLLYWOOD, CALIFORNIA
FRANK LLOYD WRIGHT, ARCHITECT

amplify and transform a cabinet into a realm, a room into bewildering vistas and avenues: a single unit into unlimited areas of color, pattern and form.

The Mirror is seen in Nature in the surfaces of lakes in the hollows of the mountains and in the pools deep in shadow of the trees; in winding ribbons of the rivers that catch and give back the flying birds, clouds and blue sky. A dreary thing to have that element leave the landscape. It may be as refreshing and as beautifying in architec-

—all these are good uses to which the architect may put the mirror. As a matter of fact he never uses plate-glass in his windows or indoors inside his buildings that he does not employ the same element in his architecture that the limpid pool presents in the landscape—susceptible to reflections. And this opportunity is new. It is a subtle beauty of both exterior and interior, as may be readily seen in the effect of the exterior if a poor quality of cylinder glass be substituted for polished plate-glass. Perhaps

PLAY HOUSE, COONLEY RESIDENCE, RIVERDALE, ILLINOIS
FRANK LLOYD WRIGHT, ARCHITECT

no one other change in the materials in which any building is made could so materially demoralize the effect of the whole as this substitution.

In the openings in my buildings, the glass plays the effect the jewel plays in the category of materials. The element of pattern is made more cheaply and beautifully effective when introduced into the glass of the windows than in the use of any other medium that architecture has to offer. The metal divisions become a metal screen of any pattern—heavy or light, plated in any metal, even gold or silver—the glass a subordinate, rhythmical accent of any emotional significance whatever, or vice versa. The pattern may be calculated with refer-

ence to the scale of the interior and the scheme of decoration given by, or kept by, the motif of the glass pattern.

I have used opalescent, opaque, white and gold in the geometrical groups of spots fixed in the clear glass. I have used, preferably, clear primary colors, like the German flashed-glass, to get decorative effects, believing the clear emphasis of the primitive color interferes less with the function of the window and adds a higher architectural note to the effect of *light* itself. The kinder-symphony in the windows in the Coonley play-house is a case in point. The sumac windows in the Dana dining-room another. This resource may be seen in most of my work, varied to suit conditions. This is a

GLASS AND CONCRETE
FRANK LLOYD WRIGHT, ARCHITECT

resource commonly employed in our buildings but usually overdone or insufficiently conventionalized. Nothing is more annoying to me than any tendency toward realism of form in window-glass, to get mixed up with the view outside. A window pattern should stay severely "put." The magnificent window-painting and plating of the windows of the religious edifice is quite another matter. There the window becomes primarily a gorgeous painting—painting with light itself—enough light being diffused to flood the interior dimly. This is an art in itself that reached its height in the Middle Ages. Probably no greater wealth of pictorial color-effect considered as pure decoration exists in the world than in the great rose-windows and pointed-arches of the cathedral.

But, the glass and bronze building is the most engaging of possibilities in modern architecture. Imagine a city iridescent by day, luminous by night, imperishable! Buildings—shimmering fabrics—woven of rich glass—glass all clear or part opaque and part clear—patterned in color or stamped to form the metal tracery that is to hold all together to be, in itself, a thing of delicate beauty consistent with slender steel construction—expressing the nature of that construction in the mathematics of structure which are the mathematics of music as well. Such a city would clean itself in the rain, would know no fire alarms—nor any glooms. To any extent the light could be reduced within the rooms by screens, a blind, or insertion of opaque glass. The heating problem would be no greater than with the rattling windows of the imitation masonry structure, because the fabric now would be mechanically perfect—the product of the machine shop instead of the makeshift of the field.

I dream of such a city, have worked enough on such a building to see definitely its desirability and its practicability.

Beauty always comes to and by means of a perfect practicability in architecture. That does not mean that the practicability may not find idealization in realization. On the contrary. Because that is precisely what architecture does and is when it is really architecture. Architecture finds idealization in realization or the reverse if you like.

Then, too, there is the lighting fixture—made a part of the building. No longer an appliance nor even an appurtenance, but really architecture.

This is a new field. I touched it early in my work and can see limitless possibilities of beauty in this one feature of the use of glass. Fortunately this field has been more developed than any other. The sense of integral

GLASS AND BRASS BARS
A WINDOW IN THE DANA HOUSE
1899
FRANK LLOYD WRIGHT, ARCHITECT

lighting seems to come more easily and naturally because there was no precedent to impede progress. And as it is now with the lighting feature, so will it soon be a disgrace to an architect to have left anything of a physical nature whatsoever, in his building unassimilated in his design as a whole.

Integral lighting began with this ideal in mind in my work thirty-one years ago, as may be seen in the play-room ceiling and in the dining room ceiling of my former house in Oak Park. Also in the ceiling of my studio library in that building. Perhaps it might be said to have begun earlier than that in the Auditorium by Adler and Sullivan where the electric lights became features of the plaster ornamentation. The lights were not incorporated, but they were provided for in the decoration as accents of that decoration.

Glass and light—two forms of the same thing!

Modern architecture is beckoned to a better reckoning by this most precious of the architect's new material. As yet, little has been done with it but the possibilities are large.

This great gift of glass is of the machine,—for today mechanical-processes are as much the Machine as any other of its factors.

AUGUST 1928

IN THE CAUSE OF ARCHITECTURE

BY FRANK LLOYD WRIGHT

VII. THE MEANING OF MATERIALS—CONCRETE

I AM WRITING this on the Phoenix plain of Arizona. The ruddy granite mountain-heaps, grown "old," are decomposing and sliding down layer upon layer to further compose the soil of the plain. Granite in various stages of decay, sand, silt and gravel make the floor of the world here.

Buildings could grow right up out of the "ground" were this "soil," before it is too far "rotted," cemented in proper proportions and beaten into flasks or boxes—a few steel strands dropped in for reinforcement.

Cement may be, here as elsewhere, the secret stamina of the physical body of our new world.

And steel has given to cement (this invaluable ancient medium) new life, new purposes and possibilities, for when the coefficient of expansion and contraction was found to be the same in concrete and steel, a new world was opened to the Architect. The Machine in giving him steel-strands gave concrete the right-of-way.

Yet three-fourths of the dwellings here are of wood and brick brought from great distances and worked up into patterns originated, east, thirty years ago. The "houses" are quite as indigenous as a cocked-hat, and almost as deciduous; one-half the cost of the whole—freight.

The Indian did better in the adobe dwelling he got from Mexico and built in the foot-hills. Even the few newer concrete buildings imitate irrelevant "styles"—although more relevant Mexico is coming north at the moment, to the rescue, in little ways. So funny, they will be architectural comedy ten years later.

It is only natural that the Architect, at first, should do as he has always done—reproduce badly in the new material the forms of the old Architecture or whatever he had instead, which were probably, themselves reproductions, as false.

Let us frankly admit that these human-processes of thought move more by habit and indirection than by intellectual necessity and attach to the established order with tenacity worthy of a nobler thing.

The Architect, by profession, is a conservative of conservatives. His "profession" is first to perceive and conform and last to change this order.

Yet gradually the law of gravitation has its way, even with the profession: natural tendency in even so humble a thing as a building-material will gradually but eventually force the architect's hand and overcome even his "profession."

Then after it has had its way, will come its sway, so that when a newer material condition enters into life, it, in turn, will have just as hard a time of it, until "the nature of the thing," by gravity, conquers "professional resistance" once more: a resistance compounded of ignorance, animal fear and self-interest.

* * * *

The literature of concrete, as a conglomerate, now fills libraries. Its physical properties are fairly well understood.

Aesthetically it has neither song nor story.

Nor is it easy to see in this conglomerate a high aesthetic property, because, in itself it is amalgam, aggregate, compound. And cement, the binding medium, is character-less in itself. The net result is, usually, an artificial stone at best, or a petrified sand heap at worst.

Concrete would be better named "conglomerate," as concrete is a noble word

LIVING ROOM UNIT AND STAIRWAY
FREEMAN HOUSE, LOS ANGELES
FRANK LLOYD WRIGHT, ARCHITECT

UPPER LEVEL, STREET FRONT
FREEMAN HOUSE, LOS ANGELES
FRANK LLOYD WRIGHT, ARCHITECT

which this material fails to live up to. It is a mixture that has little quality in itself.

If this material is to have either form, texture or color in itself, each must artificially be given to it, by human imagination.

Thus it is one of the insensate brute materials that is used to imitate others.

"Concrete"—so called—must submit to the "artistic" at the hands of any parlor-architect or interior desecrator and, consequently seldom have life of its own worthy a substance so obedient and useful.

As a material it is its misfortune to project as wooden beams, travel molded as cornices. Yet it will faithfully hang as a slab, stand delicately perforated like a Persian faience screen or lie low and heavily in mass upon the ground. Again, unluckily, it will stand up and take the form (and texture too) of wooden posts and planks. It is supine, and sets as the fool, whose matrix receives it, wills.

When, and as, he has made up his mind to his "*taste*," it will set into whatever shape may be, and will then go to work with steel strands for sinews, and do mighty things. When aged it becomes so stubborn that it would cost more to remove the structure often, than the ground upon which it stands might be worth.

Surely, here, to the creative mind, is temptation. Temptation to rescue so honest a material from degradation. Because here in a conglomerate named "concrete" we find a plastic material, that as yet has found no medium of expression that will allow it to take plastic form. So far as it is now used it might be tallow, cast-iron or plaster, poured into molds and at the mercy of their shape.

Therefore its form is a matter of this process of casting rather than a matter of anything at all derived from its own nature. Because it is thus, universally, at the mercy of demoralizing extraneous influences, it is difficult to say what is "concrete" form and what is not.

But certain truths regarding the material are clear enough. First, it is a mass-material; second, an impressionable one as to surface; third, it is a material which may be continuous or monolithic within certain very wide limits; fourth, it is a material that may be chemicalized, colored or rendered impervious to water: it may be dyed or textured in the stuff; fifth, it is a willing material while fresh, fragile when still young, stubborn when old, lacking always in tensile strength.

What then should be the Aesthetic of Concrete?

Is it Stone? Yes and No.

Is it Plaster? Yes and No.

Is it Brick or Tile? Yes and No.

Is it Cast Iron? Yes and No.

Poor Concrete! Still looking for its own at the hands of Man.

Perhaps the term "concrete" popularly meaning conglomerate, in this connection, denotes it the mongrel, servile as such, destined to no more than the place of obedient servant in the rank of materials.

Terra cotta, the fanciful, however, though less artificial, is not much more fortunate in character and make-up. The two materials have much in common. Terra cotta having the great advantage of standing up to be modelled and becoming indestructible, colorful and glazed when fired, a comparatively expensive process.

The chief difference between stone and concrete lies in the binding medium which, in the case of stone, is of the stone itself—a chemical affinity.

In the case of concrete it is a foreign substance that binds the aggregate. There is little or none other than a mechanical affinity in concrete.

But for this difference concrete would be, in fact, a true natural stone. And taking this difference for granted it is more truly an artificial stone than it is anything else; the nature of the artifice enabling the artificer to enter at the time the mixture is in a state of flux, to give it whatever shape he may desire.

USE OF PLAIN AND PATTERNED BLOCKS FOR INTERIOR WALLS
LA MINIATURA, PASADENA, CALIFORNIA
FRANK LLOYD WRIGHT, ARCHITECT

Yes, artificial stone it is that concrete usually becomes.

But the essential difference between stone and concrete is still unconsidered. And that essential difference is the plasticity of the material itself as distinguished from natural stone which has none at all.

I should say that in this plasticity of concrete lies its aesthetic value. As an artificial stone, concrete has no great, certainly no independent, aesthetic value whatever. As a plastic material—eventually becoming stone-like in character—there lives in it a great aesthetic property, as yet inadequately expressed.

To design a concrete pattern for a casting that would feature this flow of the material might be possible and so allow its plastic

To avoid all interference with the fabrication of the light-giving exterior screen the supporting pylons are set back from the lot line, the floors carried by them thus becoming cantilever slabs. The extent of the cantilever is determined by the use for which the building is designed. These pylons are continuous through all floors and in this instance exposed as pylons at the top. They are enlarged to carry electrical, plumbing, and heating conduits, which branch from the shafts, not in the floor slabs, but into piping designed into visible fixtures extending beneath each ceiling to where the outlets are needed in the office arrangement. All electrical or plumbing appliances may thus be disconnected and relocated at short notice with no waste at all in time or material.

Being likewise fabricated on a perfect unit system, the interior partitions may all be made up in sections, complete with doors, ready to set in place and designed to match the general style of the outer wall screen.

These interior partition-units thus fabricated may be stored ready to use, and any changes to suit tenants made over night with no waste of time and material.

The increase of glass area over the usual skyscraper fenestration is only about ten per cent (the margin could be increased or diminished by expanding or contracting the copper members in which it is set), so the expense of heating is not materially increased. Inasmuch as the copper mullions are filled with insulating material and the window openings are tight, being mechanical units in a mechanical screen, this excess of glass is compensated.

The radiators are cast as a railing set in front of the lower glass unit of this outer screen wall, free enough to make cleaning easy.

The walls of the first two stories, or more, may be unobstructed glass—the dreams of the shop-keeper in this connection fully realized.

The connecting stairways necessary between floors are here arranged as a practical fire-escape forming the central feature, as may be seen at the front and rear of each section of the whole mass, and though cut off by fire-proof doors at each floor, the continuous stairway thus made discharges upon the sidewalk below without obstruction.

The construction of such a building as this would be at least one-third lighter than anything in the way of a tall building yet built—and three times stronger in any disturbance, the construction being balanced as the body on the legs, the walls hanging as the arms from the shoulders, the whole, heavy where weight insures stability.

But of chief value as I see it is the fact that the scheme as a whole would legitimately eliminate the matter of "architecture," that now vexes all such buildings, from field construction, all such elements of architecture "exterior" or interior becoming a complete shop-fabrication—assembled only in the field.

The shop in our mechanical era is ten to one, economically efficient over the field, and will always increase over the field in economy and craftsmanship.

The mere physical concrete construction of pylons and floors is here non-involved with any interior or exterior, is easily rendered indestructible, and is made entirely independent of anything hitherto mixed up with it in our country as "Architecture." In the skyscraper as practised at present the "Architecture" is expensively involved but is entirely irrelevant. But here it is entirely relevant but uninvolved.

Also the piping and conduits of all appurtenance-systems may be cut in the shop, the labor in the field reduced to assembling only, "fitting" or screwing up the joints being all that is necessary.

Thus we have, literally, a shop-made building all but the interior supporting posts and floors, which may be rein-

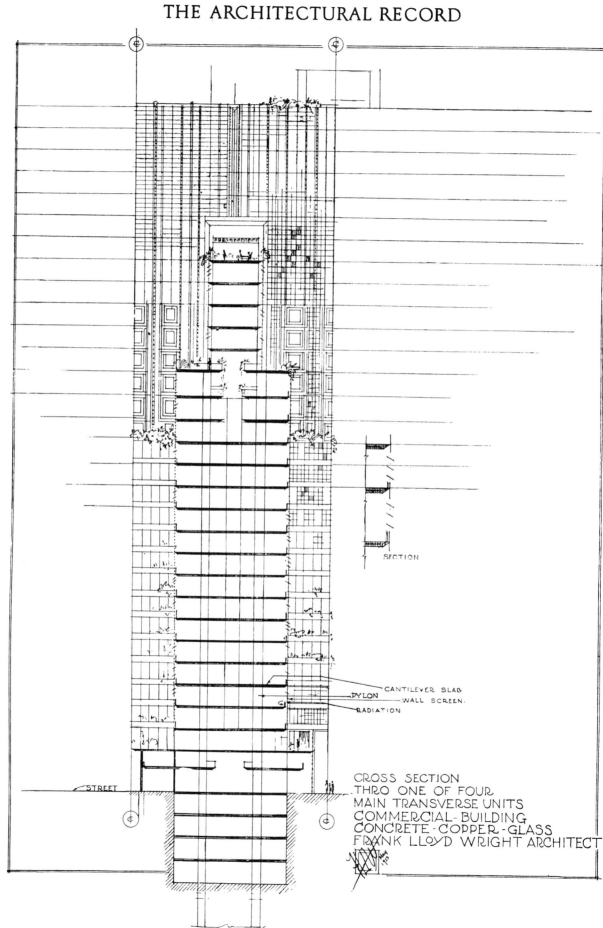

SECTION

CANTILEVER SLAB
PYLON
WALL SCREEN
RADIATION

STREET

CROSS SECTION
THRO ONE OF FOUR
MAIN TRANSVERSE UNITS
COMMERCIAL-BUILDING
CONCRETE-COPPER-GLASS
FRANK LLOYD WRIGHT ARCHITECT

forced concrete or concrete-masked steel.

In this design, architecture has been frankly, profitably and *artistically* taken from the field to the factory—standardized as might be any mechanical thing whatsoever, from a penny-whistle to a piano.

There is no unsalable floor space in this building created "for effect," as may be observed.

There are no "*features*" manufactured "for effect."

There is nothing added to the whole merely for this desired "effect."

To gratify the landlord, his lot area is now salable to the very lot-line and on every floor, where ordinances do not interfere and demand that they be reduced in area as the building soars.

What architecture there is in evidence here is a light, trim, practical commercial fabric—every inch and pound of which is "in service." There is every reason why it should be beautiful. But it is best to say nothing about that, as things are now.

The present design was worked out for a lot three hundred feet by one hundred feet, the courts being open to the south.

There is nothing of importance to mention in the general disposition of the other necessary parts of the plan. All may be quite as customary.

My aim in this fabrication employing the cantilever system of construction which proved so effective in preserving the Imperial Hotel at Tokyo, was to achieve absolute scientific utility by means of the Machine—to accomplish—first of all—a true standardization which would not only serve as a basis for keeping the life of the building true as architecture, but enable me to project the whole, as an expression of a valuable principle involved, into a genuine living-architecture of the present.

I began work upon this study in Los Angeles in the winter of 1923 having had the main features of it in mind for many years. I had the good fortune to explain it in detail to "lieber-meister" Louis H. Sullivan, some months before he died.

Gratefully I remember—and proudly too —"I have had faith that it would come," he said. "This Architecture of Democracy— I see it in this building of yours, a genuine, beautiful thing. I knew what I was talking about all these years—you see. I never could have done this building myself, but I believe that, but for me, you could never have done it."

I am sure I should never have reached it, but for what he was and what he did.

This design is dedicated to him.

DECEMBER 1928

IN THE CAUSE OF ARCHITECTURE

BY FRANK LLOYD WRIGHT

IX. THE TERMS

ENOUGH, by now, has been said of materials to show direction and suggest how far the study of their natures may go. We have glanced at certain major aspects of the more obvious of building-materials only, because these studies are not intended to do more than fire the imagination of the young architect and suggest to him a few uses and effects that have proved helpful in my own work. The subject has neither bottom, sides nor top, if one would try to exhaust "the nature of materials"! How little consideration the modern architect has yet really given them. Opportunity has languished in consequence and is waiting, still.

Perhaps these articles have been guilty of "poetic" interpretation now and then, turning these "materials" over and over in the hand. The imagination has caught the light on them, in them as well, and tried to fix a ray or two of their significance in the sympathetic mind.

POETRY, POETIC, ROMANTIC, IDEAL.

These words now indicate disease or crime because a past century failed with them and gave us the *language* of form—instead of the significant form itself.

So if we are not to fall into the category of "language" ourselves, I owe an explanation of the meaning of these words, for I shall continue to use them.

It has been common practice among artists to apply the terms qualifying one art to another art—say, those of Music to Architecture or vice-versa. This may be done because certain qualities in each are common to all. It may be helpful to make comparisons between them to bring out particular significance, as our English vocabulary is poor at best in all the words we have with which to express shadings of qualities or of our feeling in dealing with qualities.

We can hack away at the thing with our body-terms and get the subject anywhere or nowhere except misunderstood.

Nor do we speak a common tongue in the use we have come to make of these main words. We may pack into each of them more or less, and differently, than another would dream of doing, or could do. So it is well to clean them up—for now we are going to write about the uses and purposes of "materials" in creating this thing we name Architecture.

"Poetry of Form," for instance, is a phrase that will now make almost any sensible man sick.

The word "poetry" is a dangerous word to use, and for good reason. Carl Sandburg once said to me,—"Why do you use the words 'poetry,' 'beauty,' 'truth' or 'ideal' any more? Why don't you just get down to tacks and talk about boards and nails and barn doors?"

Good advice. And I think that is what I should do. But I won't, unless I can get an equivalent by doing so. That equivalent is exactly what I cannot get. Those words—romance, poetry, beauty, truth, ideal—are not precious words—nor should they be *specious* words. They are elemental human symbols and we must be brought back again to respect for them by using them significantly if we use them at all, or go to jail.

Well, then—our lot being cast with a hod of mortar, some bricks or stone or concrete and the Machine, we shall talk of the thing we are going to do with these things in the terms that are sensible enough when we speak of the horse-hair, cat-gut, fine wood, brass and keys, the "things" that make up the modern orchestra. By the way, that orchestra is New. Our possibilities in building with the Machine are New in just the same sense.

Although Architecture is a greater art than Music (if one art can be greater than another) this architect has always secretly envied Bach, Beethoven and the great Masters of Music. They lifted their batons after great and painful concentration on creation and soared into the execution of their designs with a hundred willing minds—the orchestra—and that means a thousand fingers quick to perform every detail of the precise effect the Master wanted.

What a resource!

And what facility they were afforded by forms—they made them—moving according to mood from fugue to sonata, from sonata to concerto—and from them all to the melodic grandeur and completeness of the symphony.

I suppose it is well that no architect has anything like it nor can ever get it.

But as a small boy, long after I had been put to bed, I used to lie and listen to my father playing Beethoven—for whose music he had conceived a passion—playing far into the night. To my young mind it all spoke a language that stirred me strangely, and I've since learned it was the language, beyond all words, of the human heart.

To me, architecture is just as much an affair of the human heart.

And it is to architecture in this sense that we are addressing ourselves. We are pleading here in that cause.

What, then, is Poetry of Form?

The term has become a red rag or a reproachful tag to architects at home and abroad. And, too, it is something that clients would rather not hear about. For all clients are, to some degree, infected by this contact with architects. And some of the best among them fall ill with Neo-Spanish that was itself Neo-Italian or some kind of Renaissance of the Renaissance, or linger along Quasi-Italian, or eventually die outright of Tudor or Colonial.

It is a new form of the plague—"this poison of good taste," as Lewis Mumford has precisely called it. This "poison" has cursed America for generations to come. And this happened to the good people who spoke the language of "Poetry of Form" and hopefully sought the "Romantic" when they became clients.

"Poetry of Form," in this romantic, popular sense, has not only cost wasted billions in money but has done spiritual harm beyond reckoning to the America of the future. But the fact remains that America wanted it and sought it. The failure is less significant than the fact.

So instead of speaking of "Poetry of Form" in buildings, perhaps, after all, we would do better to say simply the natural building, naturally built, native to the region.

Such a building would be sure to be all that Poetry of Form should imply, and would mean a building as beautiful on its site as the region itself.

And that word ROMANCE, Romantic or Romanza, got itself born in literature a century ago. Later Novalis and his kind chose the blue flower as its symbol. Their Romance was rather an escape from life than any realization of the idealization of it. As the word is popularly or commonly used today, it is still something fanciful, unlike life. At least it is something exotic. "Romance" is used as a word to indicate escape from the pressure of the facts of life into a realm of the beyond—a beyond each one fashions for himself or for others as he will—or may—dream.

But in music the Romanza is only a free form or freedom to make one's own form. A musician's sense of proportion is all that governs him in it. The mysterious remains just enough a haunting quality in a whole so organic as to lose all tangible evidence of how it was made—and the organic whole lives in the harmonies of feeling expressed in sound. Translate "sounds and the ear" to "forms and the eye" and a Romanza, even, seems reasonable enough, too, in architecture.

And now that word IDEAL.

The IDEAL building? Why, only that building which is all one can imagine as desirable in every way.

And POETRY? Why, the poetry in anything is only the song at the heart of it—and in the nature of it.

Gather together the harmonies that inhere in the nature of something or anything whatsoever, and project those inner harmonies into some tangible "objective" or outward form of human use or understanding, and you will have Poetry. You will have something of the song that aches in the heart of all of us for release.

Any of these Arts called "Fine" are POETIC by nature. And to be poetic, truly, does not mean to escape from life but *does* mean *life raised to intense significance and higher power.*

POETRY, therefore, is the great potential need of human kind.

We hunger for POETRY naturally as we do for sunlight, fresh air and fruits, if we are normal human beings.

To be potentially poetic in architecture, then, means—to create a building free in form (we are using the word Romanza) that takes what is harmonious in the nature of existing conditions inside the thing and outside it and with sentiment—(beware of sentimentality)—bring it all out into some visible form that expresses those inner harmonies perfectly, *outwardly*, whatever the shape it may take.

In this visible shape or form you will see not only what was harmonious in the existing conditions inside and outside and around about the building, but you will also see, in this sentiment of the architect, a quality added from the architect himself—because this ultimate form inevitably would be *his* sense of BEAUTY living now for you in these known and visible terms of his work.

These words—Poetry, Romance, Ideal—

used in proper sense—and I believe I have given them proper expression and interpretation here—are indispensable tools in getting understood when talking of creation.

At any rate, I shall use them, always in the sense I have just given them.

And there is need of another term to express a new sense of an eternal quality in creation.

Need, really, of a new dimension?

Either a new dimension to think with or a new sense of an old one.

We have heard of the fourth dimension frequently, of late, to meet this need. Why a fourth dimension, when we so little understand the possibilities of what we already use as the three dimensions?

If we make the first two (length and width) into one, as really they are both merely surface, and then add the third (thickness) as the second, thus getting mass, we will have an empty place as third in which to put this new sense as the missing dimension I shall describe. Thus comes in the third dimension about which I have talked a good deal and written somewhat.

Or suppose we arrive at it another way by simply giving spiritual interpretation to the three dimensions we already use. Say length (the first dimension) becomes continuity, width (the second dimension) becomes that breadth of which we speak when we refer to the measure of some great man's mind or a great prospect. Then thickness (the third dimension) becomes "depth" and we give to that word, "depth," the meaning we give to it when we speak of the "profound," the organic, the integral—again we have the third dimension.

We reach the missing dimension either way, but reach it we must.

For it is necessary to find some term that will make it easy to express this missing quality in discussing creation and reaching within for understanding.

But why say fourth dimension when, by properly interpreting the three we already have and by giving them the higher sig-

PLAYHOUSE NO1 · OAK · PARK · THE "ANN BAXTER"

KINDER-SYMPHONY—PLAYHOUSE IN OAK PARK, ILLINOIS
ONE OF A GROUP OF BUILDINGS FOR THE PLAYGROUND BOARD OF OAK PARK, ILLINOIS
FRANK LLOYD WRIGHT, ARCHITECT

nificance which is theirs by nature, we may be spared the confusion of more mere numbers?

This, then, is what I mean by the third dimension. Either an interpretation of the physical third, an interpretation that signifies this quality of "at-one-ness" or integral nature in anything or everything. Or, arrive at it by naming the three dimensions as now used as actually but two, adding the third as a new concept of organic-integrity, or more properly speaking, as that *quality* that makes anything *of* the thing and never on it.

Thus came the new conception of architecture as interior-space finding utilization and enclosure as its "*members*"—as archi-

tecture. The *within* is thus made concrete realization in *form*.

This is the *integral* concept of building for which I have pleaded, am still pleading and will continue to plead, instead of the earlier one—beautiful but less great—in which a block of building material was sculptured, punctured, and ornamented into architecture.

In this matter of supplying the needed term as the third dimension I may be found guilty of making a language of my own to fit my necessity.

Perhaps that is true—although it seems obvious enough to me that the quality lacking in the thought of our modern world where creation is concerned, is simply ex-

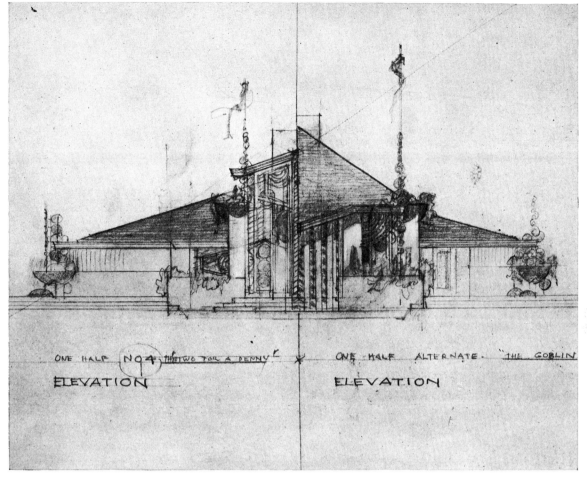

ONE HALF NO 4 THE TWO FOR A PENNY   ONE HALF ALTERNATE "THE GOBLIN

ELEVATION   ELEVATION

KINDER-SYMPHONY—PLAYHOUSES IN OAK PARK, ILLINOIS
BUILDINGS DESIGNED FOR THE PLAYGROUND BOARD OF OAK PARK, ILLINOIS
FRANK LLOYD WRIGHT, ARCHITECT

pressed in this way. I should be thankful for a better, more evident expression of this subjective element.

If I could find it I should be among the first to use it.

Until then I can only write and speak of this essence of all creative endeavor, objectively, as the third dimension. And here in this matter will be found the essential difference between what is only modern and what is truly new.

The pictorial age in which we live will no longer be satisfied to have the picture continue without this interior significance expressed in integral form. Two dimensions have characterized the work of the past centuries and two-dimension thought and work

is still modern, it seems. Is it too much to hope that the coming century will be one in which this element of the third dimension —this demand for organic significance— will characterize all the pictures that go to make up the main picture, which will be then tremendous with integrity and pregnant with new beauty?

Now, there are certain things as hard as nails, as pointed as tacks, as flat as a barn door that go to make up the technique of creation in this deepened, enlivened, more potential sense.

Since we now have materials in our hands to work with as elements, it is method that I now want to write about, believing that if I can make even the beginning of the

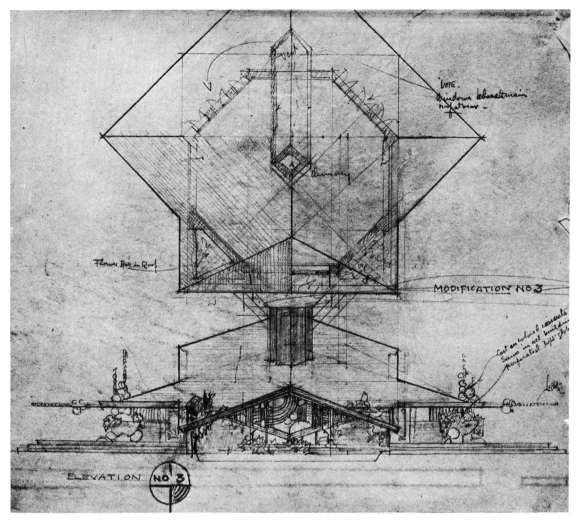

KINDER-SYMPHONY—A PLAYHOUSE IN OAK PARK, ILLINOIS
ELEVATION OF PLAYHOUSE NO. 3 AND MODIFICATIONS MADE ABOVE MAIN ROOF
FRANK LLOYD WRIGHT, ARCHITECT

matter of making true, significant buildings a little more clear, I shall have rendered real service. I would much rather build than write about building, but when I am not building, I will write about building—or the significance of those buildings I have already built.

The conception of the room *within*, the interior spaces of the building to be conserved, expressed and made living as architecture—the architecture of the *within*—that is precisely what we are driving at, all along. And this new quality of thought in architecture, the third dimension, let us say, enters into every move that is made to make it—enters into the use of every material; enters the working of every method we shall use or can use. It will characterize every form that results naturally from this integral interpretation of architecture in its demand upon us for integrity of means to ends—for integrity of the each in all and of the all in all in whatever we do—yes, from pig to proprietor, from a chicken-house to a cathedral.

One more word is indispensable to get the essence of this matter of creation visible on the surface.

That word is PRINCIPLE.

In an earlier paper, there is an attempt to

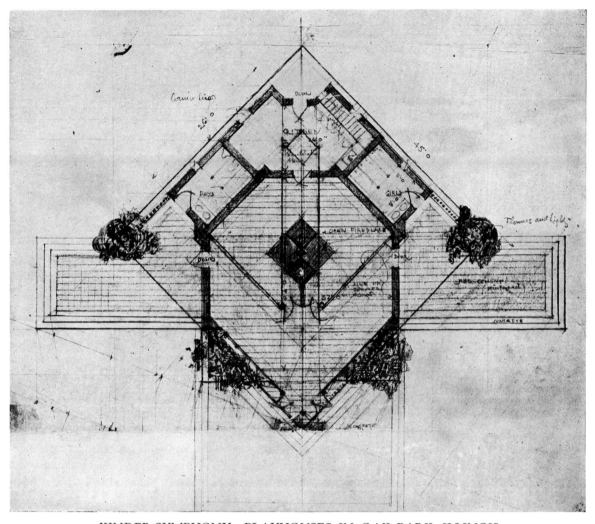

KINDER-SYMPHONY—PLAYHOUSES IN OAK PARK, ILLINOIS
GROUND PLAN. THE SAME GROUND PLAN WAS USED IN ALL FOUR BUILDINGS
FRANK LLOYD WRIGHT, ARCHITECT

define character and to throw some light on the vexed matter of style!

Principle is the working scheme, or the scheme at work in character, style, integrity, truth or beauty. It is not a motif but a means. We might say principle is the law that governs the production of any one or all of them.

The principle of anything is the law that works its being.

Natural law is principle, or the other way around, as you please. Our application of what we understand of principle is mostly expedient, seldom a genuine working of principle. That is all that is the matter with us. Principle is the tool with which the architect must consciously work to be a safe man or get great effects in his work.

He may be an artist—that is, he may be sentient to his finger-tips and be merely artistic without this command of principle, or, let us say, without this noble submission to its command, never knowing the command when seen or heard or "sensed."

In command of principle or commanded by it, only so is the artist potential in creation.

This miserable assumption of virtues, though one has them not, may be expedient but it is all the hell there is attached to this affair of getting spirit materialized in works that gratify supremely human desires—we might say, getting the Beautiful born. And then have someone pop up and say with a sneer, "Yes, but what is beauty?" as though beauty were a commodity like soap, cheese or tobacco.

Well, yes. Here, in beauty, is another word to stumble over or mumble with in this age of the pragmatic "expedient" which, after all, is only an experiment.

But, now we have them all in a row— Poetry, Romantic, Ideal, Beauty—faithful mistresses of principle which we may now name Truth. And "Integrity," "Character," "Style," are attributes, merely, of the working of the master—Principle.

What is Beauty? And Keats' "Ode to a Grecian Urn" answers—"Truth, Beauty—Beauty, Truth."

Obviously, the gifted boy was right, but the nature of either is no nearer for his statement—in the case of the young architect who wants to build something that is both true and lovely. Before we get out of this, that word "love" and the word "joy," too, will get in, I feel sure. Here they are at this moment. Very well, let them in to the distinguished company they know so well. And then let us ask them for help.

"Art is the evidence of man's joy in his work," man has said. And that love is the motivating power in creation we all know by experience.

We are talking about creating or about creations, and this motivation, "Love," is essential to any conception of it—to any beginning of it.

Conceive, then, in love, and work with principle, and what men call Beauty will be the evidence of your joy in your work. After the purity and intensity of your desire or love, then, according to the degree that you have got command of Principle or willingly obey its commands, that materialization of spirit will appear in your work in earthly form—and men will call it Beauty.

Look about you at earthly forms! Trees, flowers, the reactions to one another of the elements in sky, earth and sea. All are merely effects of the working of definite principles with definite "materials" — which are really only elements in the creative hand.

The "design" of this in the altogether is too large in pattern to be yet comprehended by man, yet for our purposes in all or in each, we may find the evidence we seek of method in creation.

Method in creation?

It is there most certainly. Principle is at work continually in this school for architects—working there with simple materials and never-failing *ideas* of form. The form is a consequence of the principle at work. It would seem that no proper excuse for "making" anything ugly need ever be accepted from an architect—with all this prima facie evidence surrounding him, evident even in his own fingers as he writes or draws. He may study forms, "types" constructed by the infallible working of interior principles in this common school. What escapes us is the original idea or ultimate purpose.

This urge to create the beautiful for love of the beautiful is an inheritance. Enough for us that because of the inheritance we have carved out for ourselves with imagination, this higher realm of Beauty.

With imagination, then, let us try to learn the method of working principle with such simple elements as are everywhere put into our hands as materials. Love in our hearts—passion, yes, is essential to success, as our motif.

Now having done our best to light up these words and discuss the relationship existing between them, we will go on to talk of those matters, as hard as nails, as pointed as tacks, as flat as a barn-door, that are involved in the method—of creation.

Love no one can give. Assuming that inspiration is in the heart, we can show facts and performances with materials according to Principle that will be helpful to others in relation to method in creation.

MAY 1952

Few realize that the principles of Wright's "organic architecture" were actually written in 1894. They were first published in an article by Wright in ARCHITECTURAL RECORD, March 1908, and are republished here (top of succeeding pages), along with his current article. His credo, dated 1894 but difficult to improve upon today, is important background for his criticism of the contemporary architectural scene.

233

ORGANIC ARCHITECTURE

LOOKS AT MODERN ARCHITECTURE

Frank Lloyd Wright

MODERN-ARCHITECTURE is the offspring of Organic-architecture: an offspring, already emasculate and commercialized, in danger of becoming a Style. Having suffered many styles since Old Colonial washed up on eastern and Mission reappeared on western shores, this country takes over another one — this time the 58th variety — derived from its own exported Organic-architecture.

Organic-architecture was Middle West. Out of the "Cradle of Democracy" at the end of the nineteenth and the beginning of the twentieth century, came this new sense of architecture. Gradually, over a fifty-year period, a period of ambiguous acceptance and university adversity, it planted and established·fertile forms and new appropriate methods for the natural (machine) use of steel, glass, plastics (like concrete) and provided more ample freedom in shelter for the free new life of these United States than any "style" had ever provided or even promised. Organic-architecture thus came of America — a new freedom for a mixed people living a new freedom under a democratic form of life. Susceptible of infinite variety, it changed the proportions of building throughout the world. The Machine was dedicated to it. Grandomania dead of it — or dying.

Organic-architecture was definitely a new sense of shelter for *humane* life. Shelter, broad and low. Roofs either flat or pitched, hipped or gabled but always comprehensive Shelter. Wide flat eaves were sometimes perforated to let trellised light through upon characteristic ranges of windows below. Ornament was non-existent unless integral. Walls became screens, often glass screens, and the new open-plan spread space upon a concrete ground-mat: the whole structure intimate and wide upon and of the ground itself. This ground-mat floor eventually covered and contained the gravity-heating system (heat rises naturally as water falls) of the spaces to be lived in: forced circulation of hot water in pipes embedded in a broken stone bed beneath the floor slabs (soon misnamed "radiant-heat"). Other new

234

*Part of the 1894
Chicago scene,
not by Wright*

In 1894, with this text from Carlyle at the top of the page —
"The Ideal is within thyself, thy condition is but the stuff thou
art to shape that same Ideal out of" — I formulated the following "propositions." I set them down here much as they were
written then, although in the light of experience they might be
stated more completely and succinctly.

I. Simplicity and Repose are qualities that measure the true
value of any work of art.

But simplicity is not in itself an end nor is it a matter of the
side of a barn but rather an entity with a graceful beauty in its

FRANK LLOYD WRIGHT'S PROPOSITIONS OF 1894

ORGANIC ARCHITECTURE LOOKS AT MODERN ARCHITECTURE

techniques, new forms adapted to our inevitable ma-
chine-methods appeared in these new structures. The
economics of continuity and cantilever-structure were
realized. Even the walls played a new role or disappeared.
Basements and attics disappeared altogether. A new
sense of space in appropriate human scale pervaded not
only the structure but the life itself lived in it was broad-
ened, made more free because of sympathetic freedom of
plan and structure. The interior space to be lived in
became *the reality of the whole performance.* Building, as
a box, was gone.

The integral character of the third dimension was born
to architecture.

Here came to America by way of its own architecture
a natural concept of cultural human growth as an integrity comparable to growth of trees or a plant to grace
the already disgraced landscape and liberate the individual from the sham of classicism.

By way of the integral quality of depth due to the
third dimension and new sense of space as contrived by
the new formulas of continuity and cantilever in devising construction, a new countenance emerged. The
clear countenance of principle. The old post-and-beam
formula was now too wasteful. Hard and clumsy, it
seemed like a rattling of the bones. The cut-slash-and-
butt construction of the old camouflaged box of the

*Some critics have called this one of the best of Wright's
early "prairie" houses — Robie house, Chicago, 1908*

integrity from which discord, and all that is meaningless, has been eliminated. A wild flower is truly simple. Therefore:

1. A building should contain as few rooms as will meet the conditions which give it rise and under which we live, and which the architect should strive continually to simplify; then the ensemble of the rooms should be carefully considered that comfort and utility may go hand in hand with beauty. Beside the entry and necessary work rooms there need be but three rooms on the ground floor of any house, living room, dining room and kitchen, with the possible addition of a "social office"; really there need be but one room, the living room, with requirements otherwise sequestered from it or screened within it by means of architectural contrivances.

2. Openings should occur as integral features of the structure and form, if possible, its natural ornamentation.

3. An excessive love of detail has ruined more fine things from the standpoint of fine art or fine living than any one human shortcoming — it is hopelessly vulgar. Too many houses, when they are not little stage settings or scene paintings, are mere notion stores, bazaars or junk-shops. Decoration is dangerous

---

Renaissance or otherwise seemed harsh or trivial. Ugly and false. Each organic building (an integument rather than a box) became as one with its site and occupancy. Nor could these buildings be imagined anywhere else nor for any other purpose whatever than where and for what they were built.

Thus by 1893–1900 a great negation transpired in America, entirely free of European influences. *But this sweeping negation was only the platform upon which to affirm* these new principles of life and economic building-construction. Naturally this negation had novel aesthetic aspects but wore the countenance of principle.

As a matter of course, these novel aspects of countenance were striking *effects:* startlingly clean, "stream-lined" "effects." Soon these effects were elsewhere seized upon, in Germany particularly, where years later they appeared at the Bauhaus.

Organic-architecture as built in America during the years 1893 to 1909 was first extensively published in Europe by Germany, 1910, owing to the insistence of Professor Kuno Francke, "Exchange Professor of Aesthetics" at Harvard. (It had been published in England years before.) Reaching Paris soon, it there became, by way of journalistic ability and our own provincial museums, again the Box. But, the box nude! Duly dedicated to Machinery.

The original and elemental affirmative characteristics or the original negation made by Organic-architecture in three dimensional structure, *the Machine dedicated to it*, now reappeared as a bare two-dimensional facade *dedicated to the Machine!* The streamlined novelty of the original negation became thus a fit fad for Fascism. But our provincials began to import it because the culture-mongrel of our country and our museums believes, and will continue to believe, that American "culture" is a bastard. "Culture comes from Europe."

Well, this import was not an affair of construction at all but a mere "aesthetic," a painter's, not an architect's. Soon a cliché. The fruitful *affirmative negation* made by Organic-architecture in three dimensions now reappeared as a two-dimensional affair. *All* ornament was scraped off. A high box would be contrasted with a long low box or square boxes were placed together alongside very tall boxes. Or on came the nude box cut open or set up in the air on posts without pants. But always, nevertheless and notwithstanding — the BOX. Thus surfaced the box was invariably painted white to emphasize the fact that it did not intend being a becoming feature of the ground upon which it was put. By maintaining a white sepulture for unthinking mass-life, individuality was soon leeched from the performance. Otherwise no such cliché could have been made so useful

Museum of Modern Art

A prairie house with a pool — the Coonley House, Riverside, Illinois, circa 1910

unless you understand it thoroughly and are satisfied that it means something good in the scheme as a whole, for the present you are usually better off without it. Merely that it "looks rich" is no justification for the use of ornament.

4. Appliances or fixtures as such are undesirable. Assimilate them together with all appurtenances into the design of the structure.

5. Pictures deface walls oftener than they decorate them. Pictures should be decorative and incorporated in the general scheme as decoration.

6. The most truly satisfactory apartments are those in which most or all of the furniture is built in as a part of the original scheme considering the whole as an integral unit.

II. There should be as many kinds (styles) of houses as there are kinds (styles) of people and as many differentiations as there are different individuals. A man who has individuality (and what man lacks it?) has a right to its expression in his own environment.

III. A building should appear to grow easily from its site and be shaped to harmonize with its surroundings if Nature is manifest there, and if not try to make it as quiet, substantial and organic as She would have been were the opportunity Hers.

FRANK LLOYD WRIGHT'S PROPOSITIONS OF 1894

ORGANIC ARCHITECTURE LOOKS AT MODERN ARCHITECTURE

to our American mass-education or serve our standard practice of quick commerce.

This sterilizing performance was duly dedicated to machinery, as any cliché should be, not *machinery dedicated to it* as in Organic-architecture. So, here came a kind of tapeworm into the entrails of Organic-architecture. Because of the novel effects of the original organic negation made for organic purposes this mixture of negation with negation is, as of today, what is called "Modern-architecture."

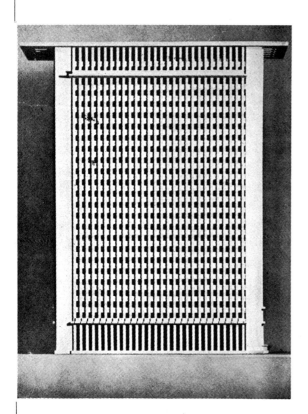

Project, never built, for an office building in San Francisco, done by Wright in 1912

Any two-dimensional cliché is too easy to commercialize or teach. To educationists and the commercial capitalist it was providential — just what both wanted because so shallow an affair of surfaces. The Box now, sometimes of glass, say, but always a post-and-beam affair even if not rattling its bones, became more and more evident in standard education. Buildings began gradually to appear intermixed with the "effects" of Organic-architecture — to be now called "Modern-architecture."

The imported cliché was not only easy to teach. "Less is more" unless less, already little, becomes less than nothing at all and "much ado about nothing."

Now, because of a much too shallow aesthetic (a painter's), the original affirmative negation made by Organic-architecture (an architect's) seems too soon in danger of losing, under the name of Modern-architecture, its humane characteristics and original poetry. Confused with architecture superficially fashioned in two dimensions we have a superficial imitation of the original profound negation made by Organic-architecture itself.

Easy to practice, easier still upon the resources of human science and imagination, the Box, ornamental camouflage (the "Classic") scraped off — *but old thought unchanged* — again rises — educational and fashionable: The cliché of a new STYLE!

Regardless, the old box comes back. The crate now consecrate.

In it we see high and low purposes all packaged or banked alike.

Architectural careers thus become quick. The true amateur, sterilized owing to this revival of the box-facade by accredited schools — and names — is thus made "safe." Grateful for this sterilization, if for no other reason, our leading universities together with realtor "developers" and our swelling bureaucratic government are all ready to "take over" "Modern-archi-

We of the Middle West are living on the prairie.* The prairie has a beauty of its own and we should recognize and accentuate this natural beauty, its quiet level. Hence, gently sloping roofs, low proportions, quiet sky lines, suppressed heavy-set chimneys and sheltering overhangs, low terraces and out-reaching walls sequestering private gardens.

IV. Colors require the same conventionalizing process to make them fit to live with that natural forms do; so go to the

Another pre-Wright
vision of Chicago

237

tecture." It goes everywhere the educational institution and especially the Museum happens to be or to go. The Museum-as-Education and Education-as-the-Museum have found just what could easily be handled in the name of culture: culture must come from abroad! That is where the cliché came from.

Now, the moral nature of the Cuckoo (to be sure) characterized much if not most of the ambitious subscribers to this go-getter rush for the band-wagon. Any honest aspirant had small chance of recognition and none

of genuine success. Any aspirant, tough or callow, could more easily exploit the Box bare than take time and pains to go deeper into the principles of Organic-architecture.

Organic-architecture based upon fundamental human and structural principles insisted upon *integral method and always significant form true to structure throughout. Or none.* It was profound — too slow for popular purposes. Therefore preparation for architectural practice would

Interior of circular library, Florida Southern College, Lakeland, Fla.

woods and fields for color schemes. Use the soft, warm, optimistic tones of earths and autumn leaves in preference to the pessimistic blues, purples or cold greens and grays of the ribbon counter; they are more wholesome and better adapted in most cases to good decoration.

V. Bring out the nature of the materials, let their nature intimately into your scheme. Strip the wood of varnish and let it alone — stain it. Develop the natural texture of the plastering and stain it. Reveal the nature of the wood, plaster, brick or stone in your designs; they are all by nature friendly and beautiful. No treatment can be really a matter of fine art when these natural characteristics are outraged or neglected.

VI. A house that has character stands a good chance of growing more valuable as it grows older while a house in the prevailing mode, whatever that mode may be, is soon out of fashion, stale and unprofitable.

Buildings like people must first be sincere, must be true and then withal as gracious and lovable as may be.

Above all, integrity. The machine is the normal tool of our civilization, give it work that it can do well — nothing is of greater importance. To do this will be to formulate new industrial ideals, sadly needed.

ORGANIC ARCHITECTURE LOOKS AT MODERN ARCHITECTURE

be not only slow but far too difficult. Also, a discerning client was needed rather than a fashionable one. There are still a few discerning ones developing in America.

Being truly individual, Organic-architecture lacked the journalist. America is nothing if not journalistic.

Writing as of 1952, the old Box — undressed — seems coming back again. The white-paint-men thrive on choice ways of setting it up on top of the ground. Regardless. They set it up tall, endwise; put it over there, down crosswise. Set it on the bias? Likely enough set it up on top of posts or anything else. Soon they will pivot it. Tyros slash and stripe its fascistic facades horizontally or vertically or checker-wise the fronts. Soon diagonally? They stamp it to look thick or stamp it to look thin: put lids on it — or none. Lids either square or askew, projecting or flush. The professors make a drum of it and beat it for dismal accord with the soulless character of an Era.

Thus Modern-architecture is Organic-architecture deprived of a soul. Therefore architecture is now so easy to grasp that any boy of three months' experience can practice it and appear with a dose of it on the front page of the local newspaper next month, or within a year (or two) be heralded in color by the market-magazines of building-materials as the new "It." The "plan-factory" now has shows in Art-Museums.

I fear the history of creative art down the ages thus repeats itself in our own modern times and again we have categories of names. Names! But now names all essentially *unlike* for performances as *alike* as any two peas.

So this is Modern-architecture! Well — if so — this affair, too, will pass as matter of intelligent choice. St. Augustine once observed, "The harvest shall not be yet." Perhaps what is left behind when we sicken of it all will be better (I so believe) than what came of similar betrayal of principles in times past. Better, because of

what is left of the character of integral form and proportion — the plastic humanitarian space in building which Organic-architecture has already made. Probably the humanly significant forms belonging to Organic-architecture now camouflaged or betrayed and called "modern" will come back from the gutter of Fashion toward which they now seem headed: come back and — deepened by experience — start all over again.

The timeless war of Principle with Expediency will go on and on, in our country especially, because more than ever human nature here is habituate. Like vegetation. Or the parasite. To really change human habituation (even to the cigarette degree) would require more than one try in any one century. While nailing up a box in different ways is so easy, why should a Get-rich-quick Society like ours take time and the extreme pains necessary to make an organism of anything? A cultural organism (like any other true organism) must *grow*. Growth *is* slow. It cannot be had like a box nailed up by the tyro internationally. The answer is yet to come.

Any "international style" would probably be a cultural calamity fit for Fascism but intolerable to democracy. Meantime so-called "Modern-architecture" runs the gamut of the old Box stripped and trying to assume forms originated by Organic-architecture. As this pretentious shell, empty of true organic significance, goes rapidly toward the gutter of fashion — let us observe . . . "there goes to the gutter the architecture of this modern era from which succeeding generations will probably perceive what was missed and begin to build again on the basis of what was lacking when the gutter was reached."

I hope. And I believe.

Frank Lloyd Wright—Taliesin West—February 1952

The Citation of
The American Institute of Architects
upon the presentation of
The Gold Medal of the Institute to
Frank Lloyd Wright
at the Eighty-first Convention
Houston, Texas
March 17, 1949

*Prometheus brought fire from Olympus and endured
the wrath of Zeus for his daring; but his torch lit other
fires and men lived more fully by their warmth.
To see the beacon fires he has kindled is the greatest*